MARIE KØLBÆK IVERSEN

HISTORIES OF PREDATION

CHANNEL 1

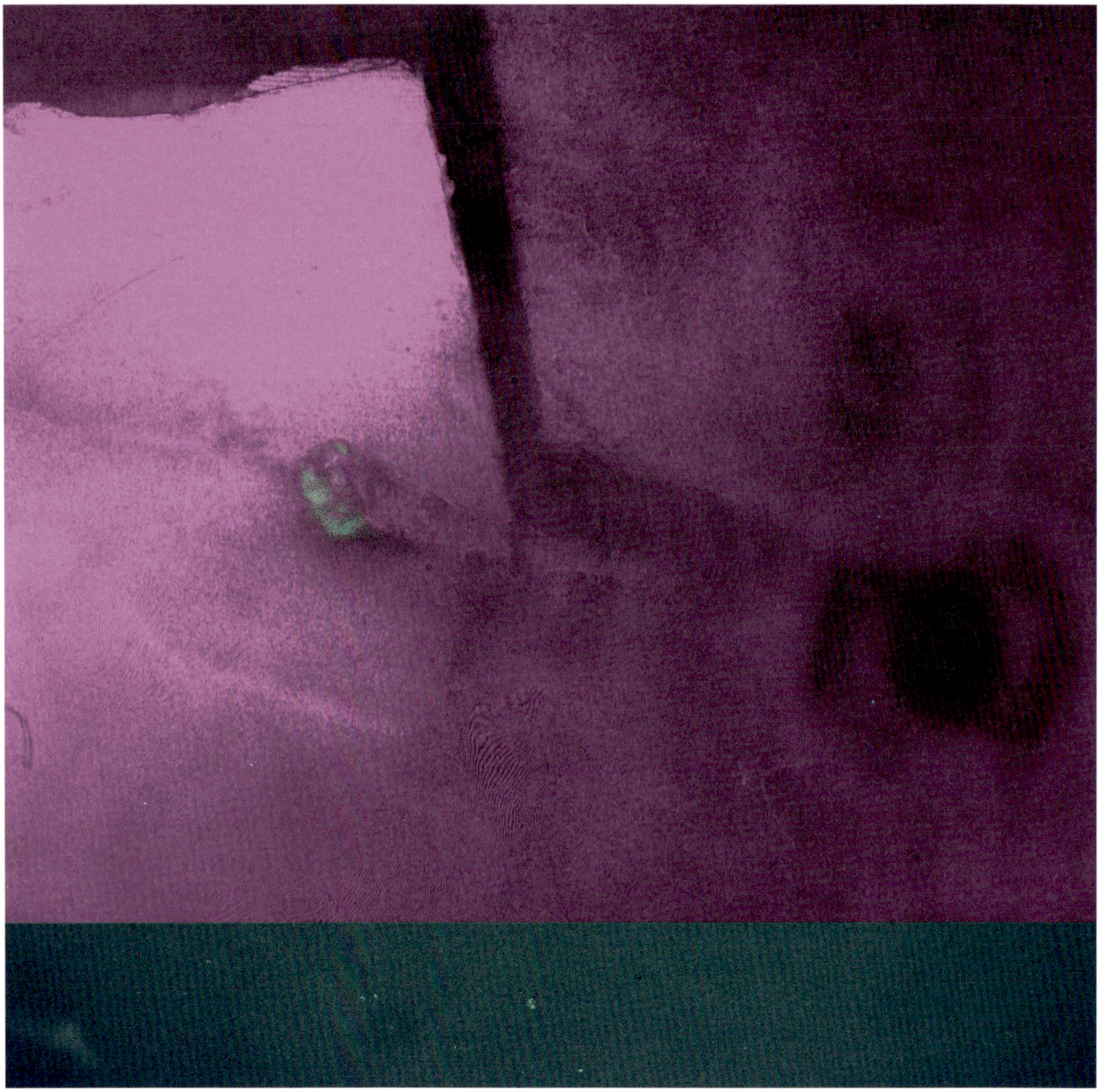

5

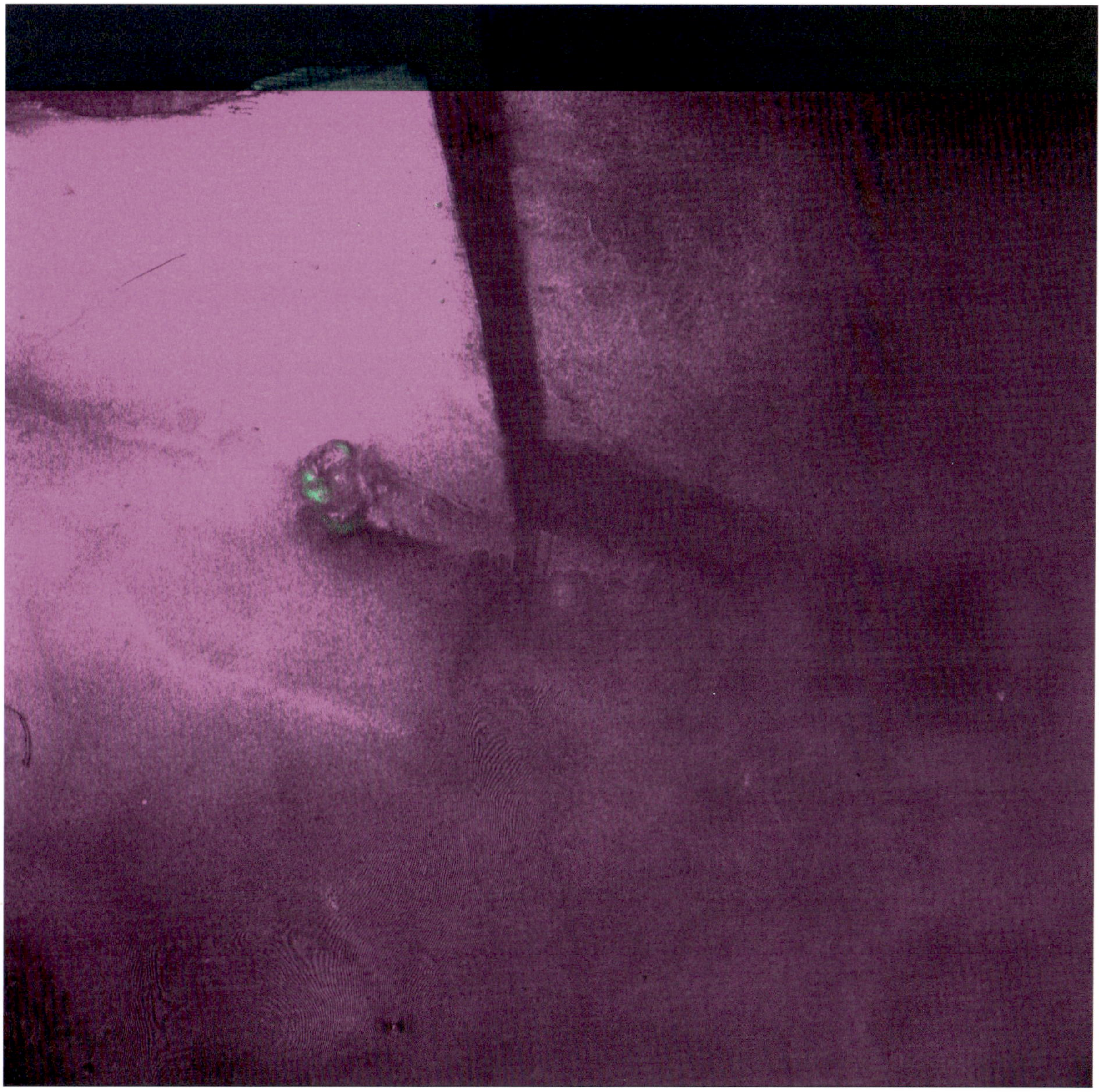

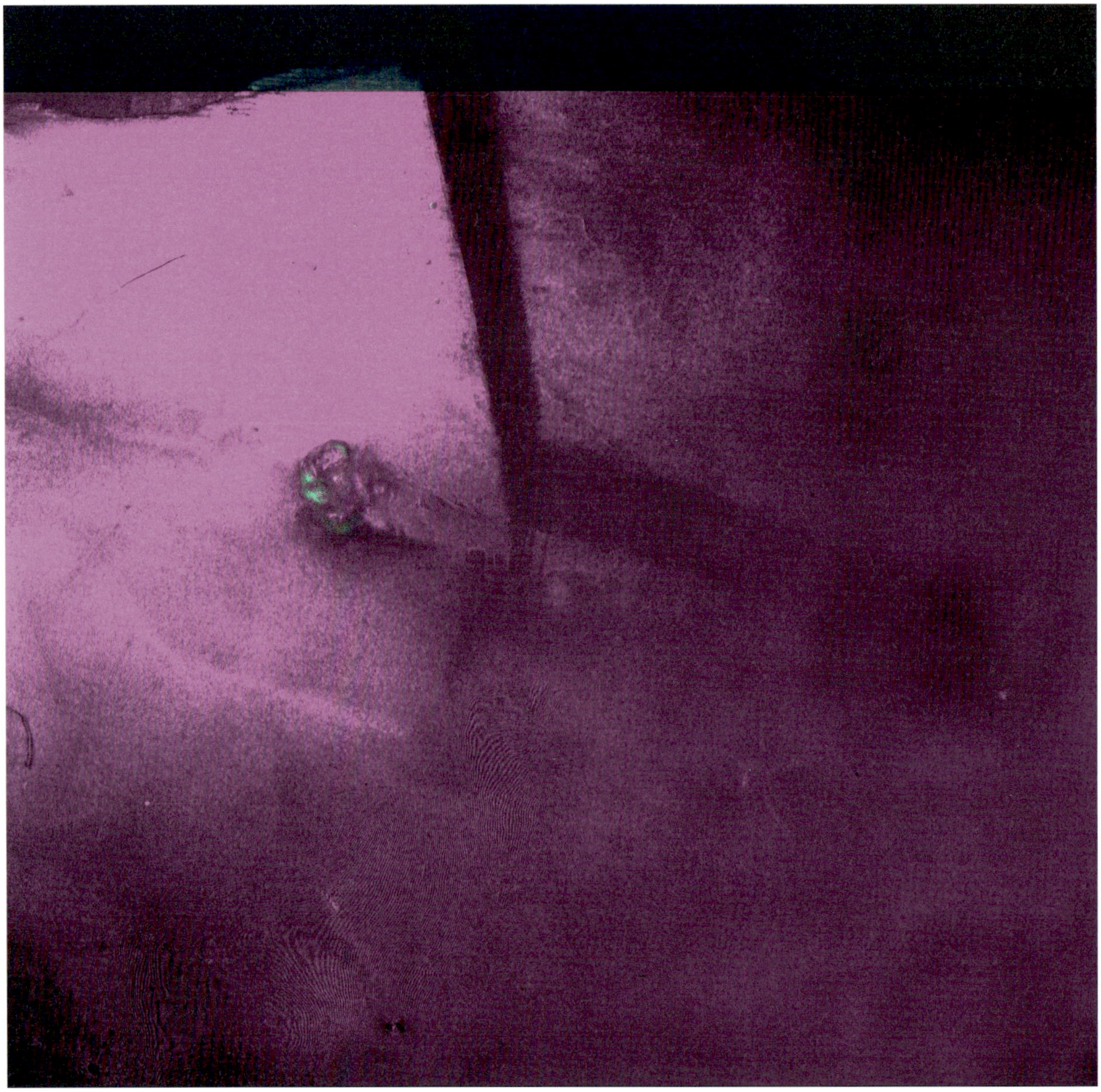

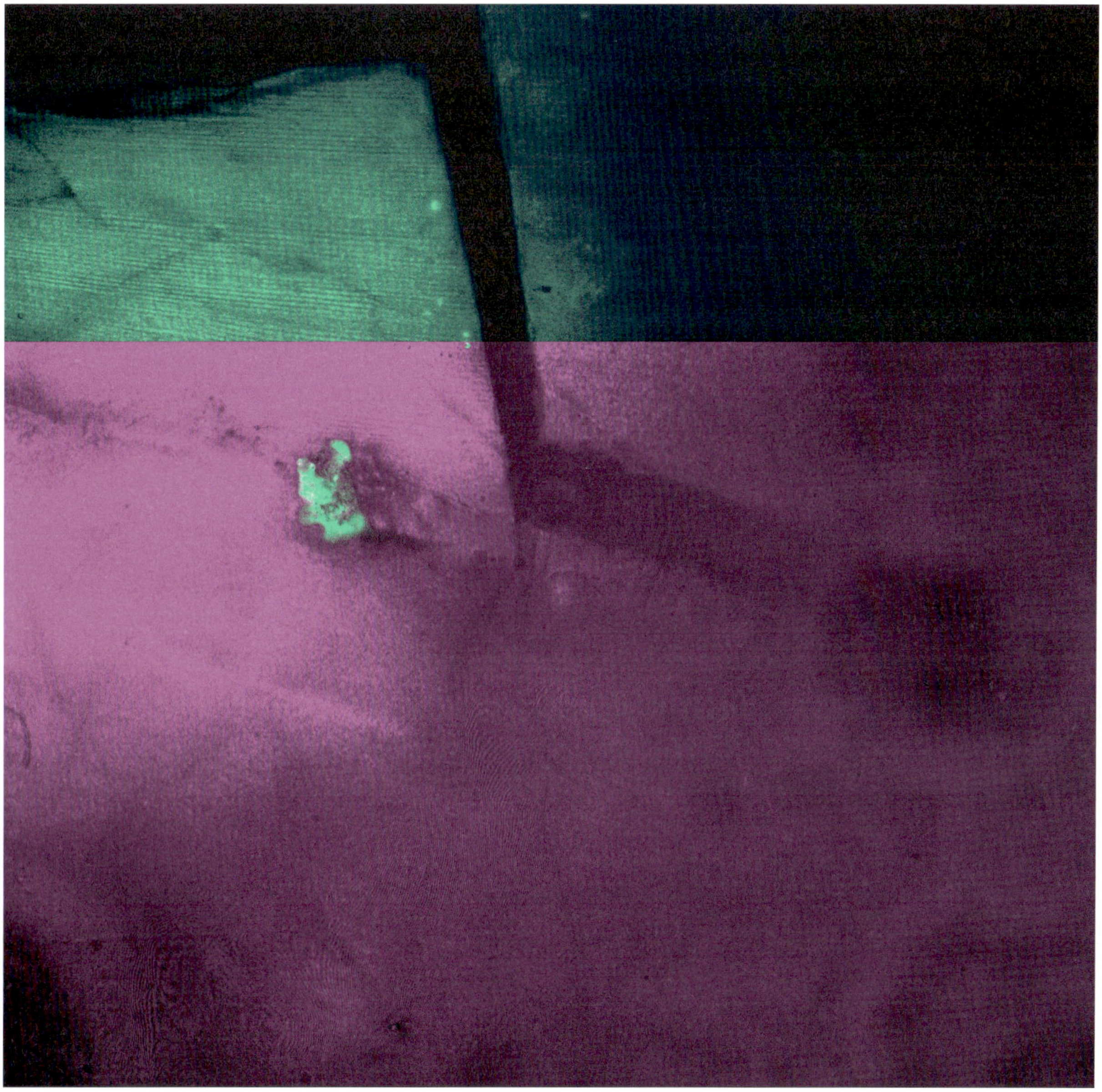

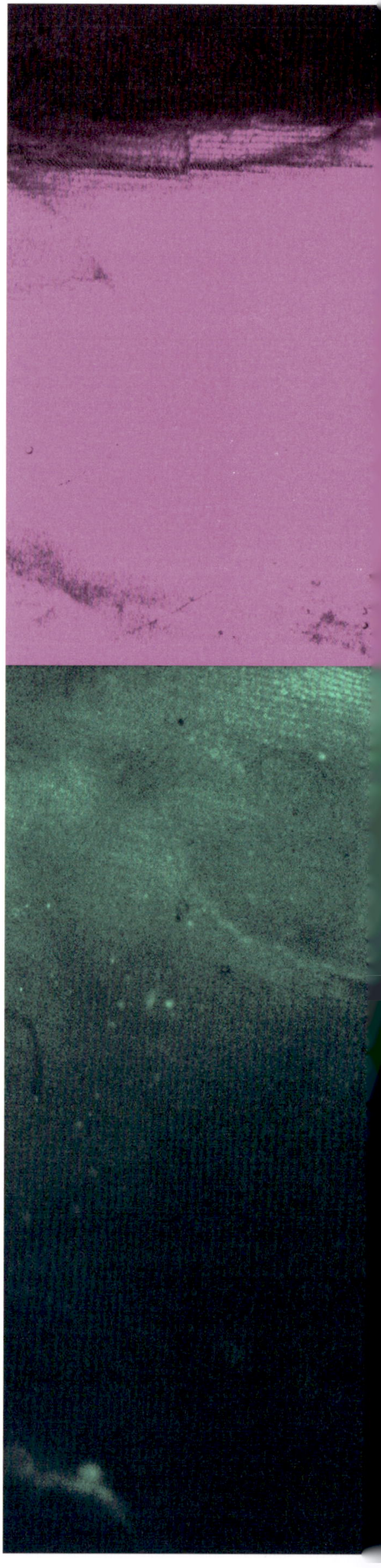

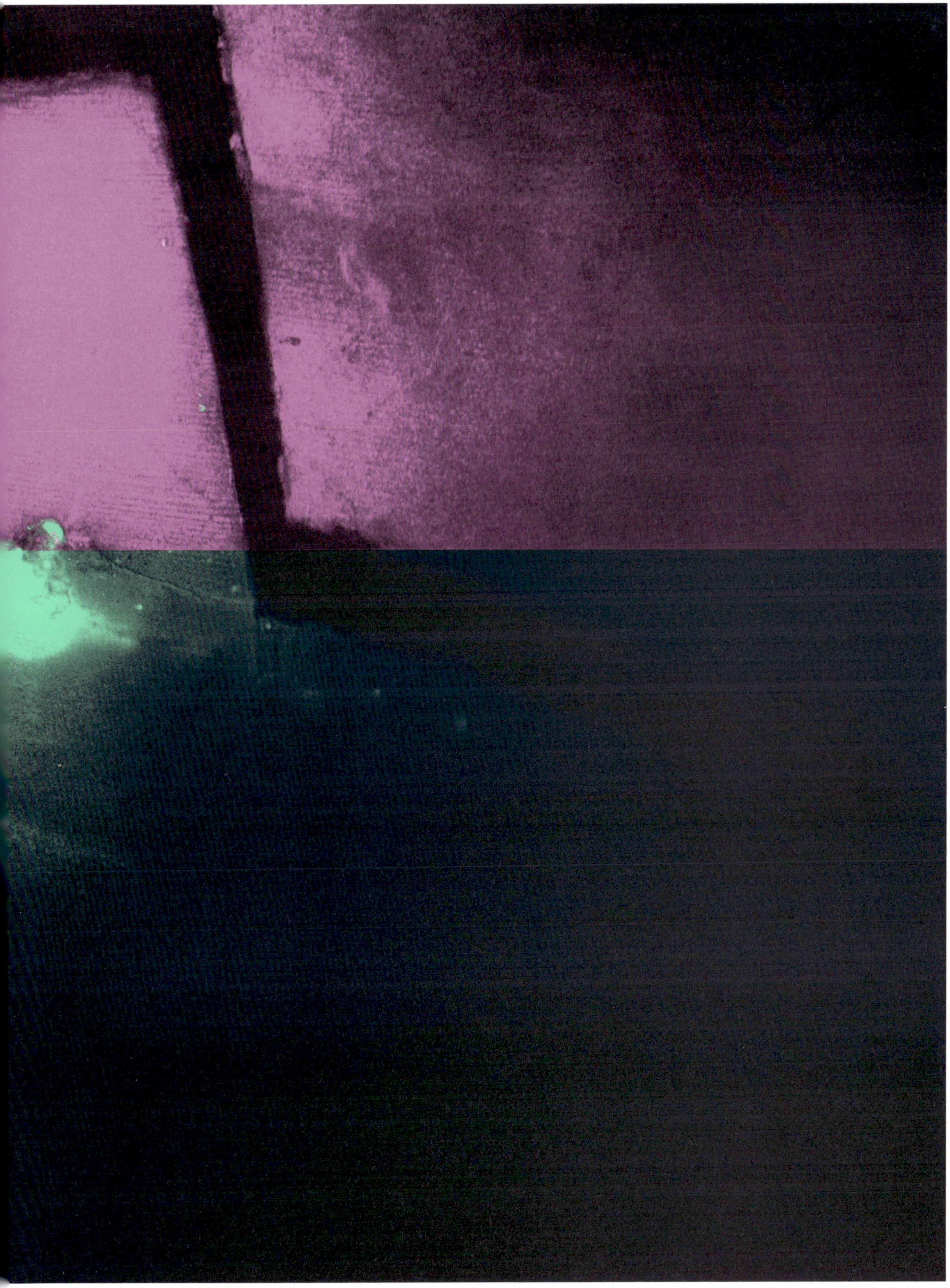

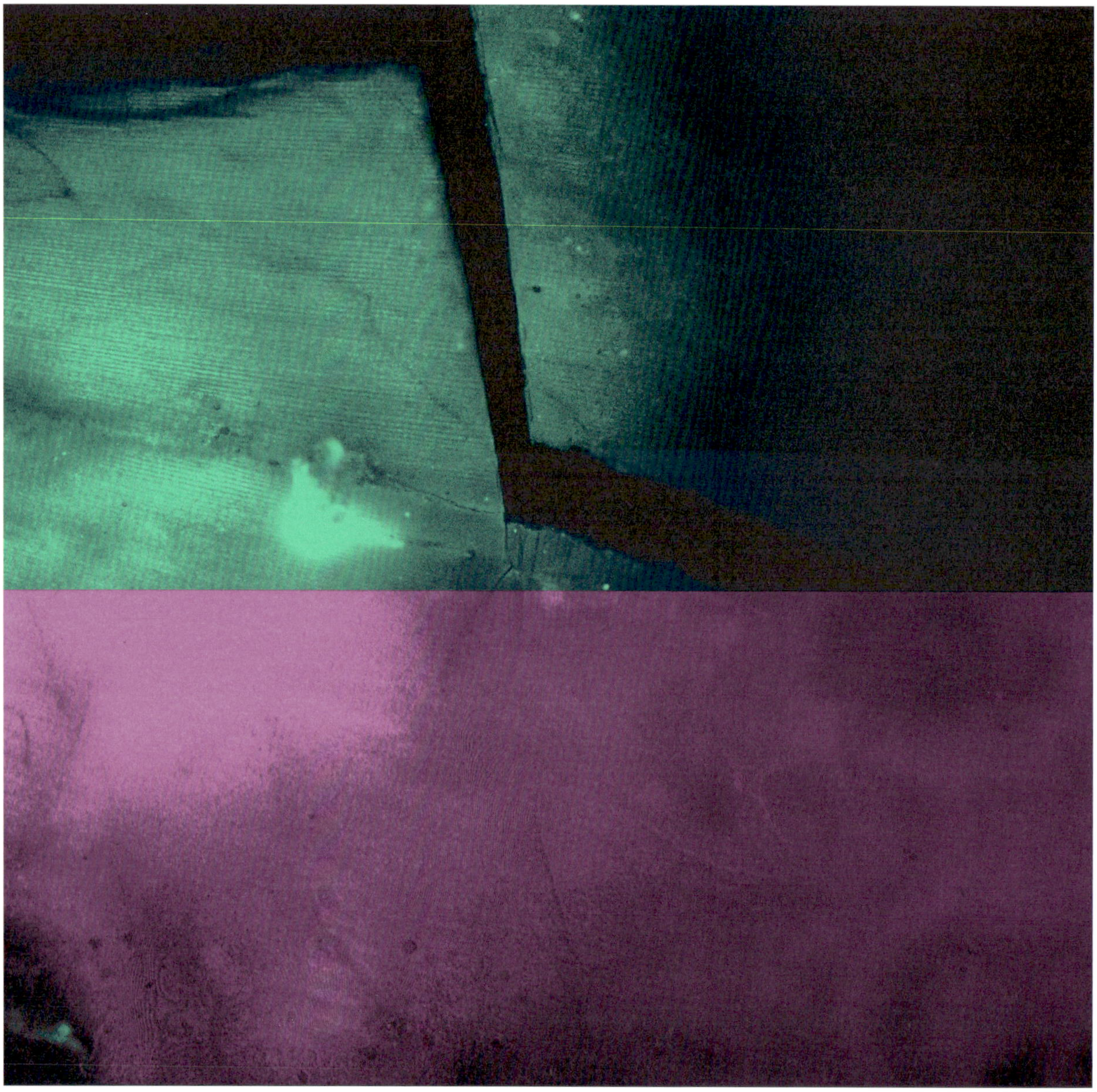

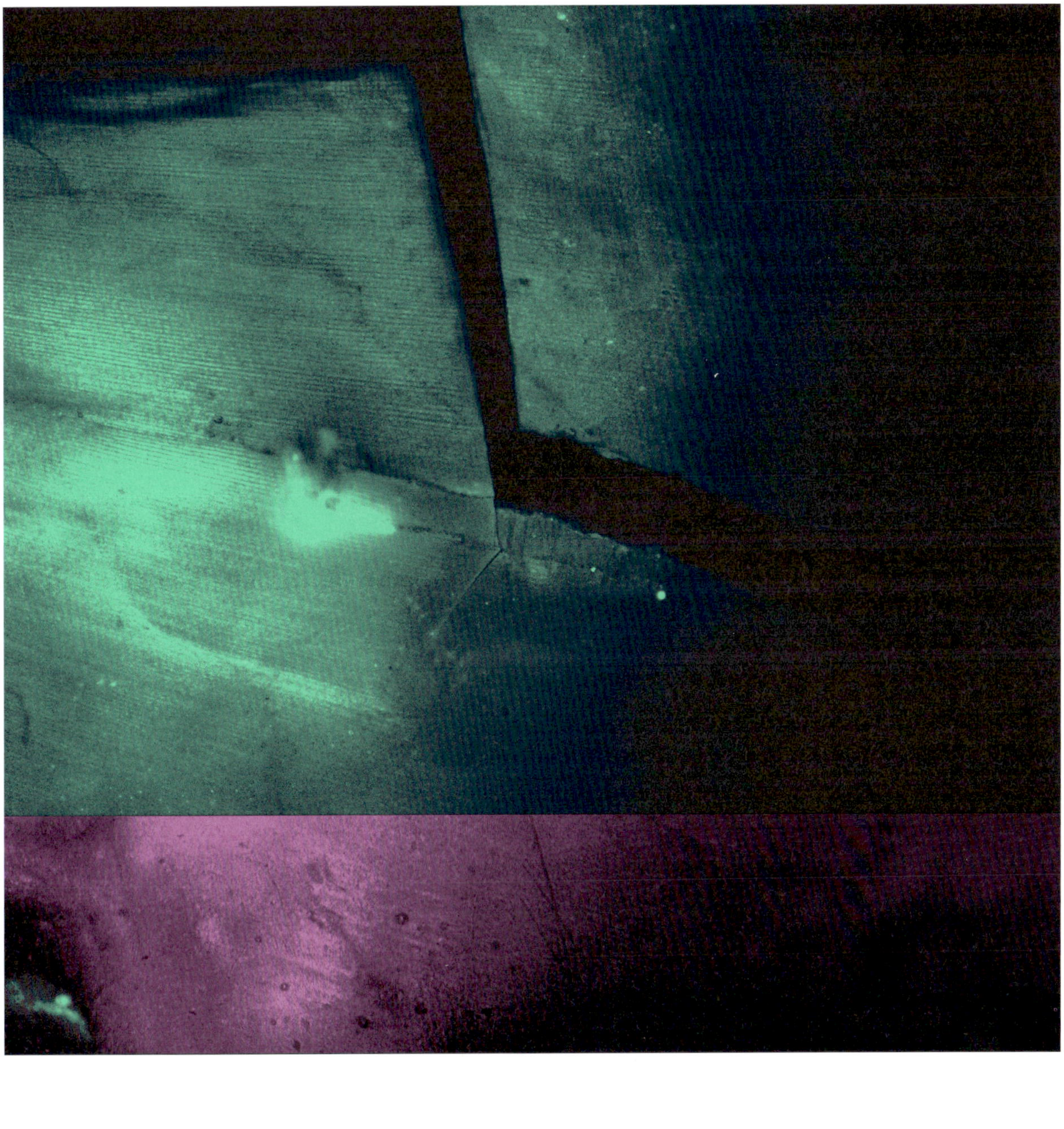

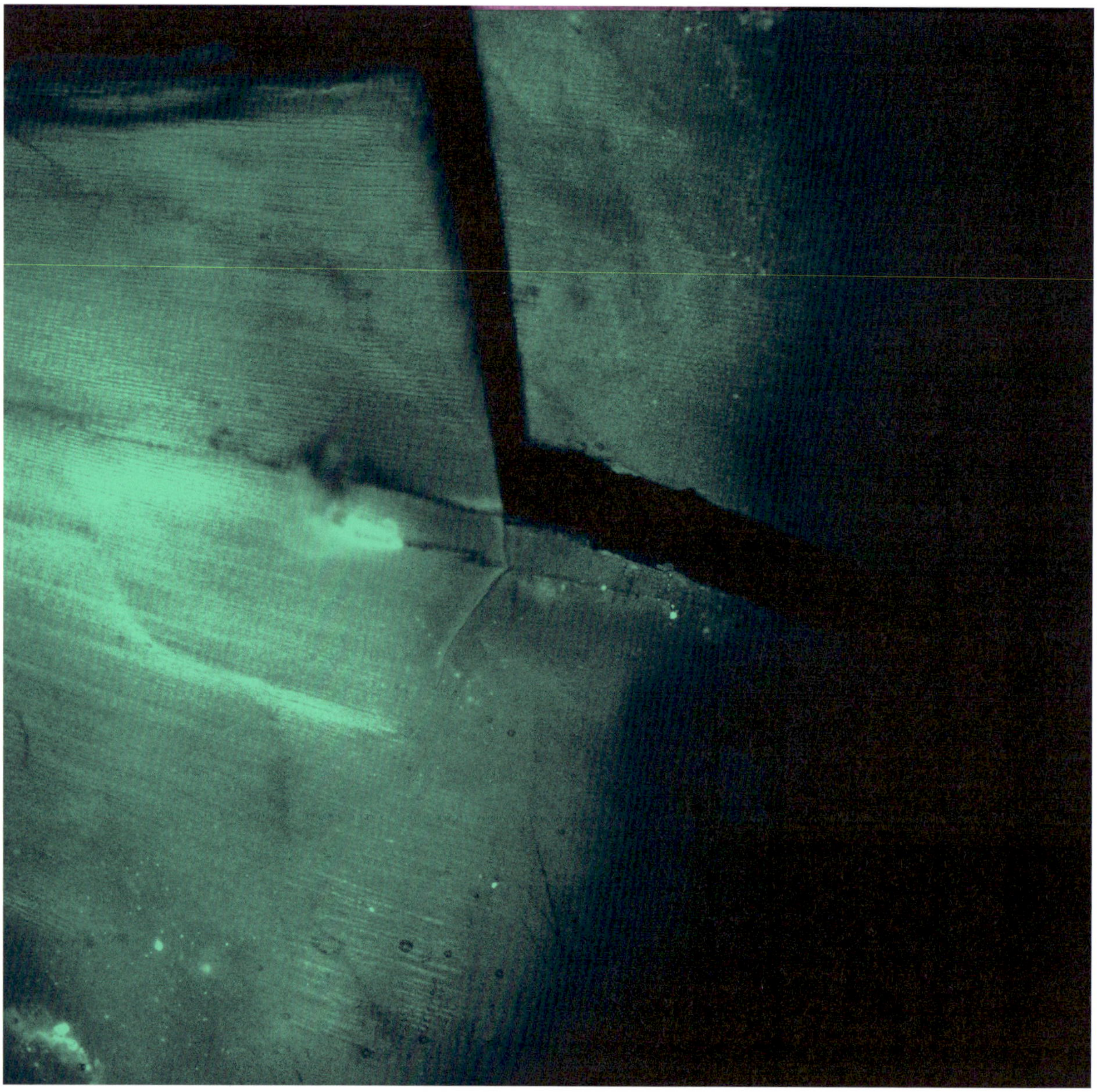

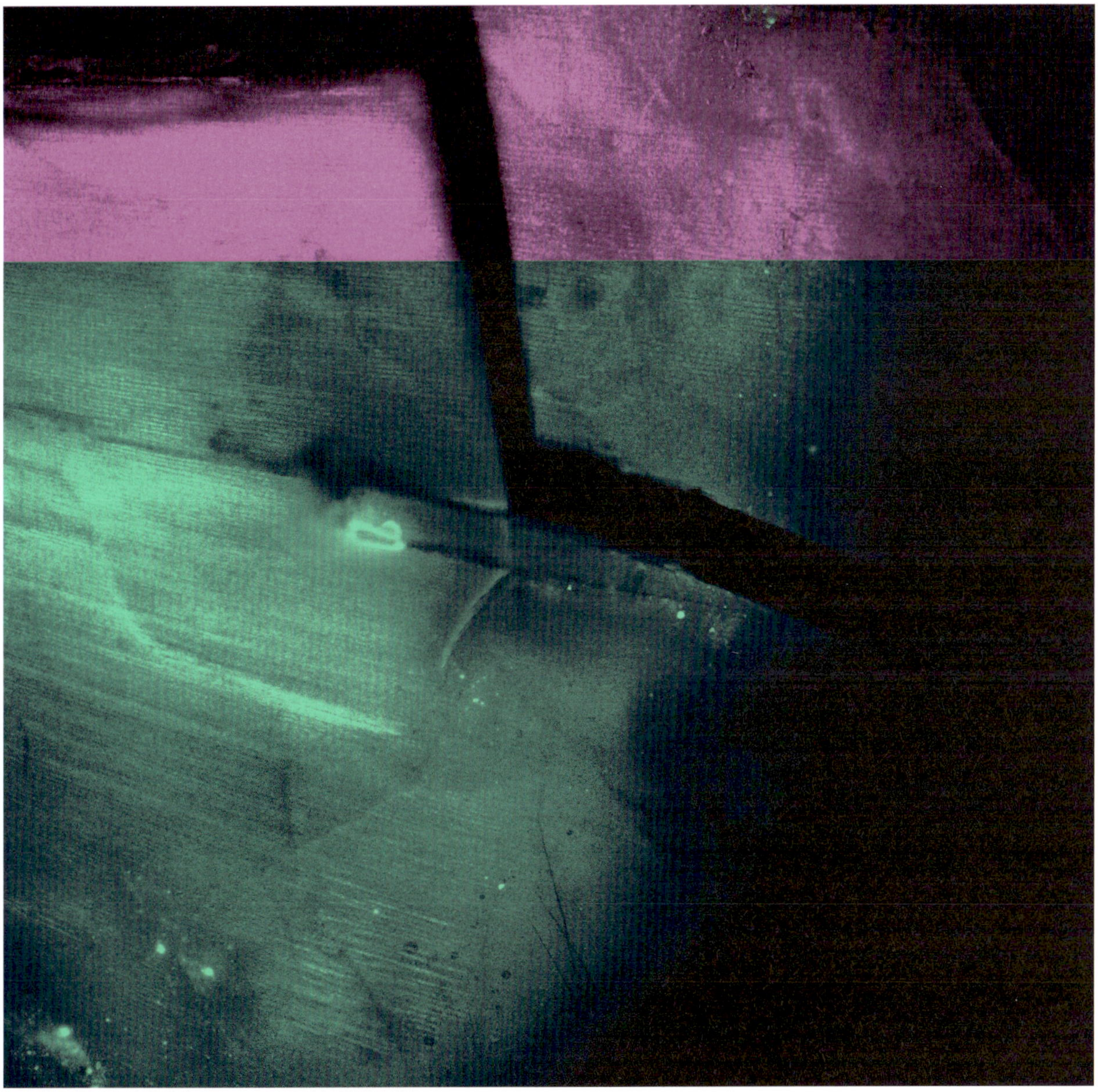

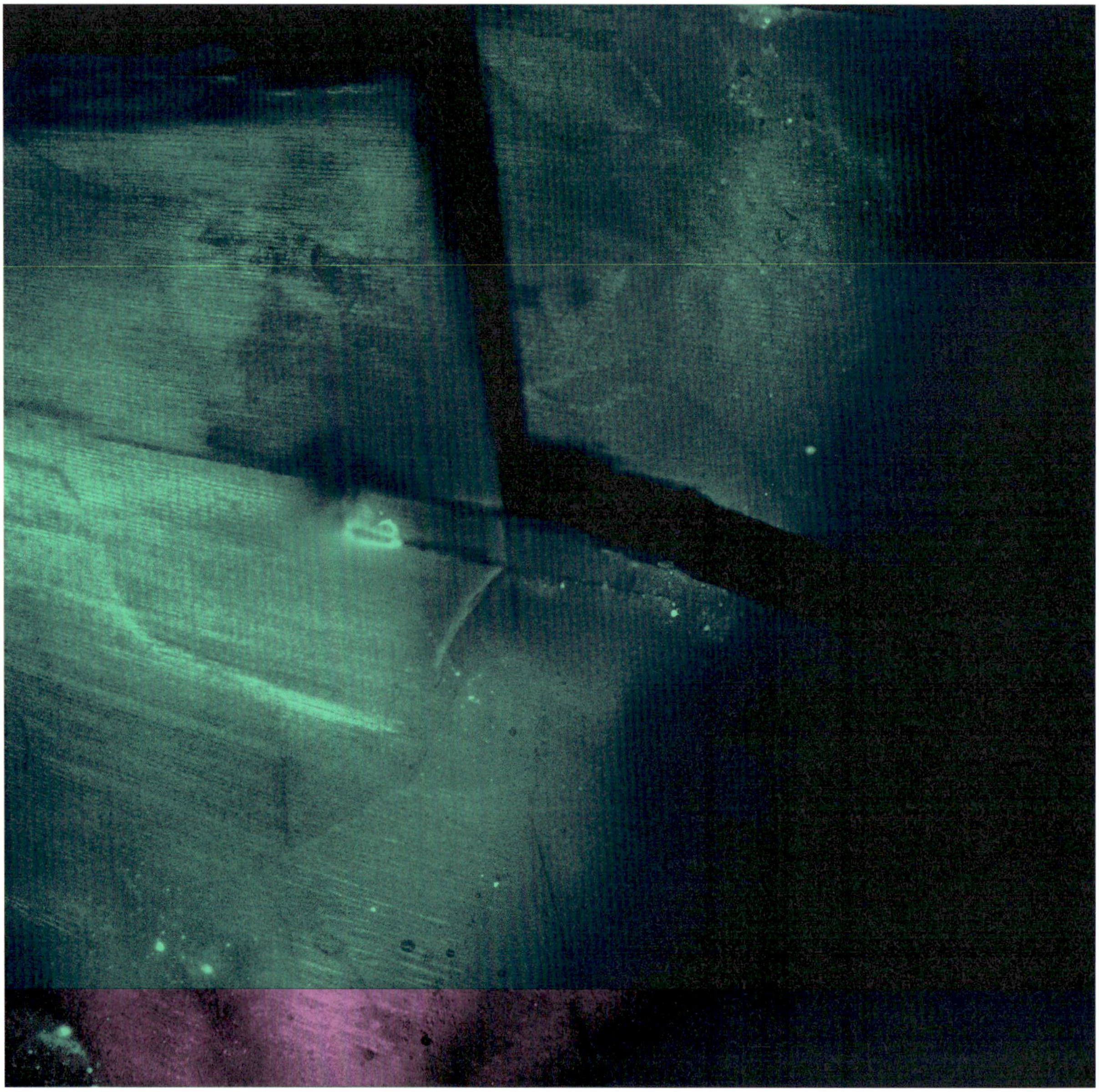

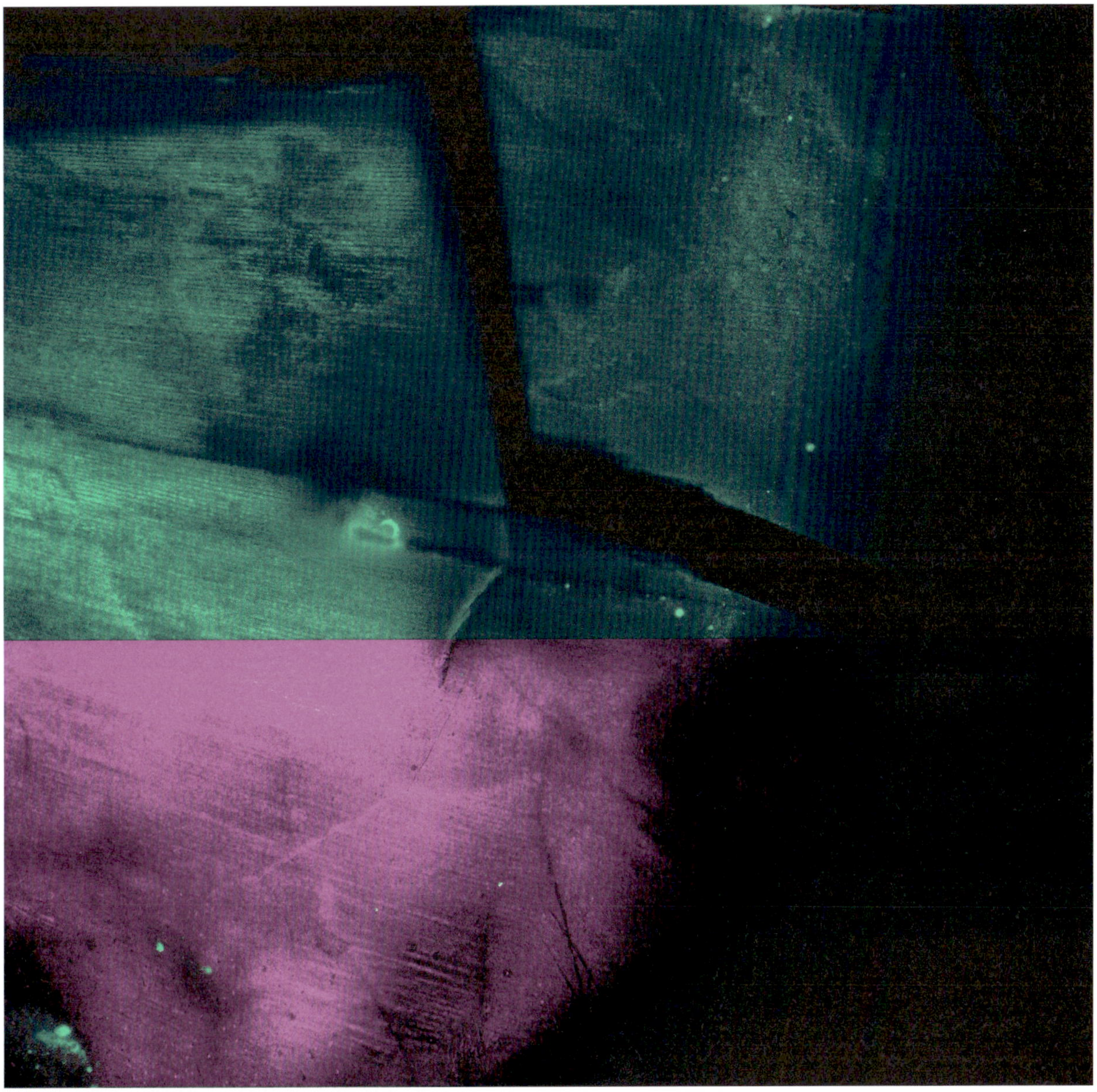

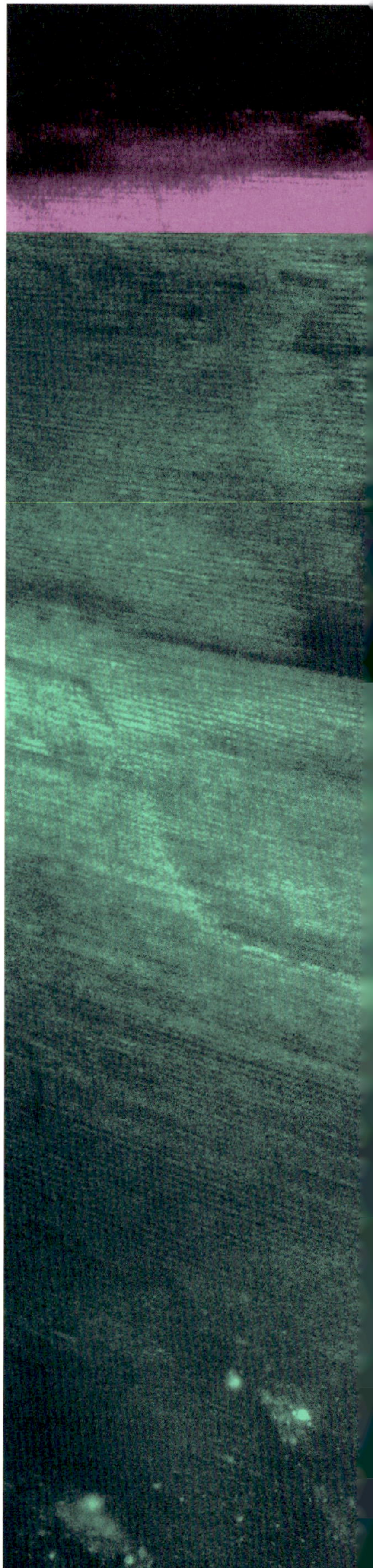

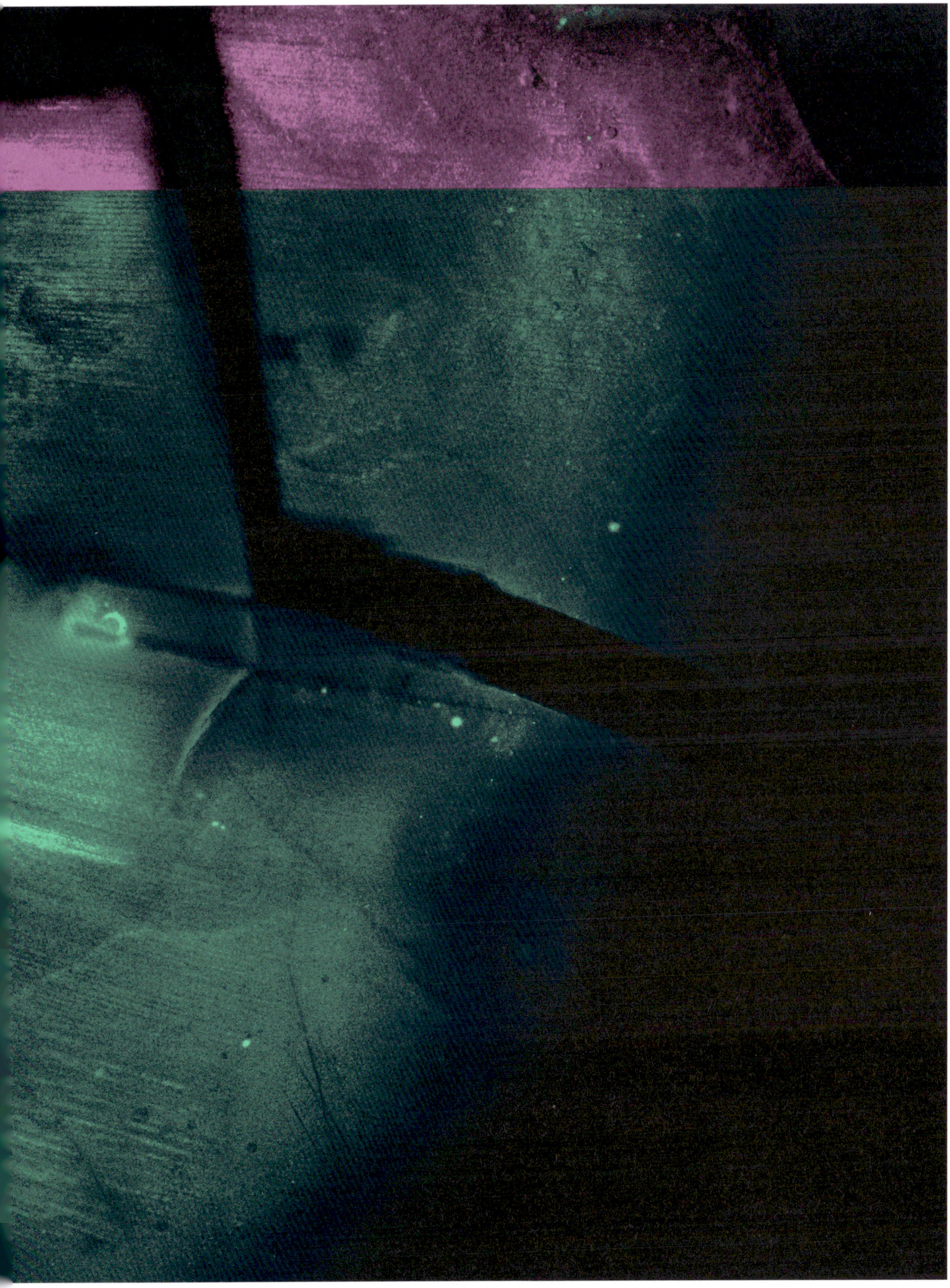

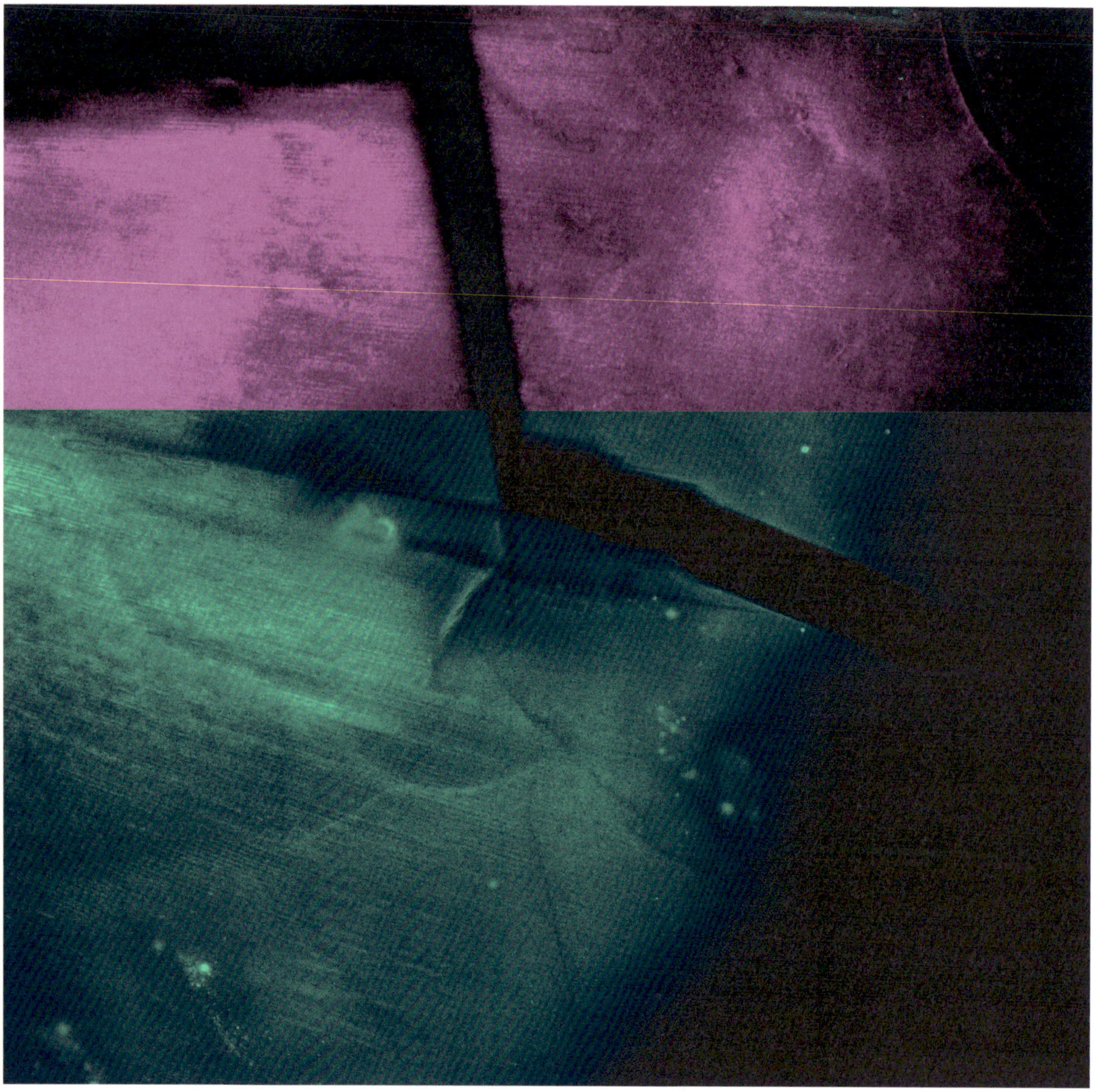

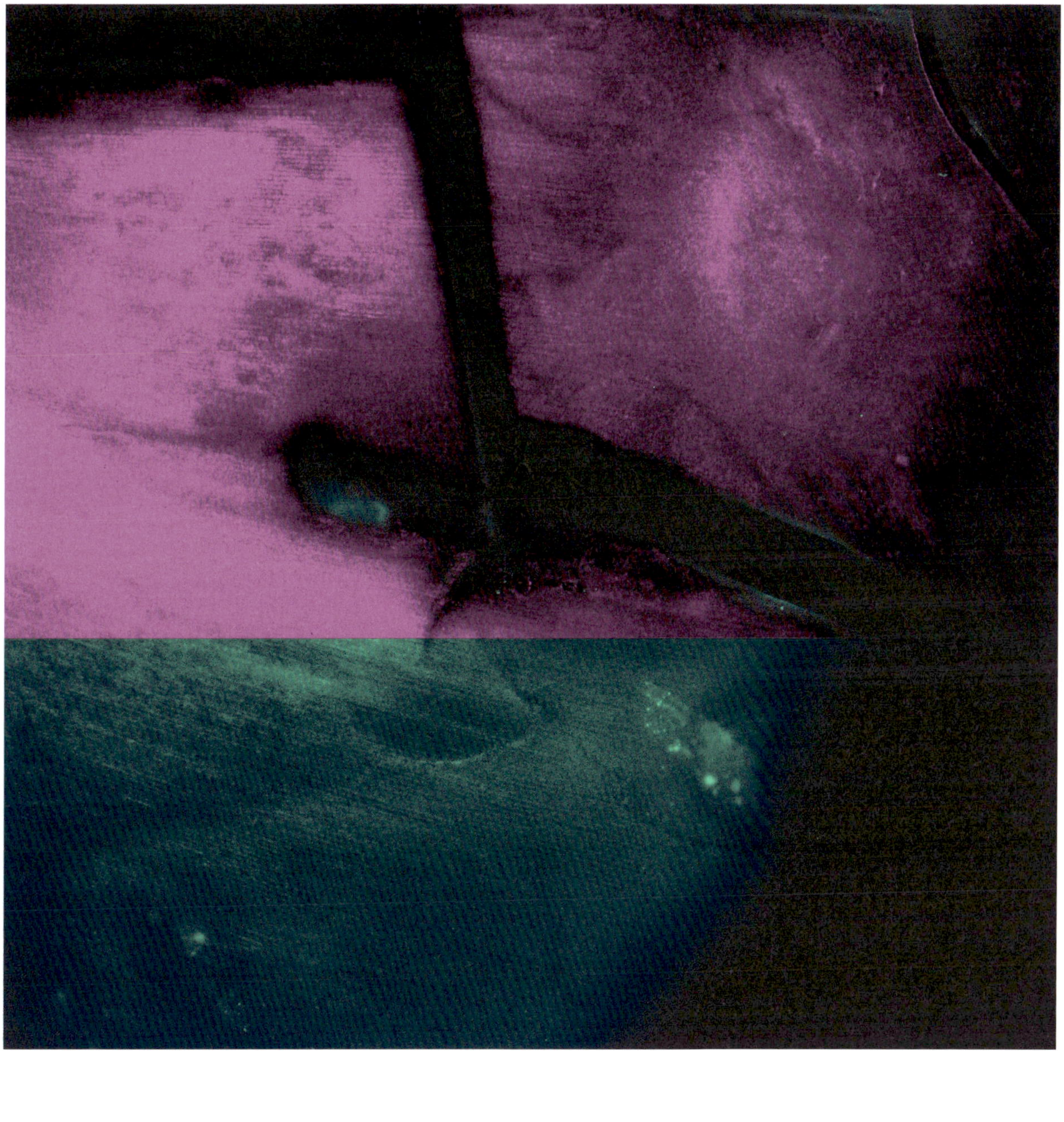

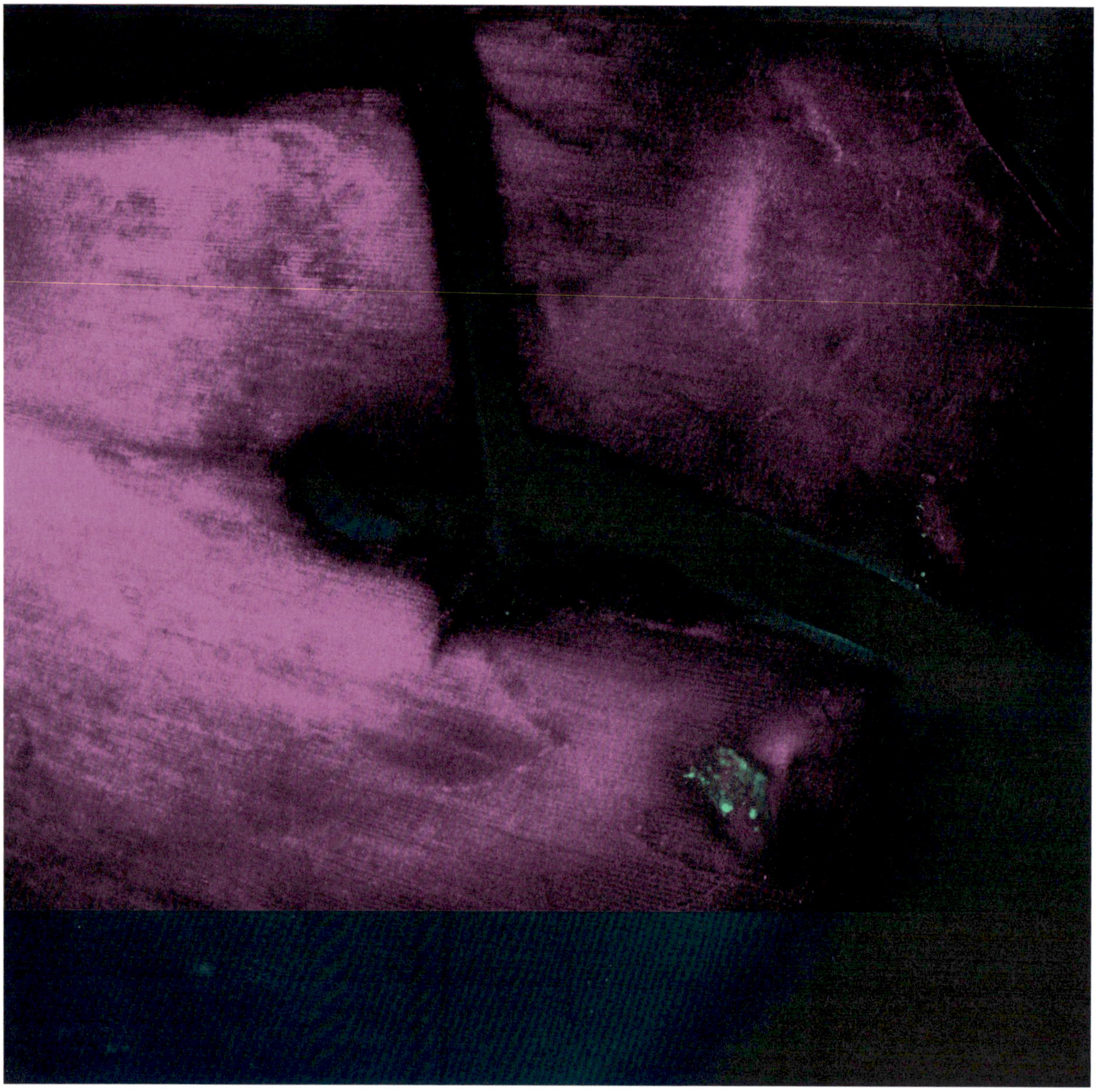

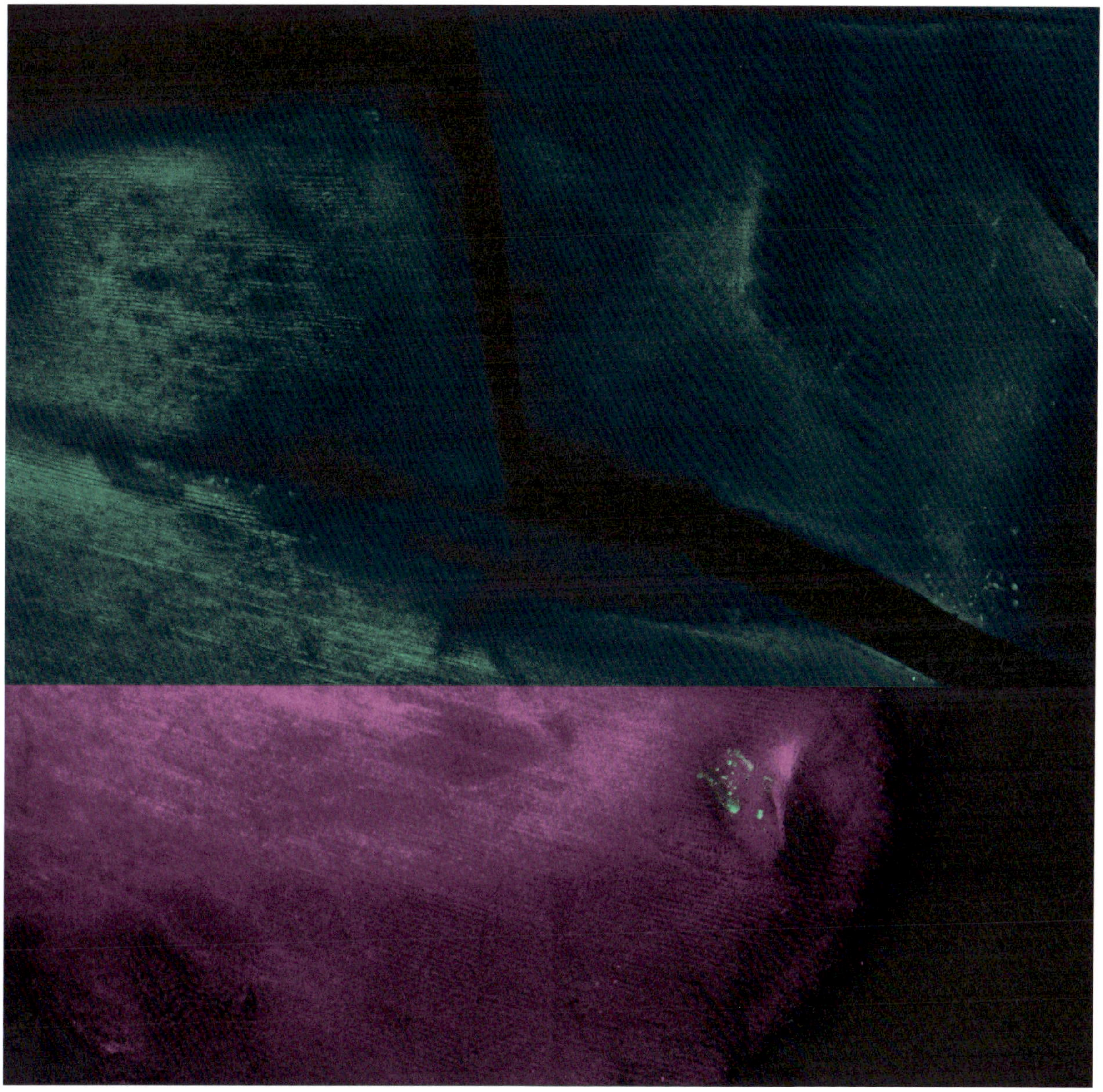

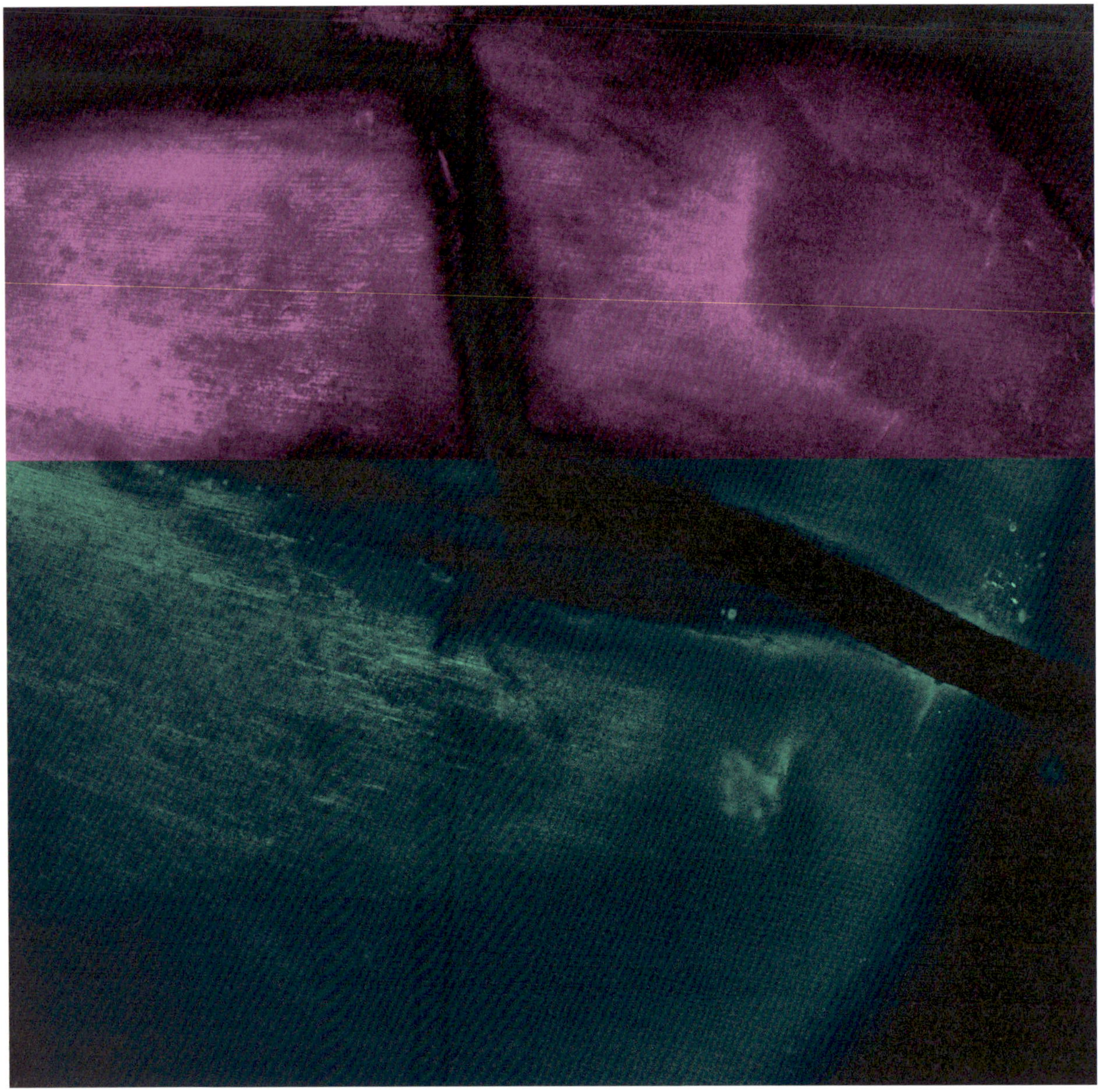

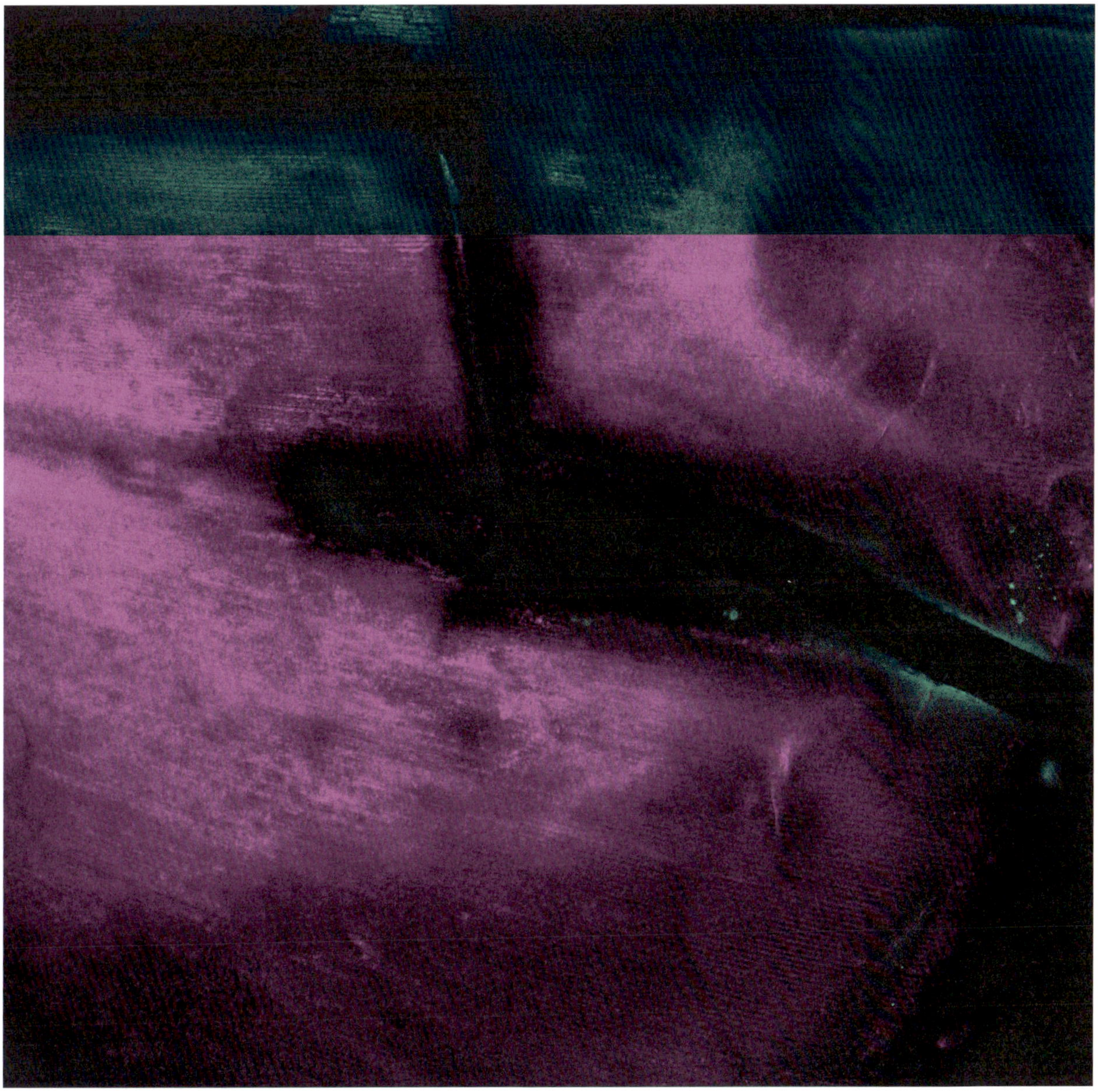

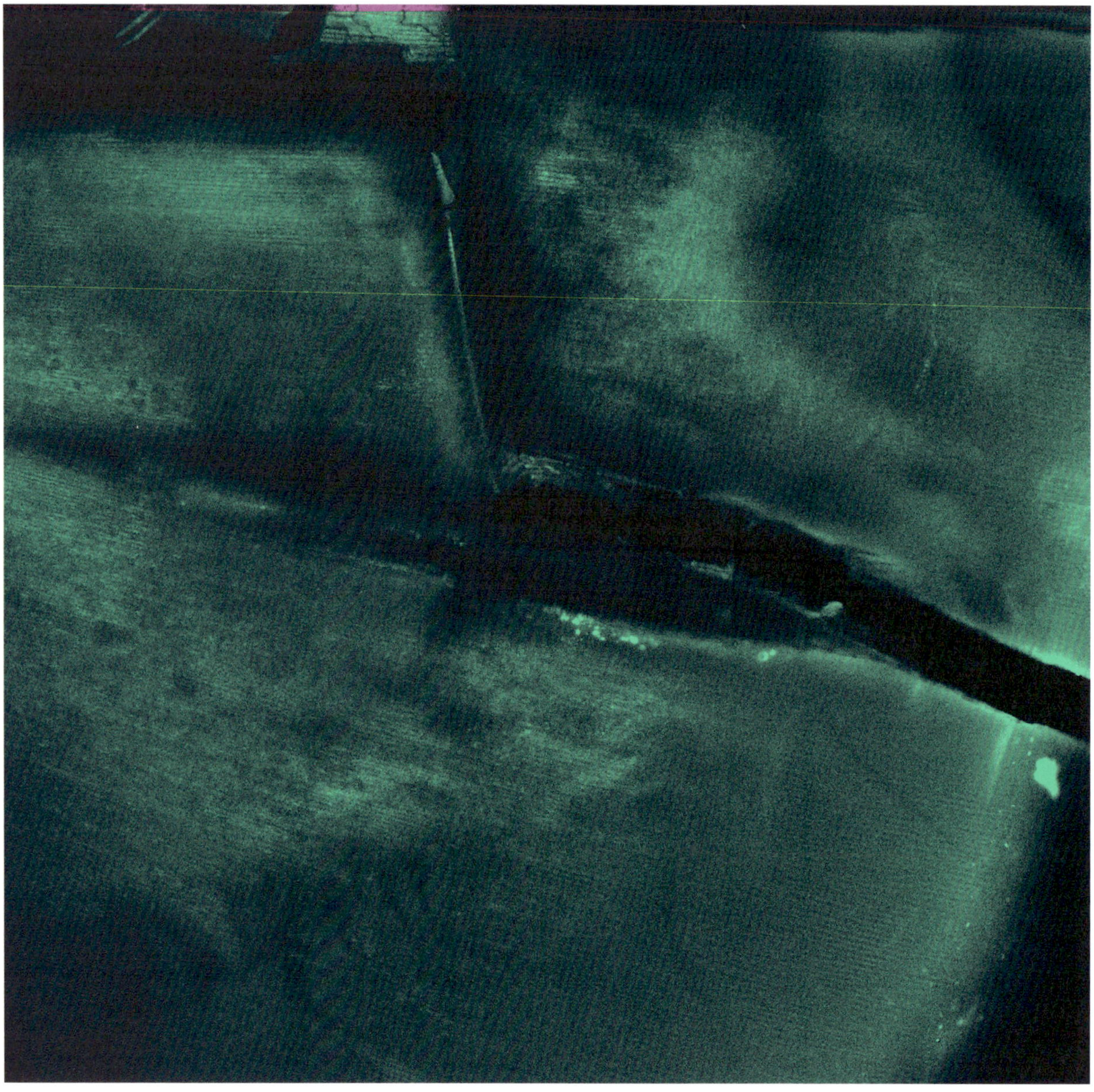

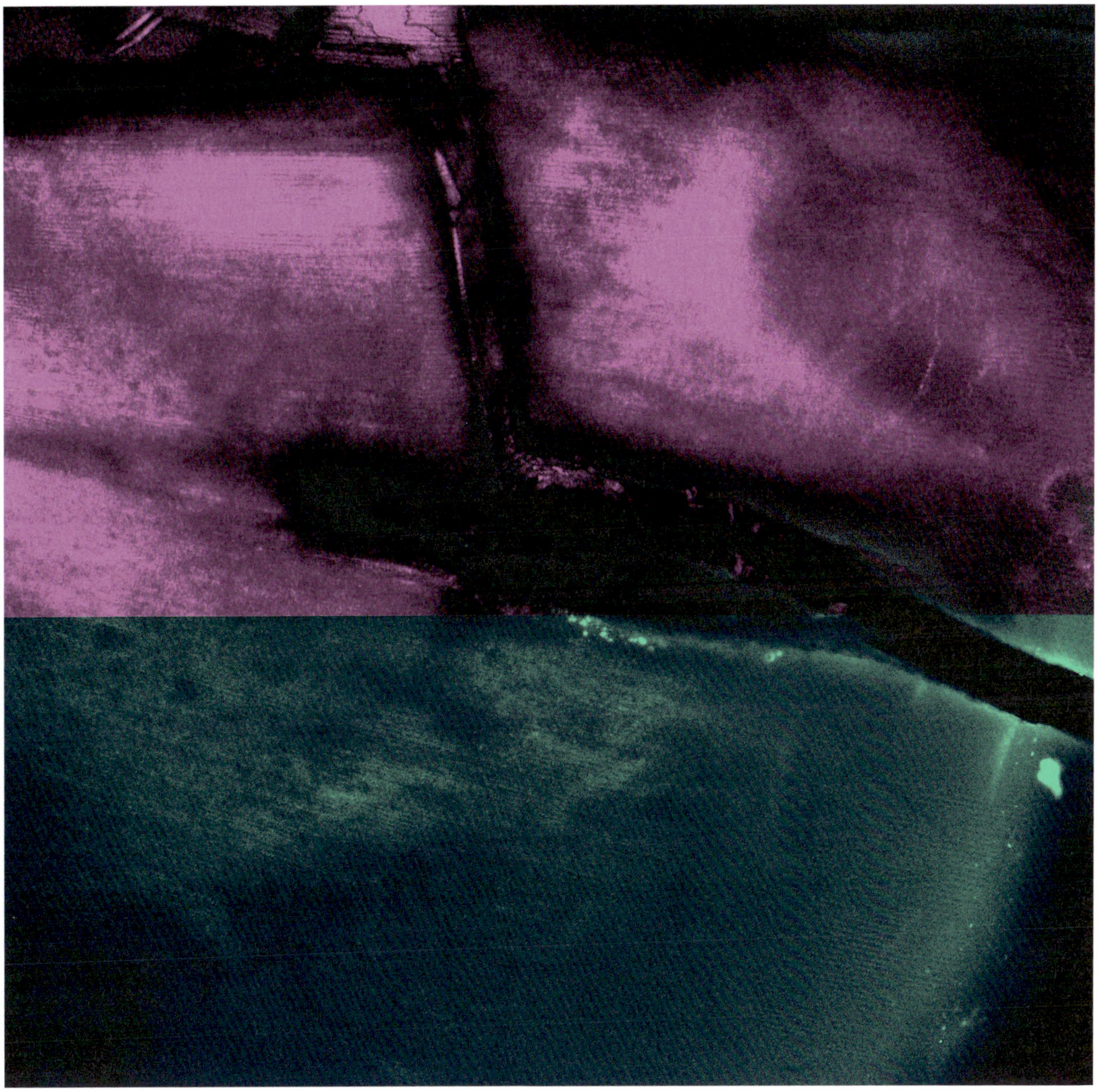

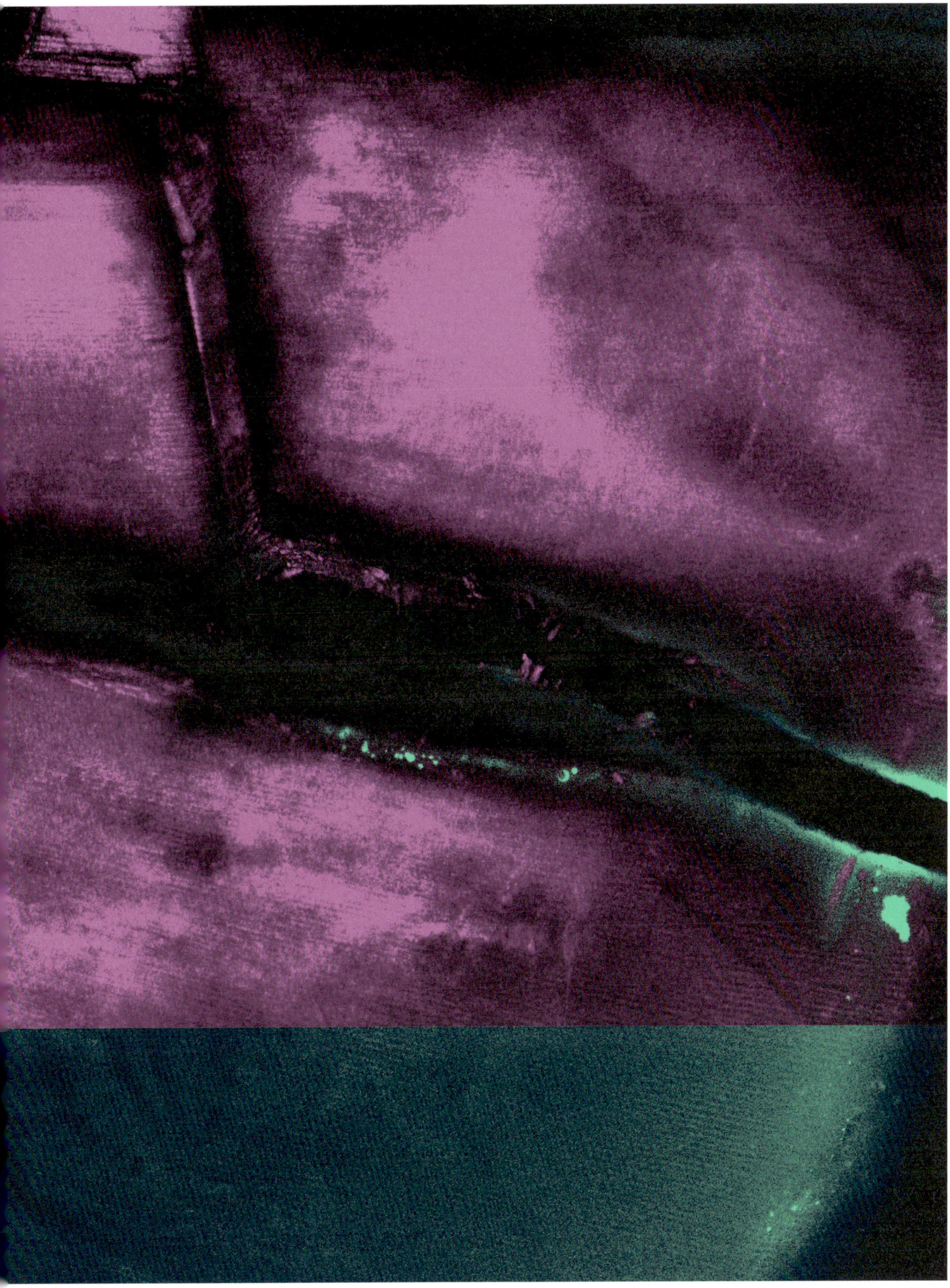

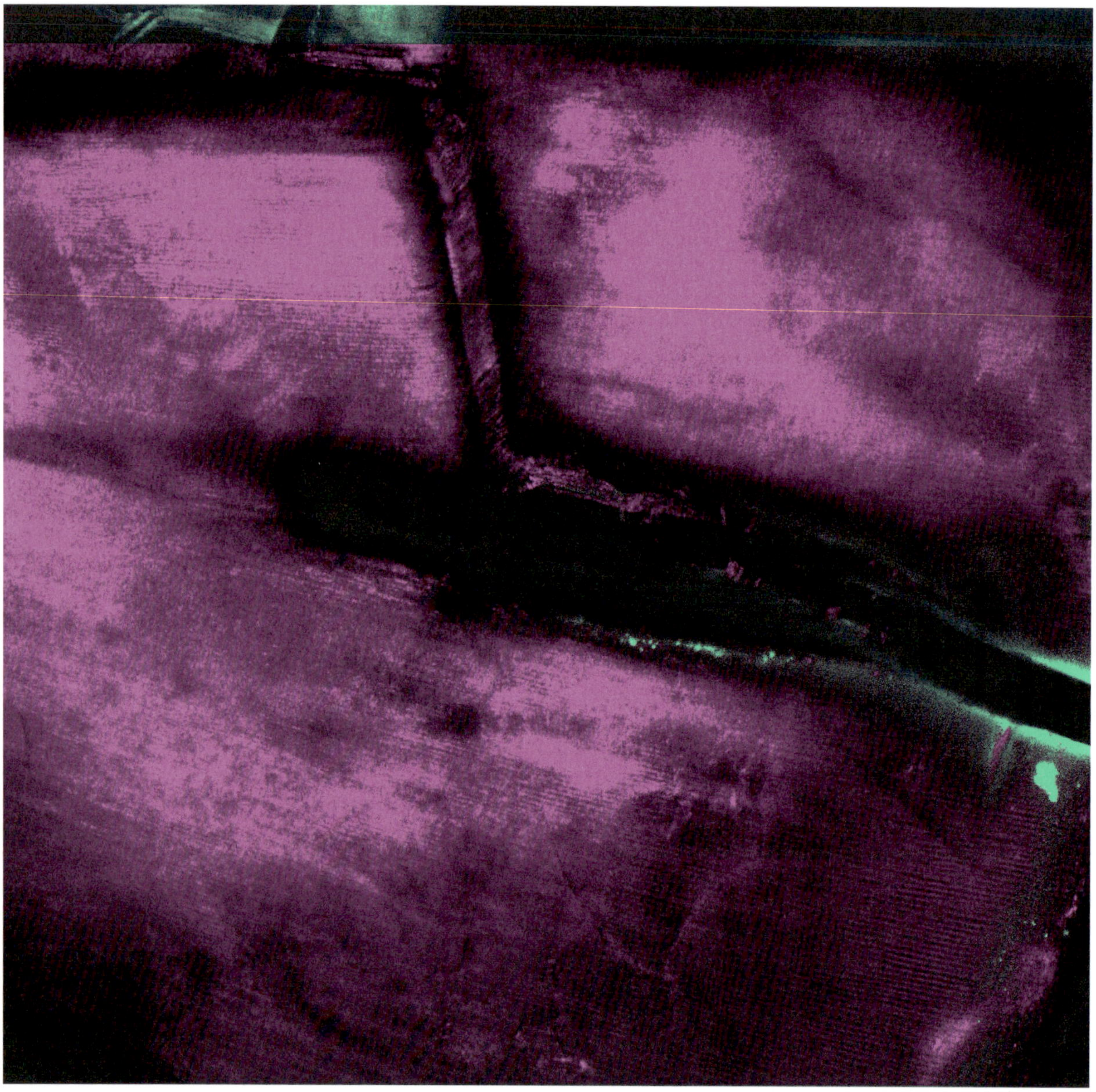

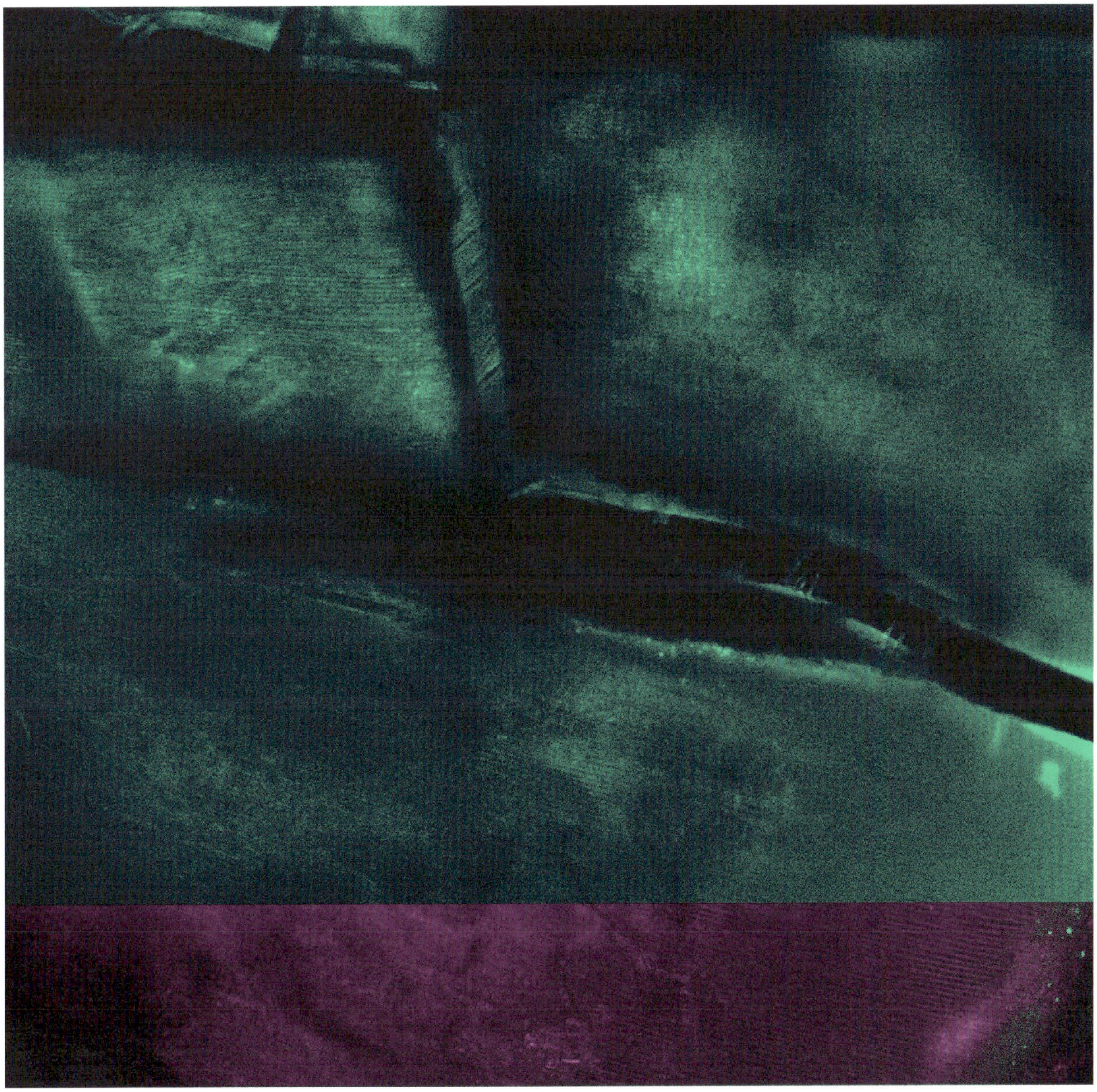

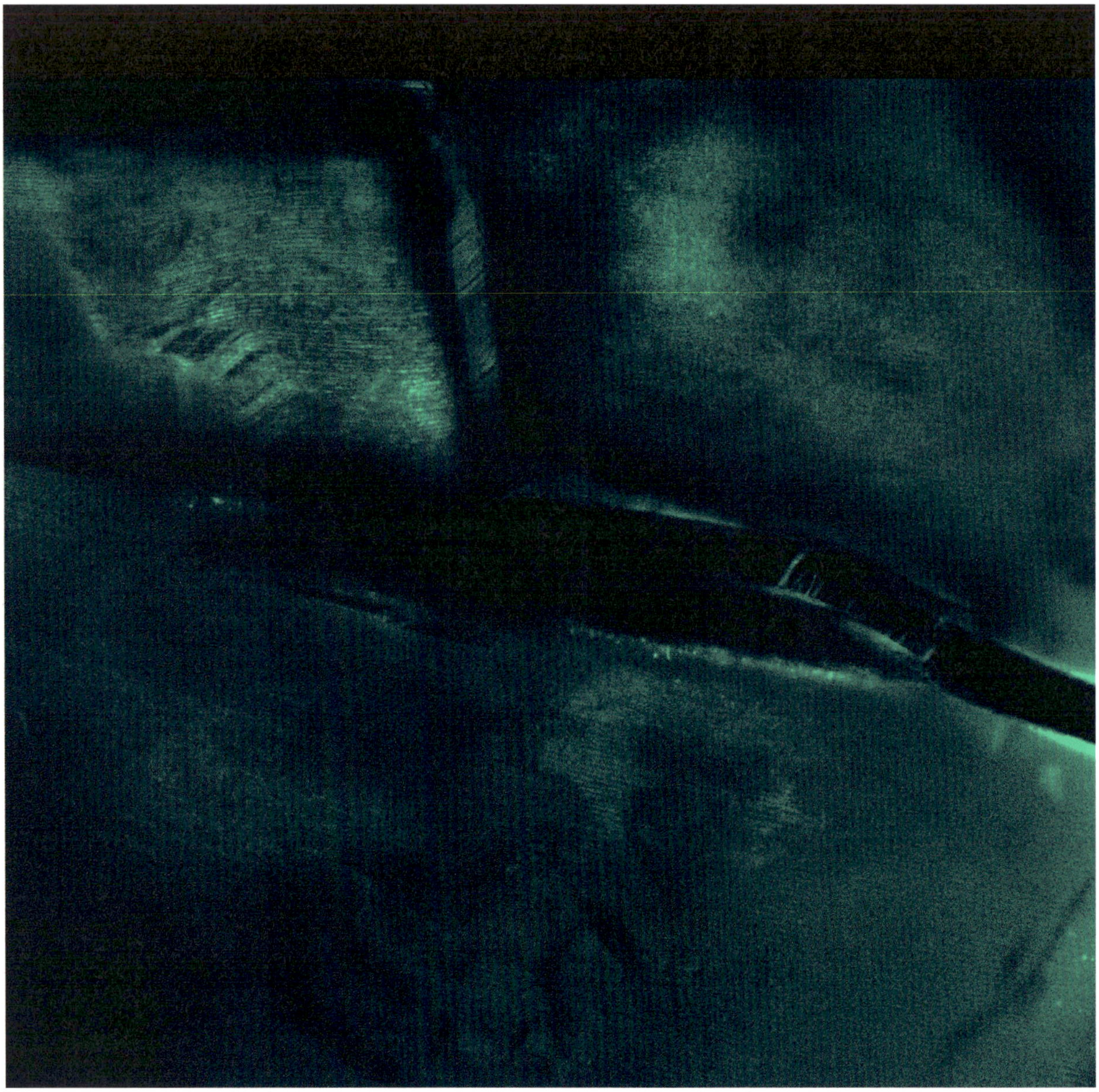

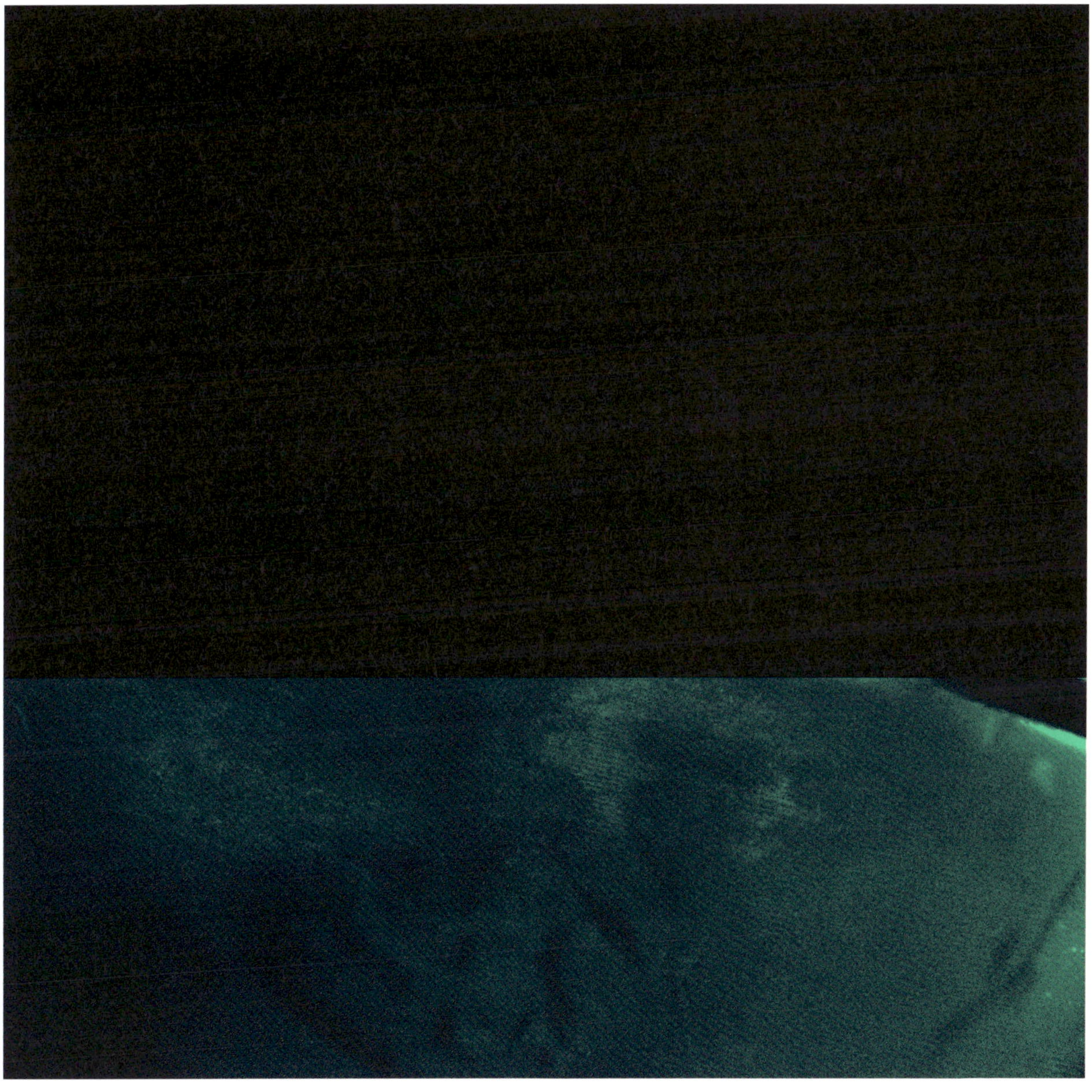

CHANNEL 2

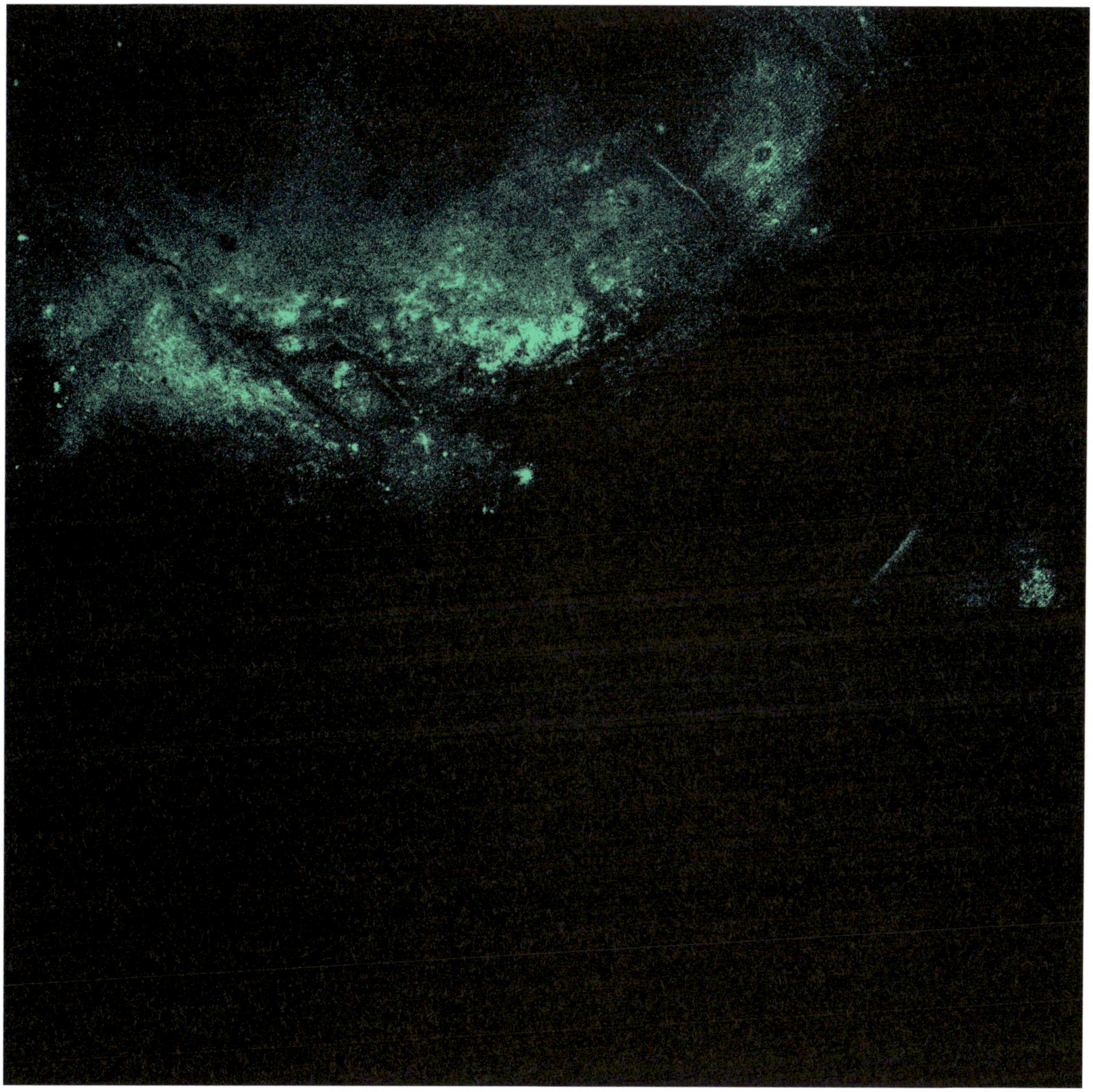

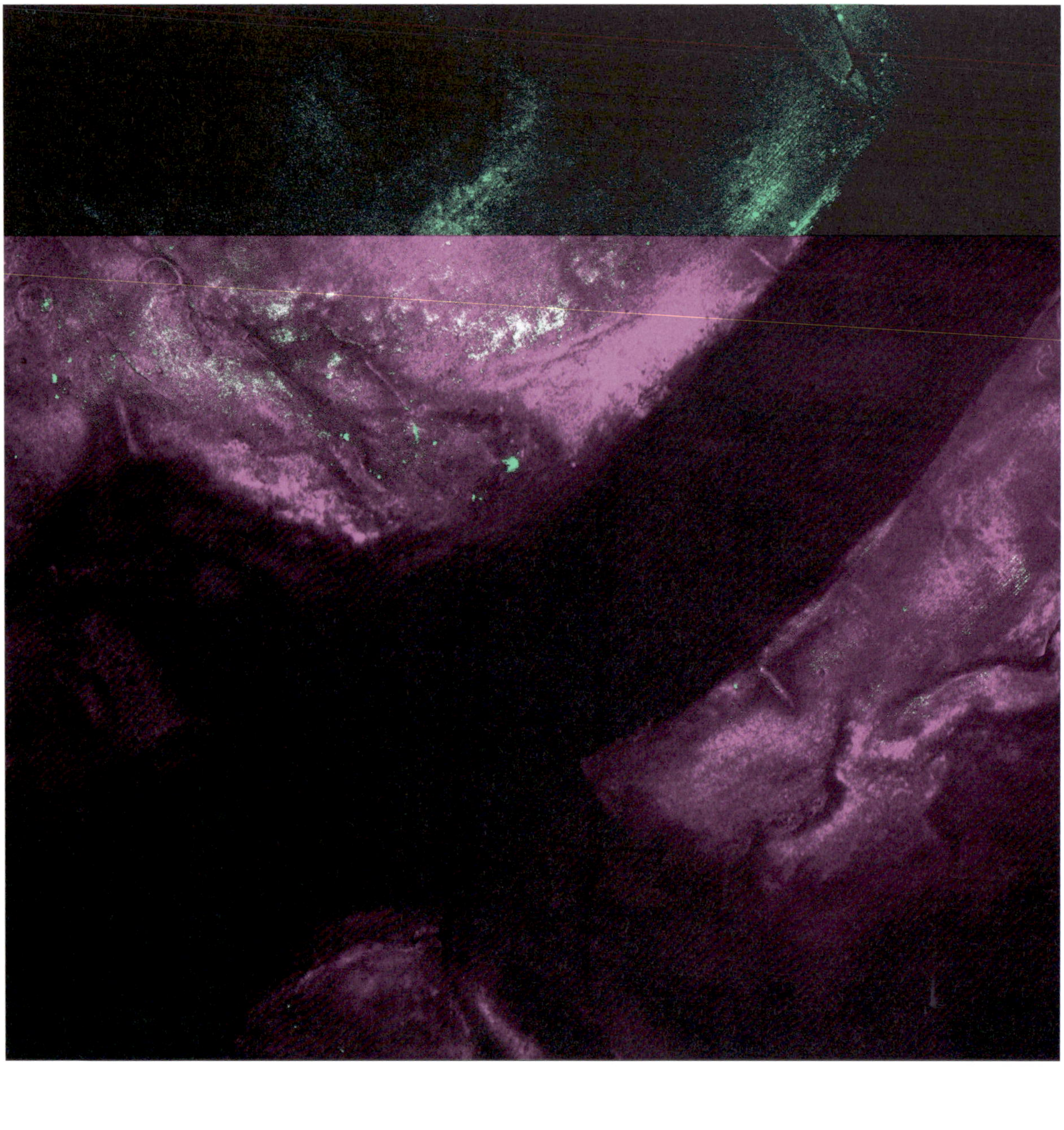

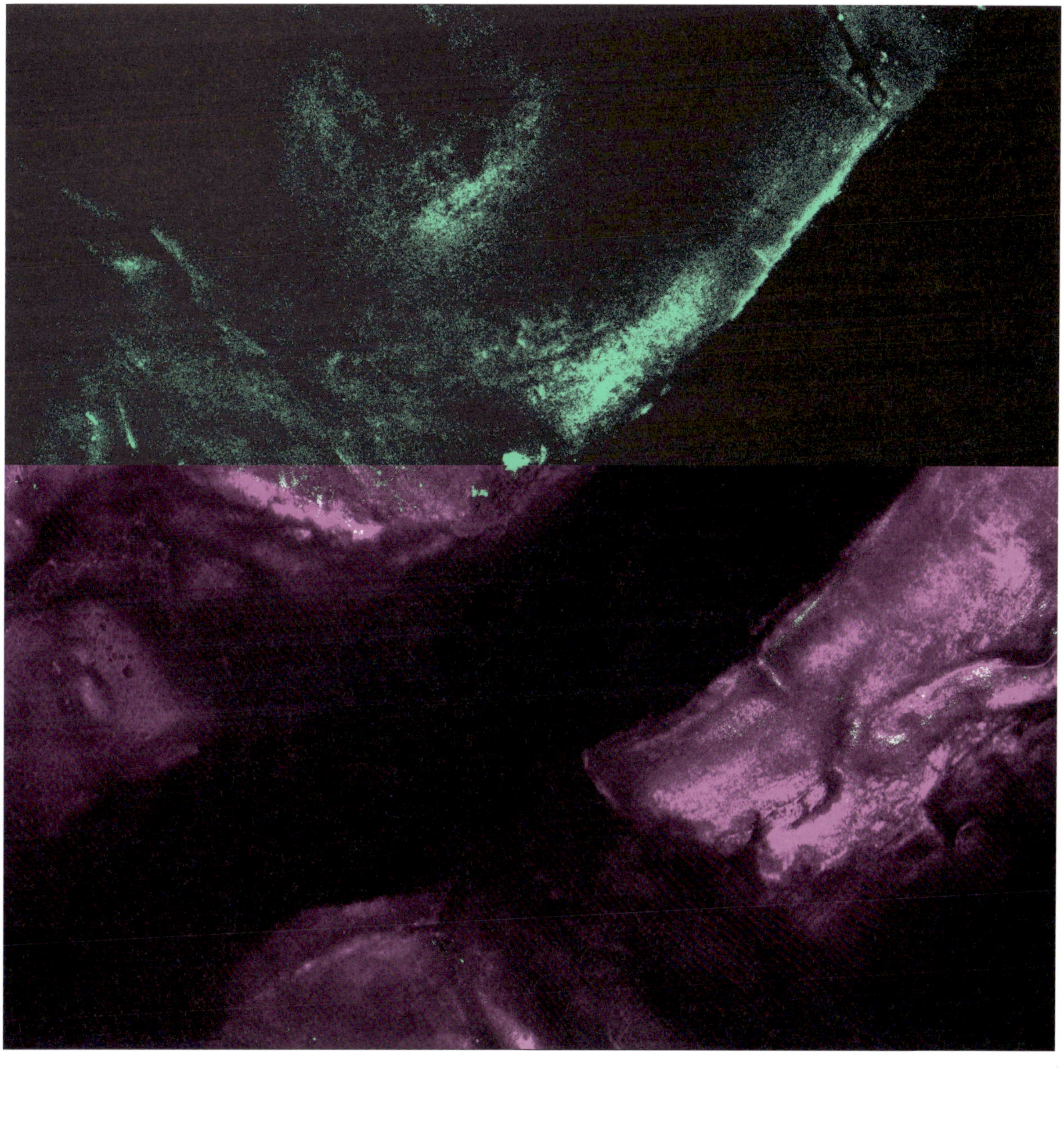

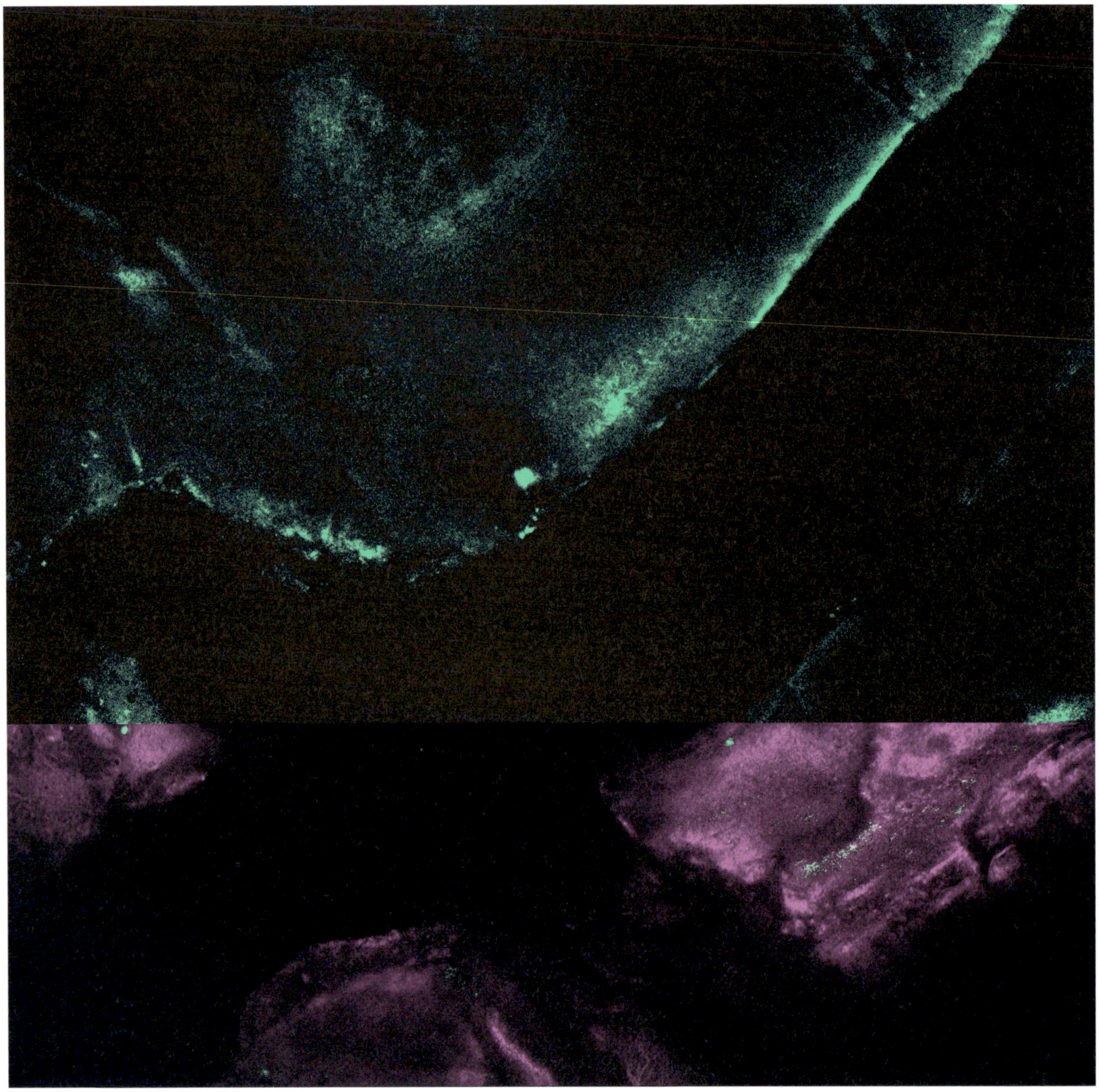

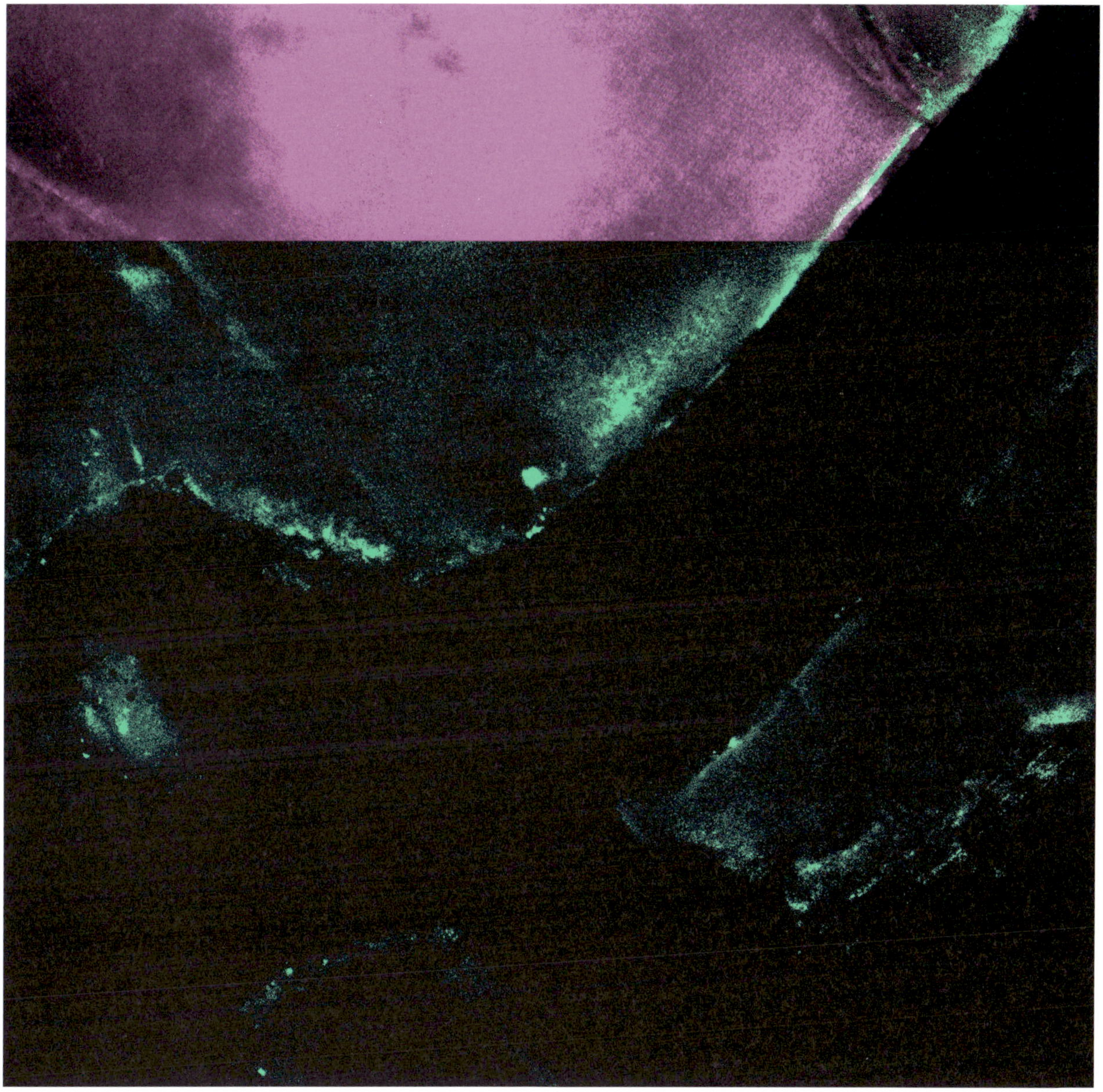

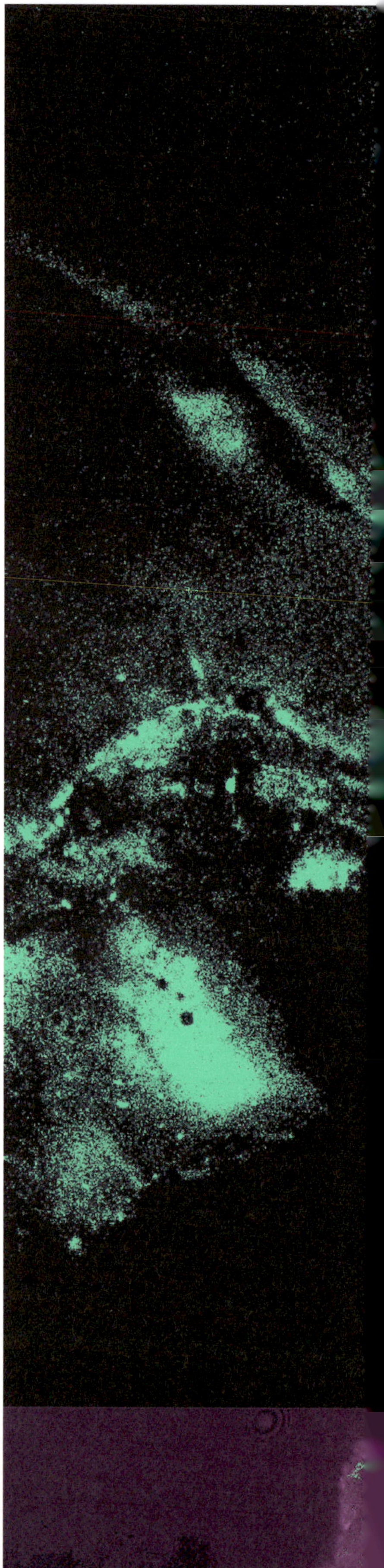

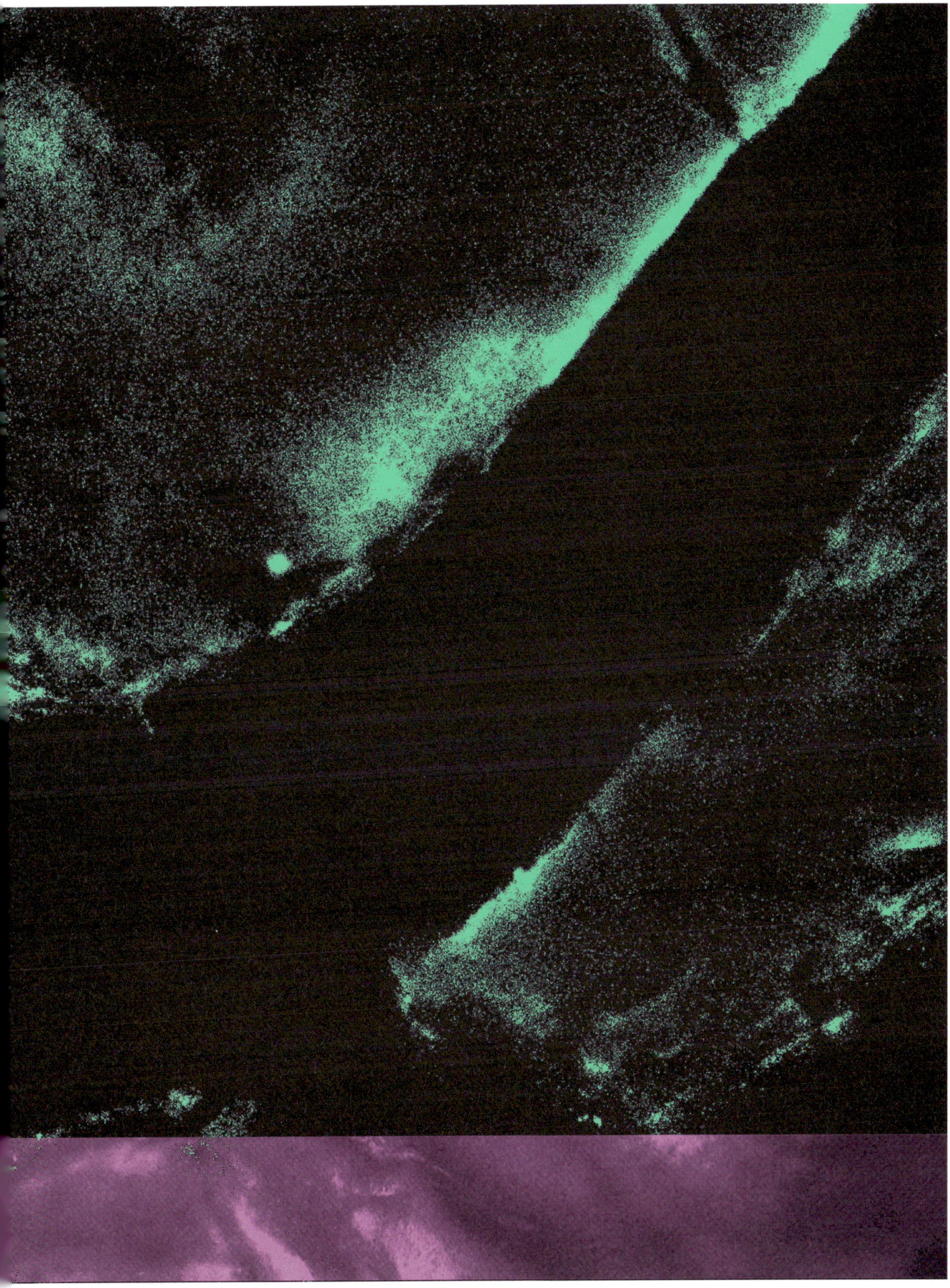

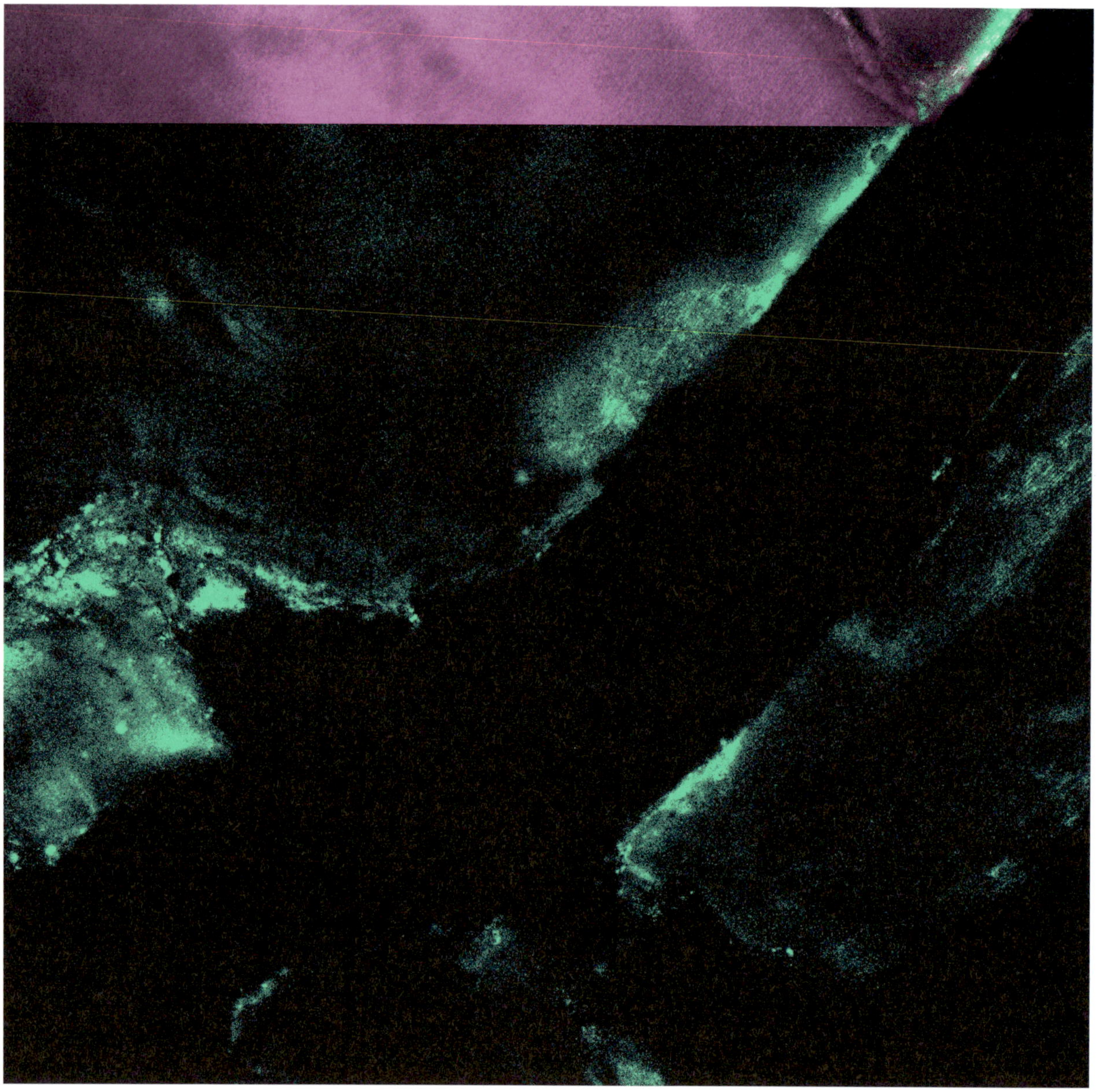

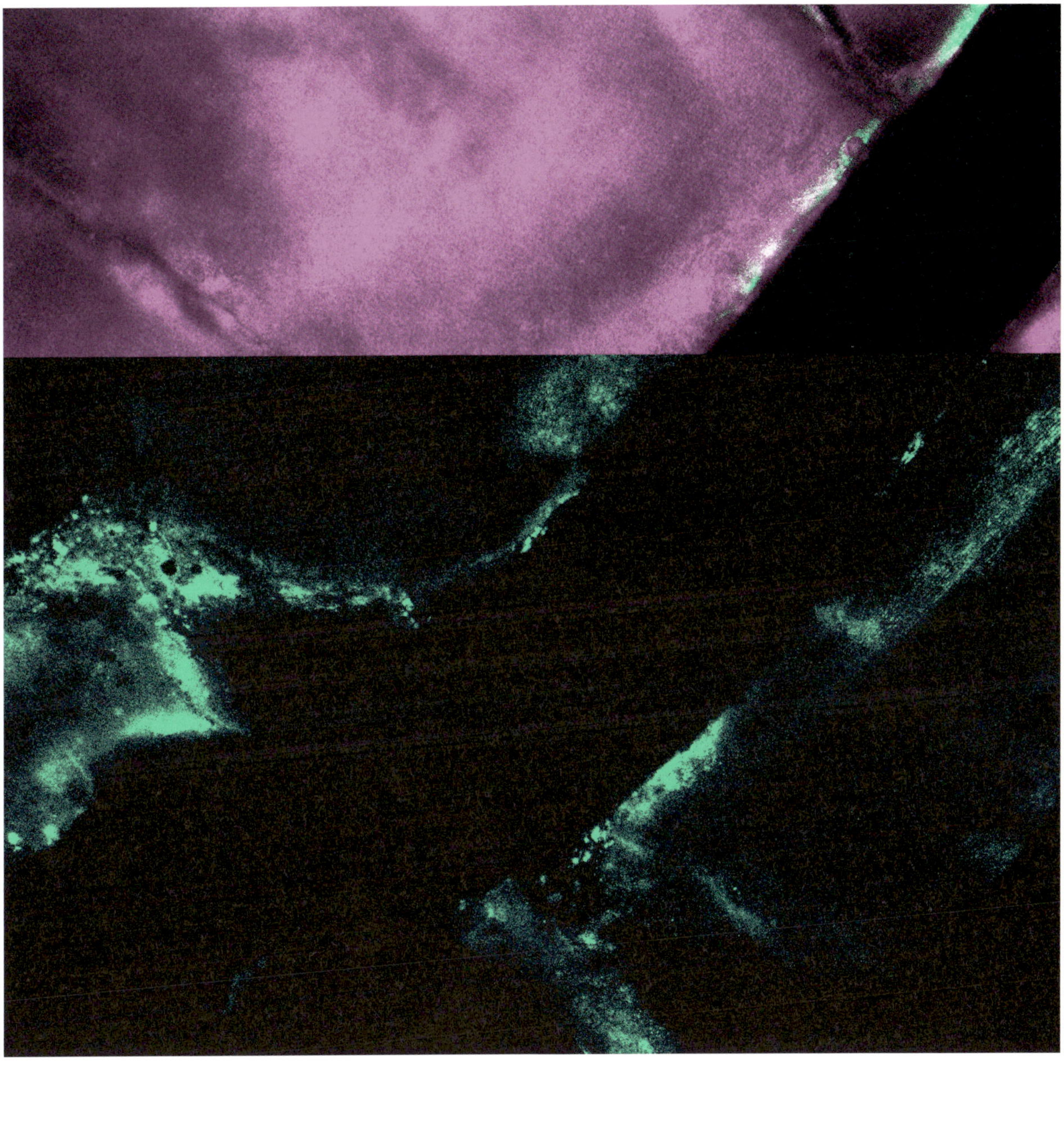

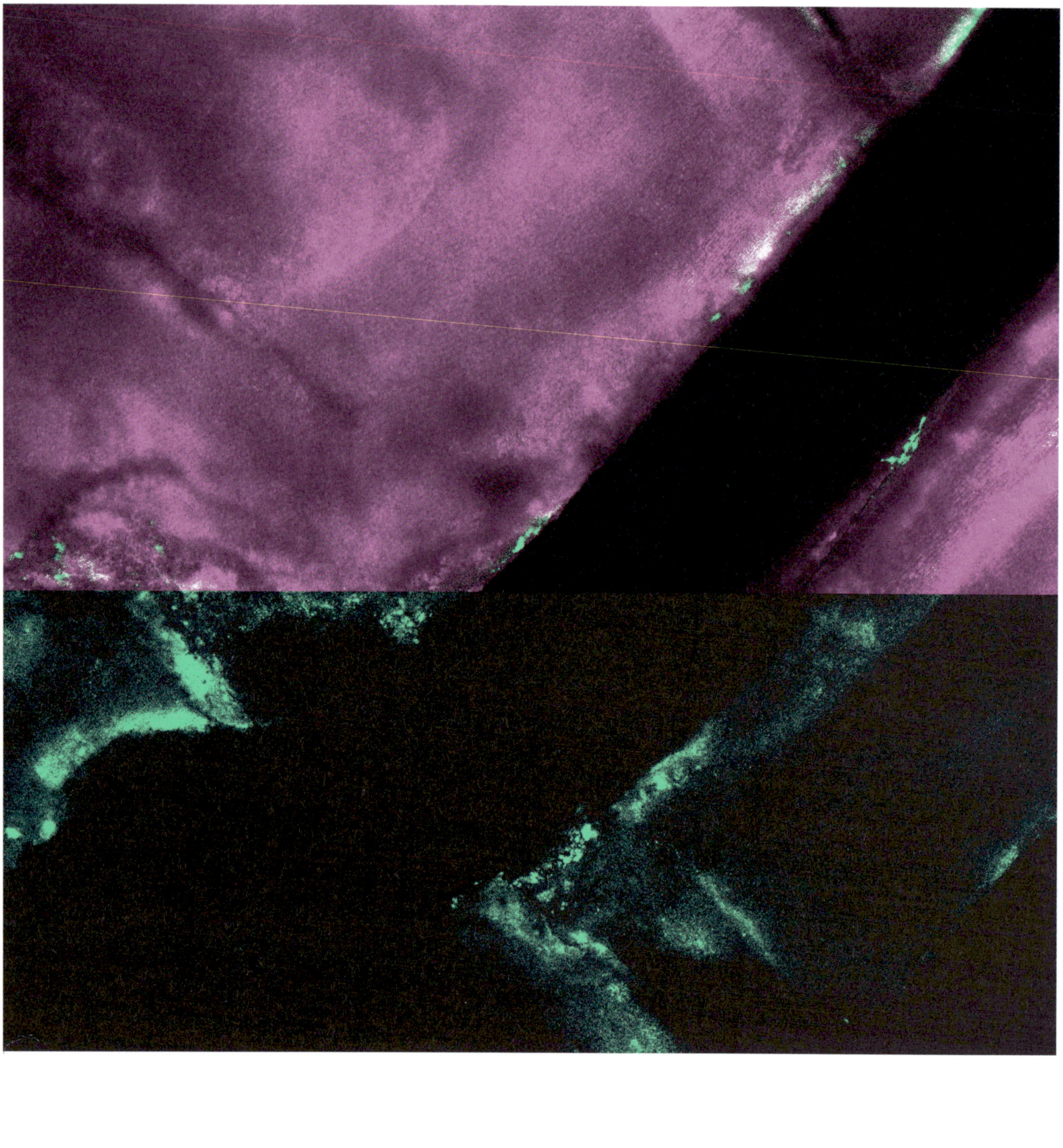

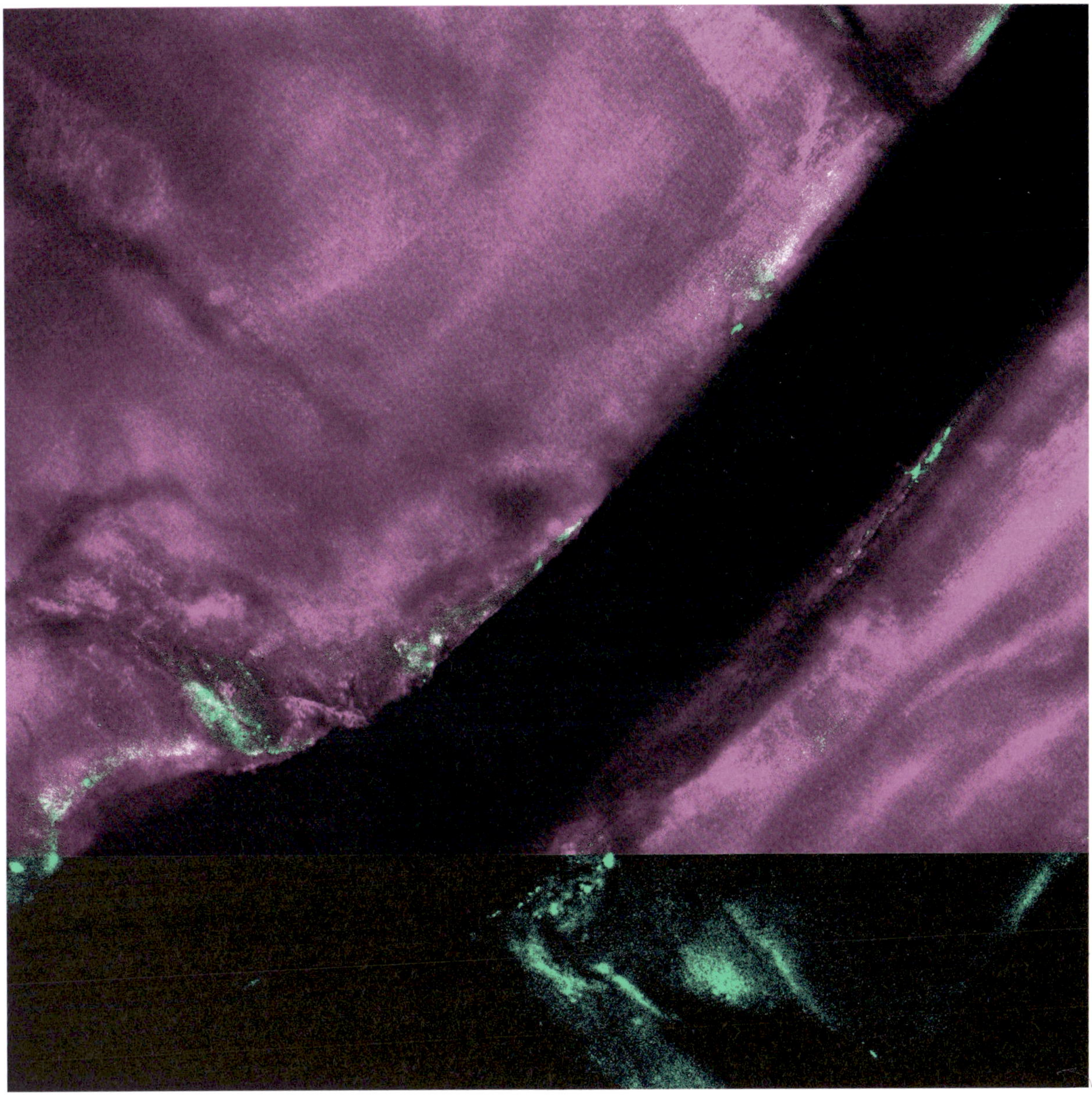

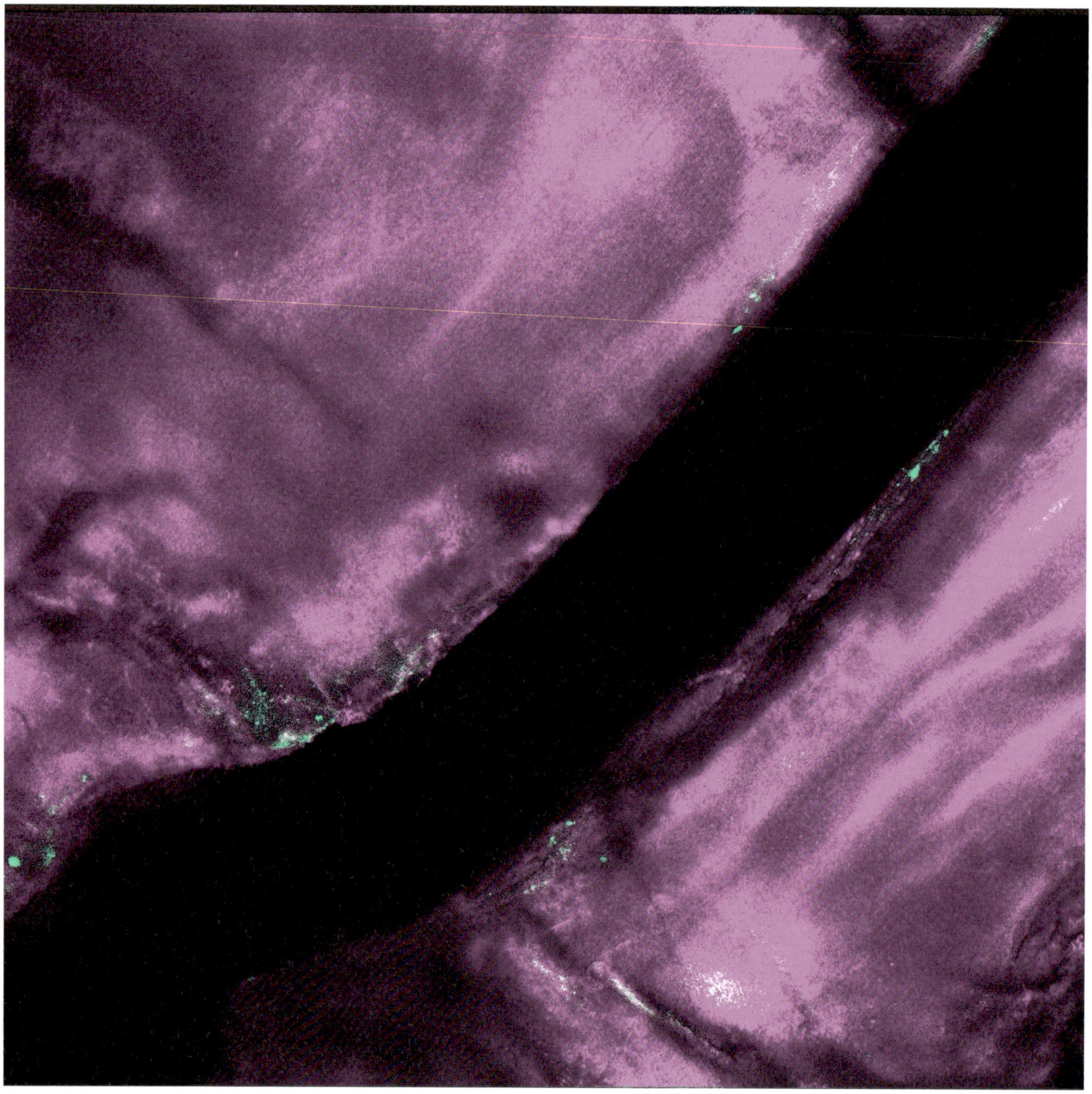

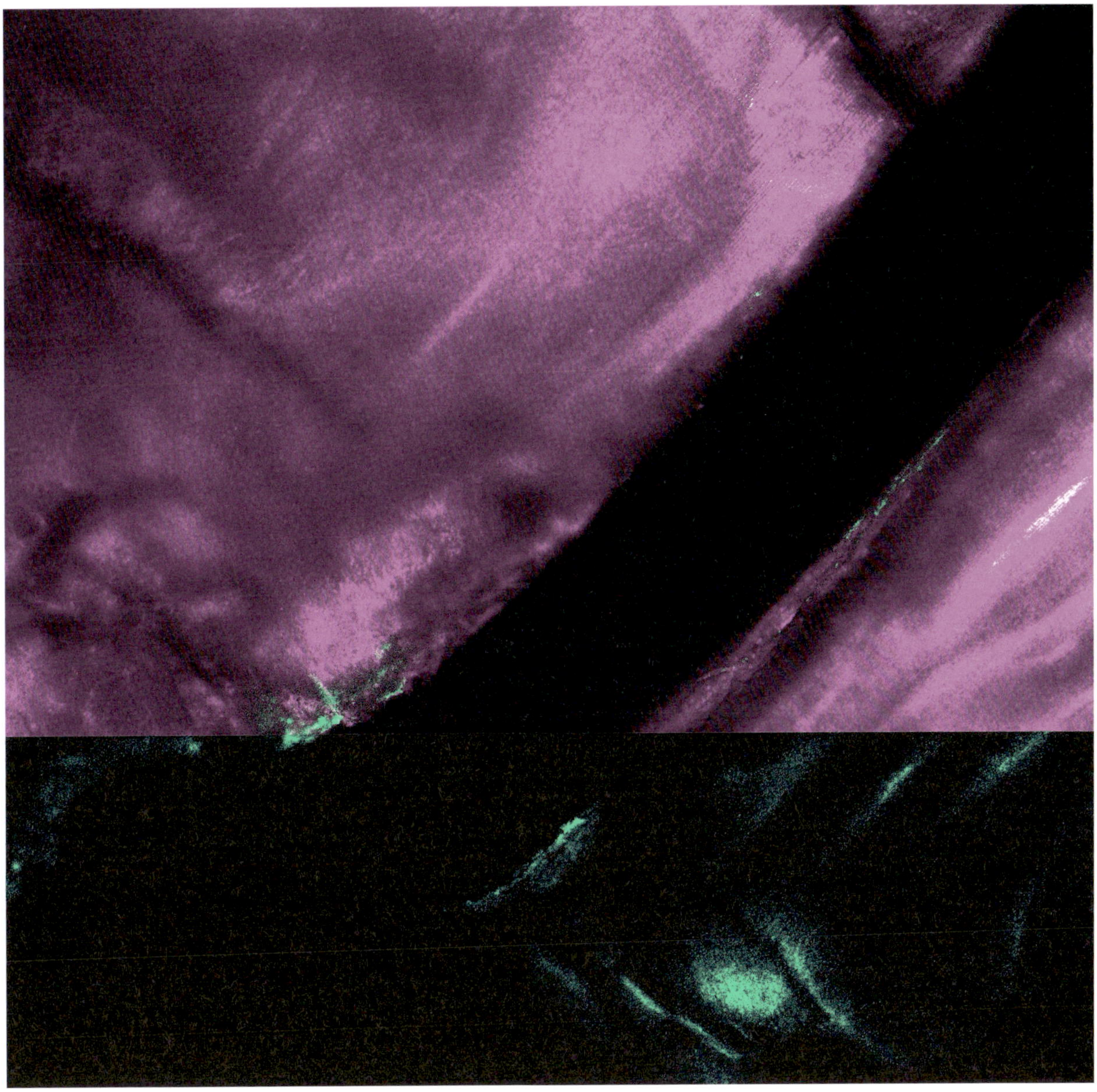

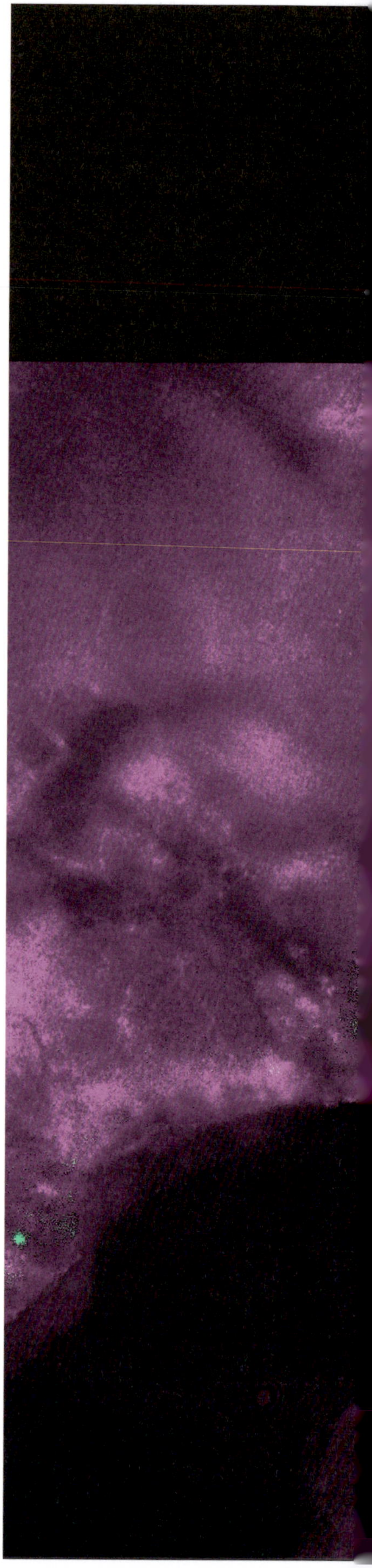

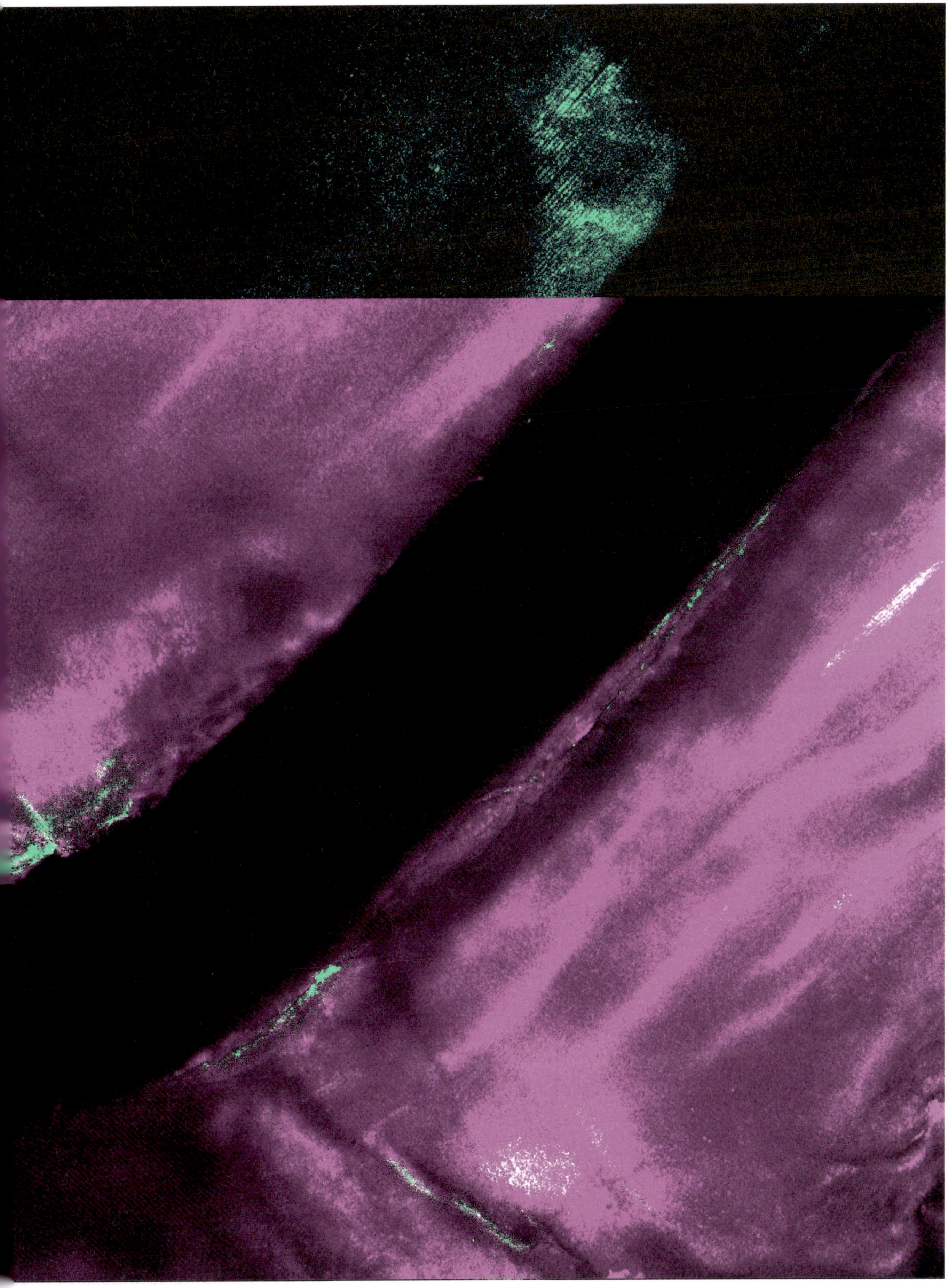

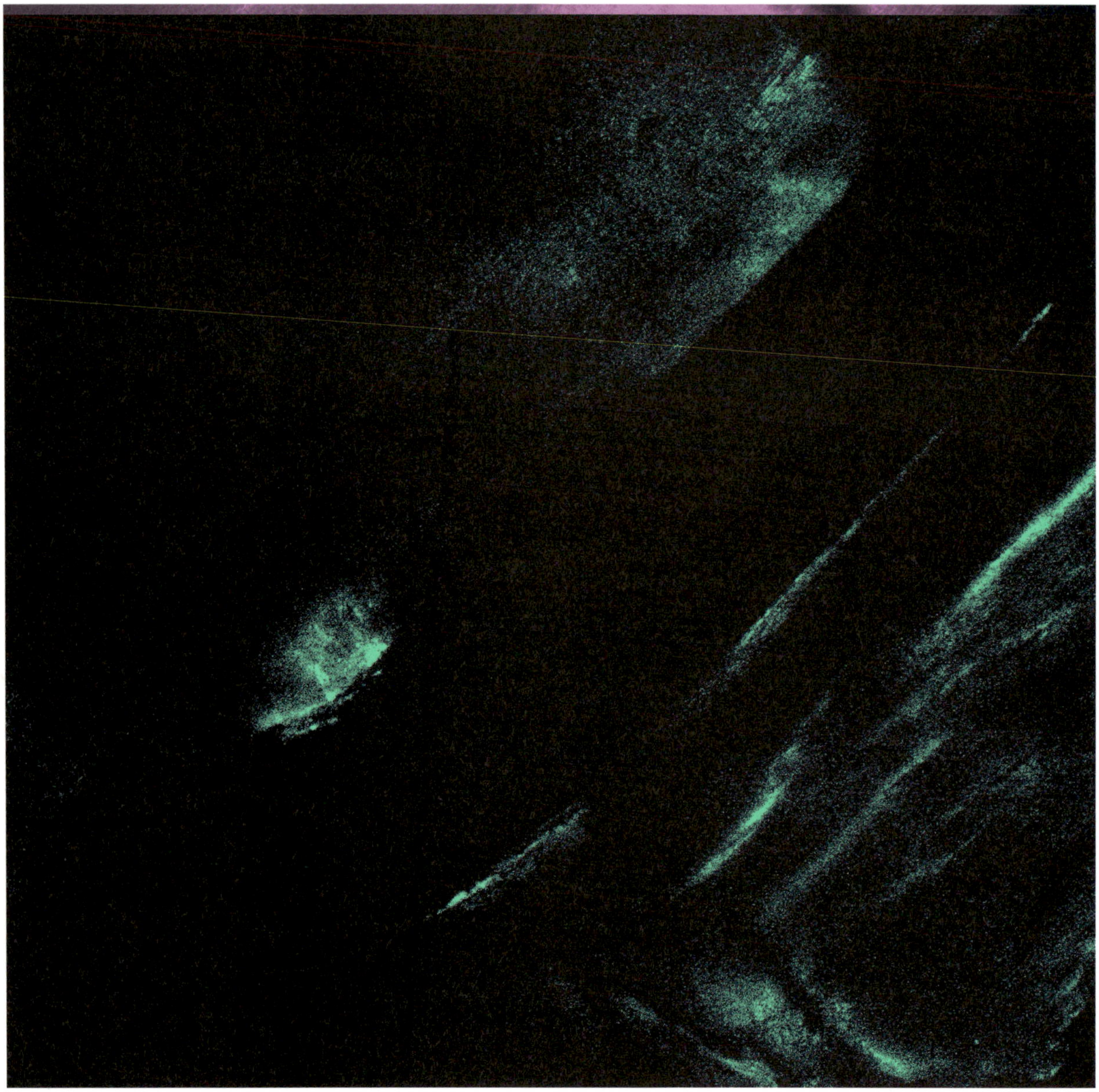

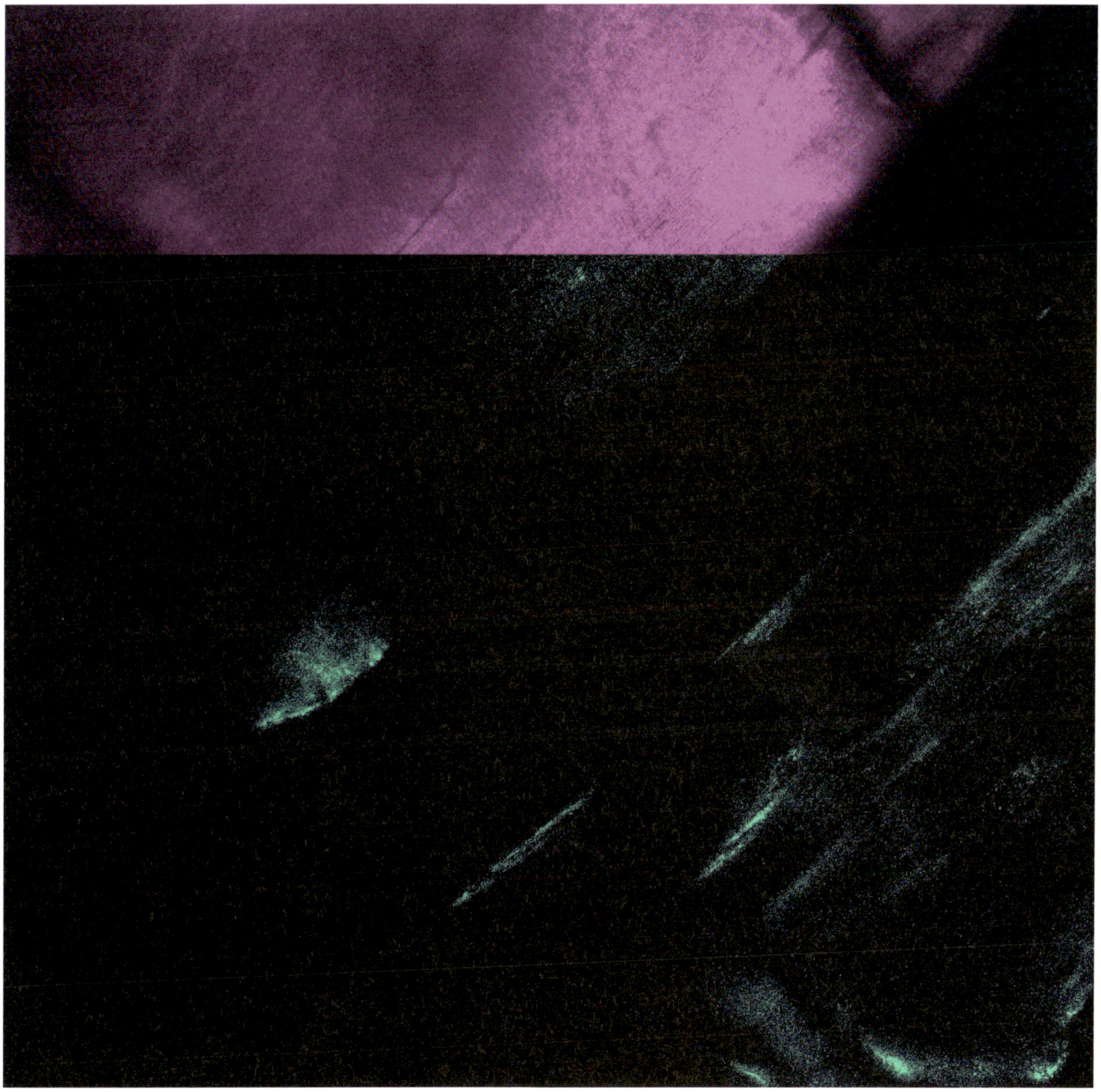

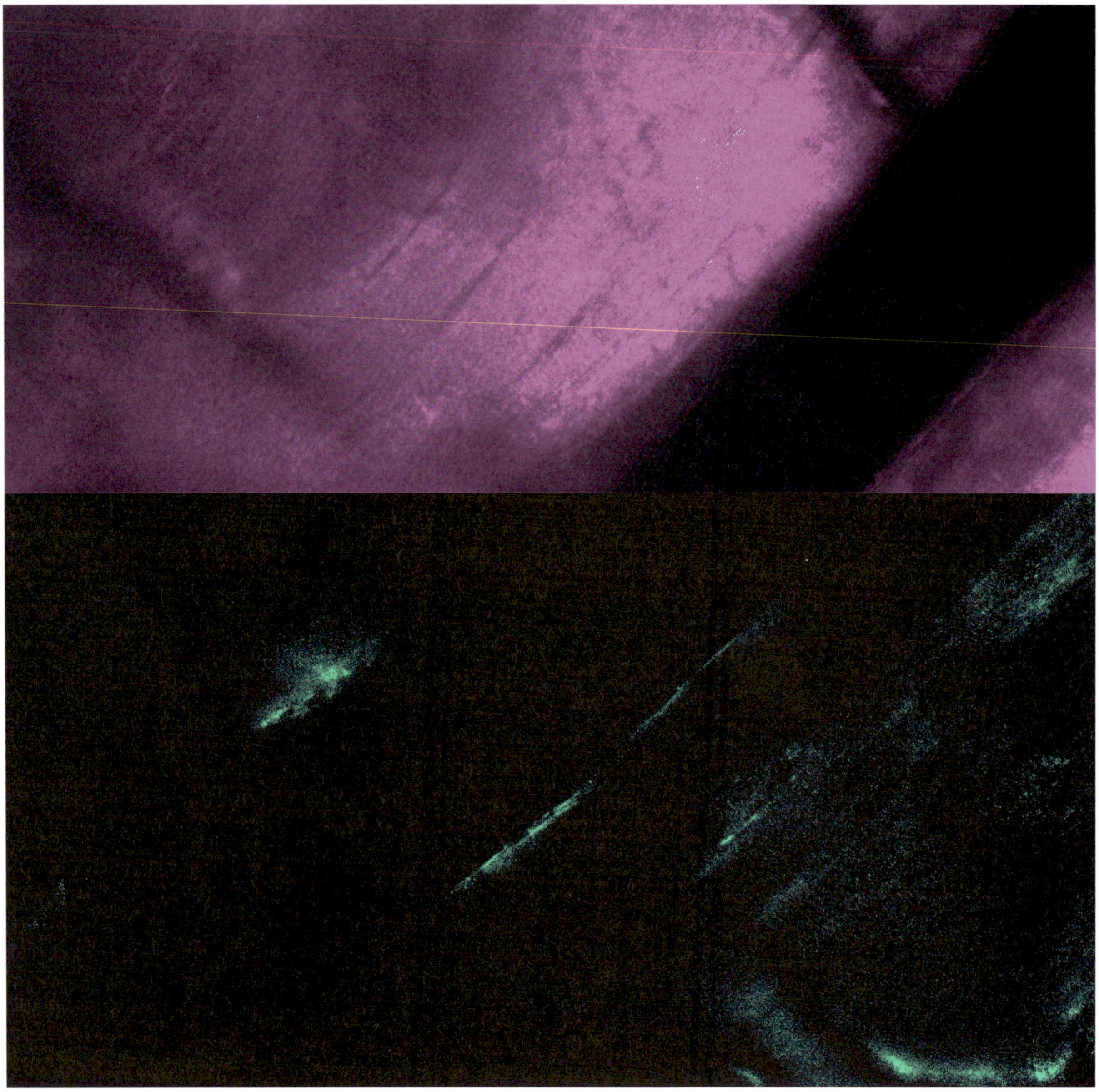

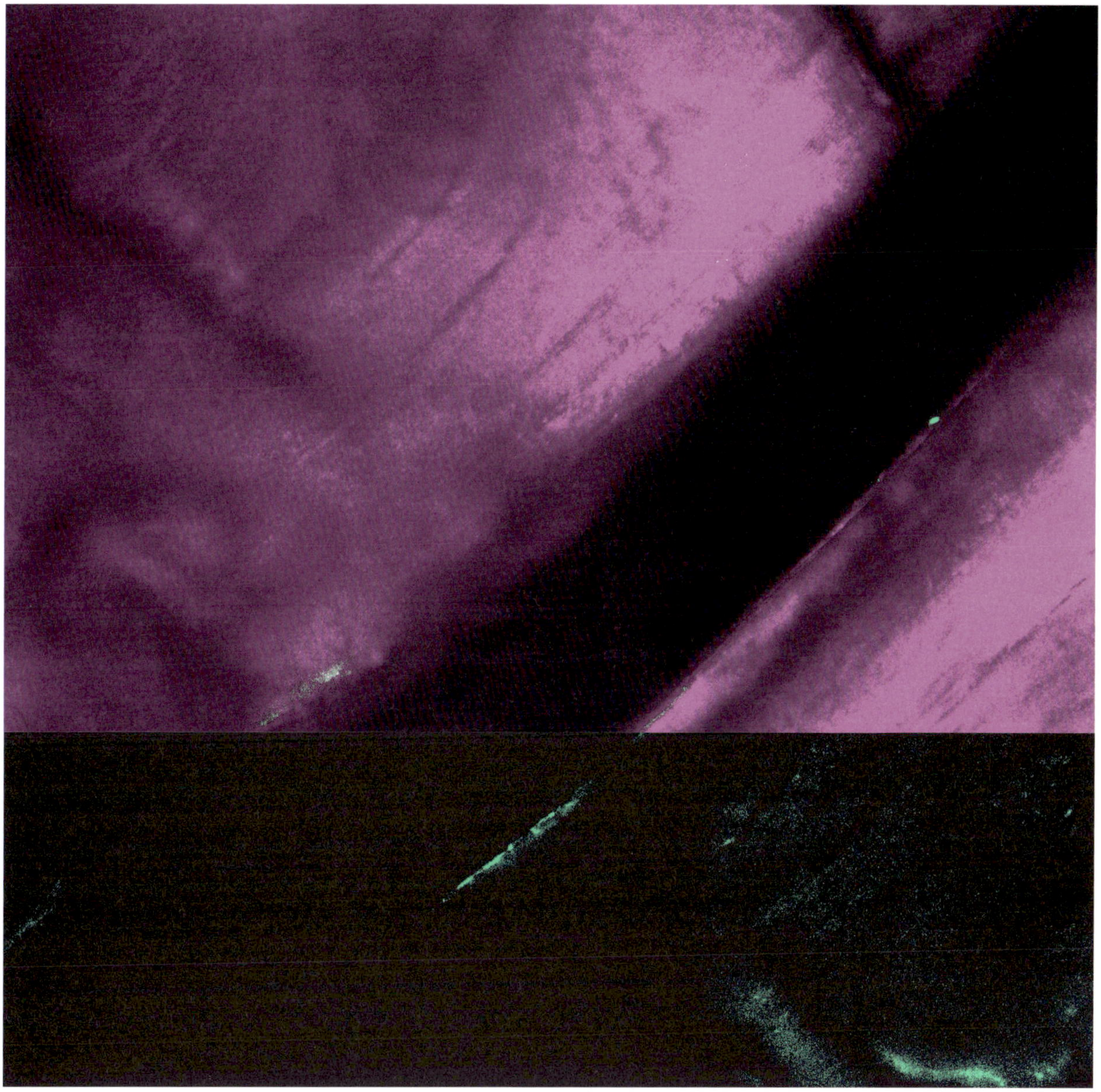

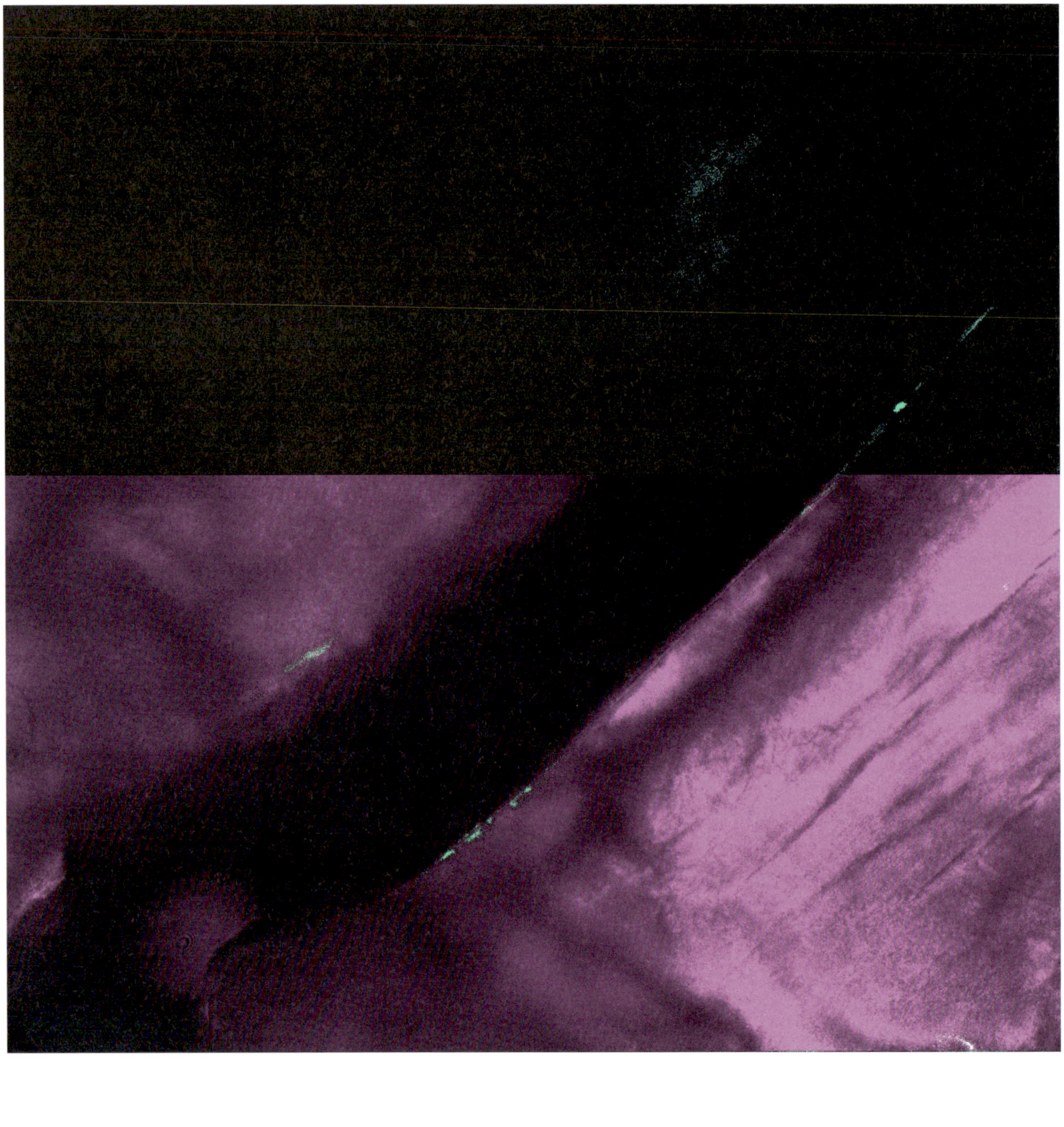

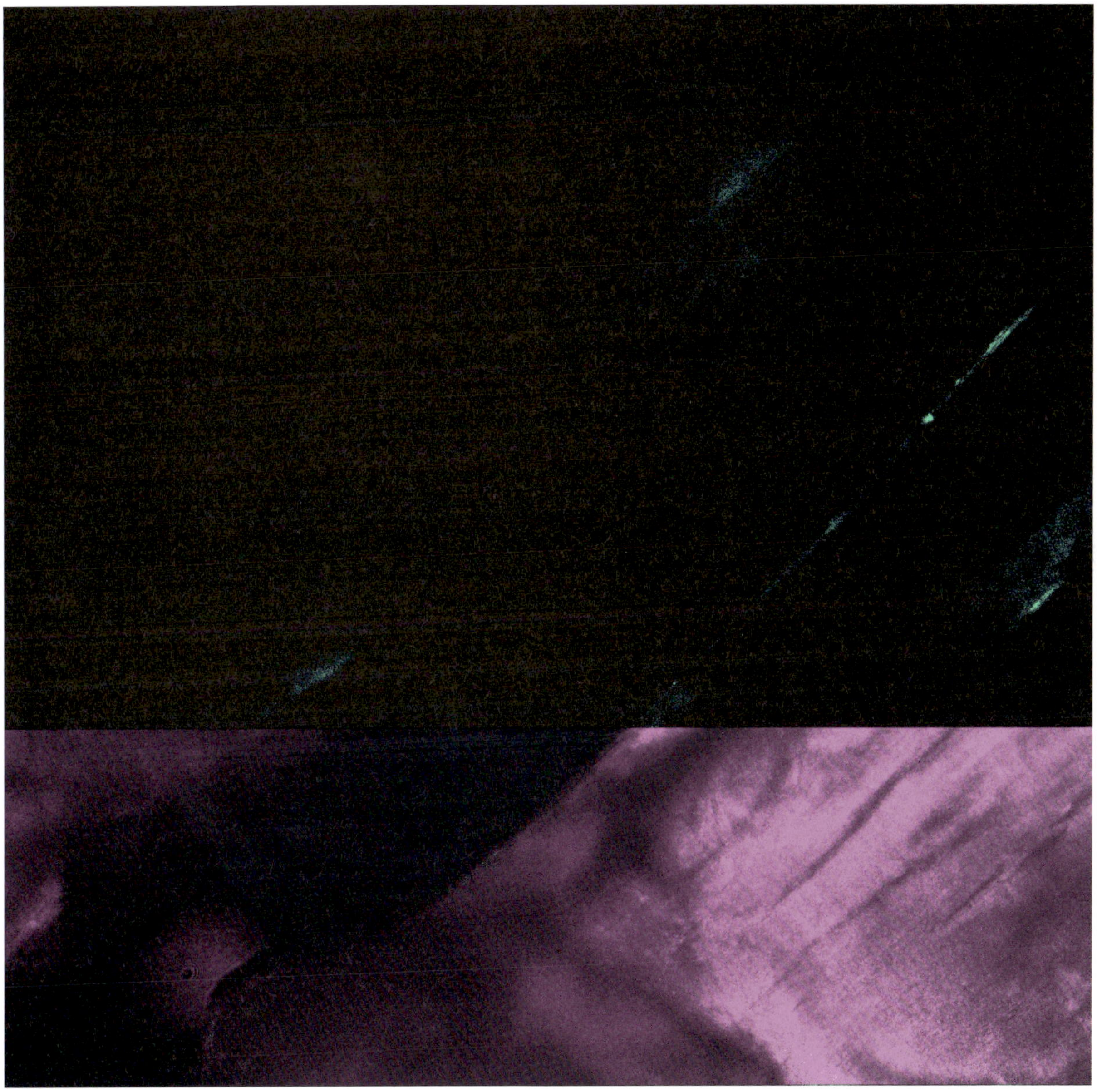

CHANNEL 3

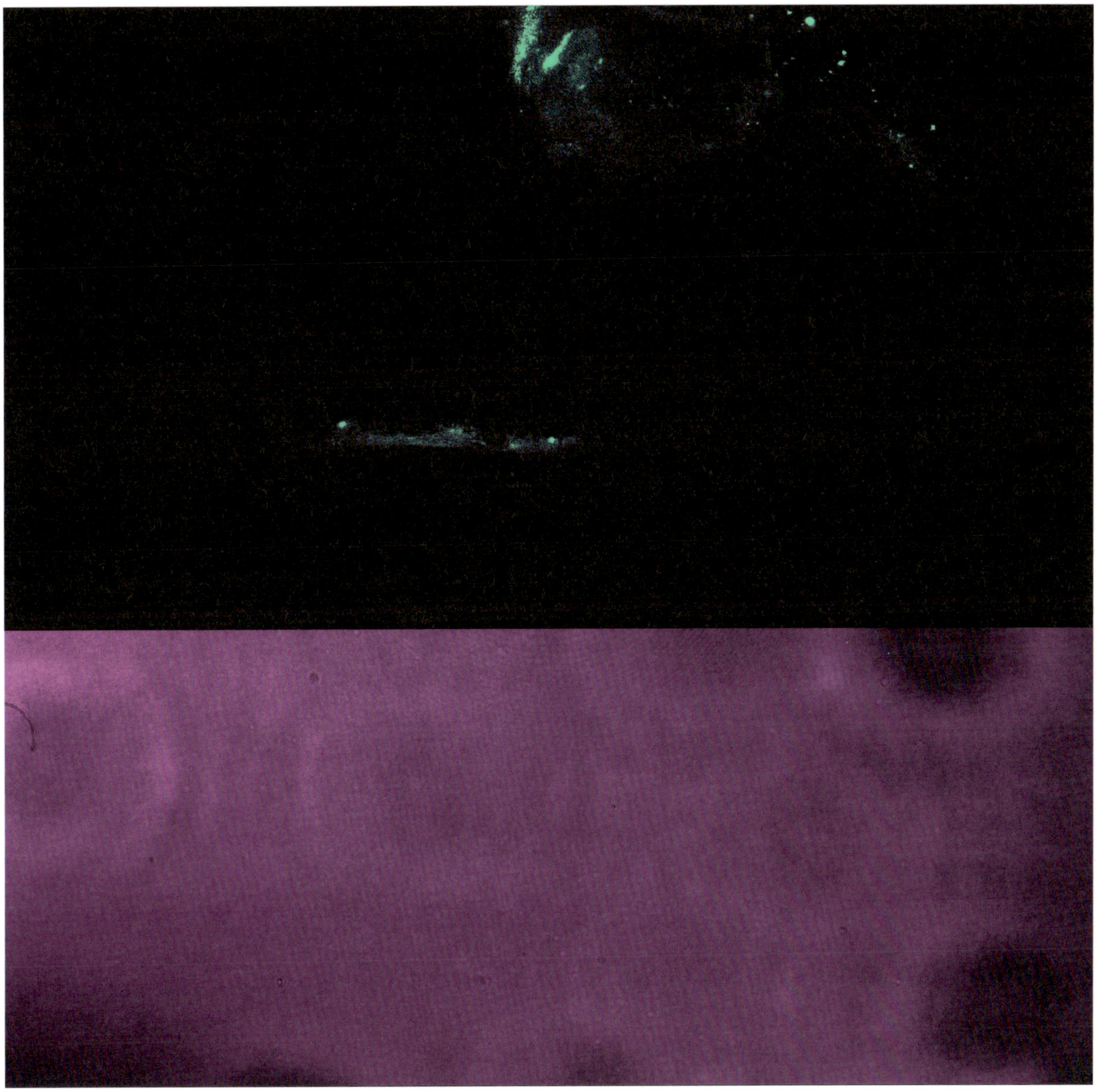

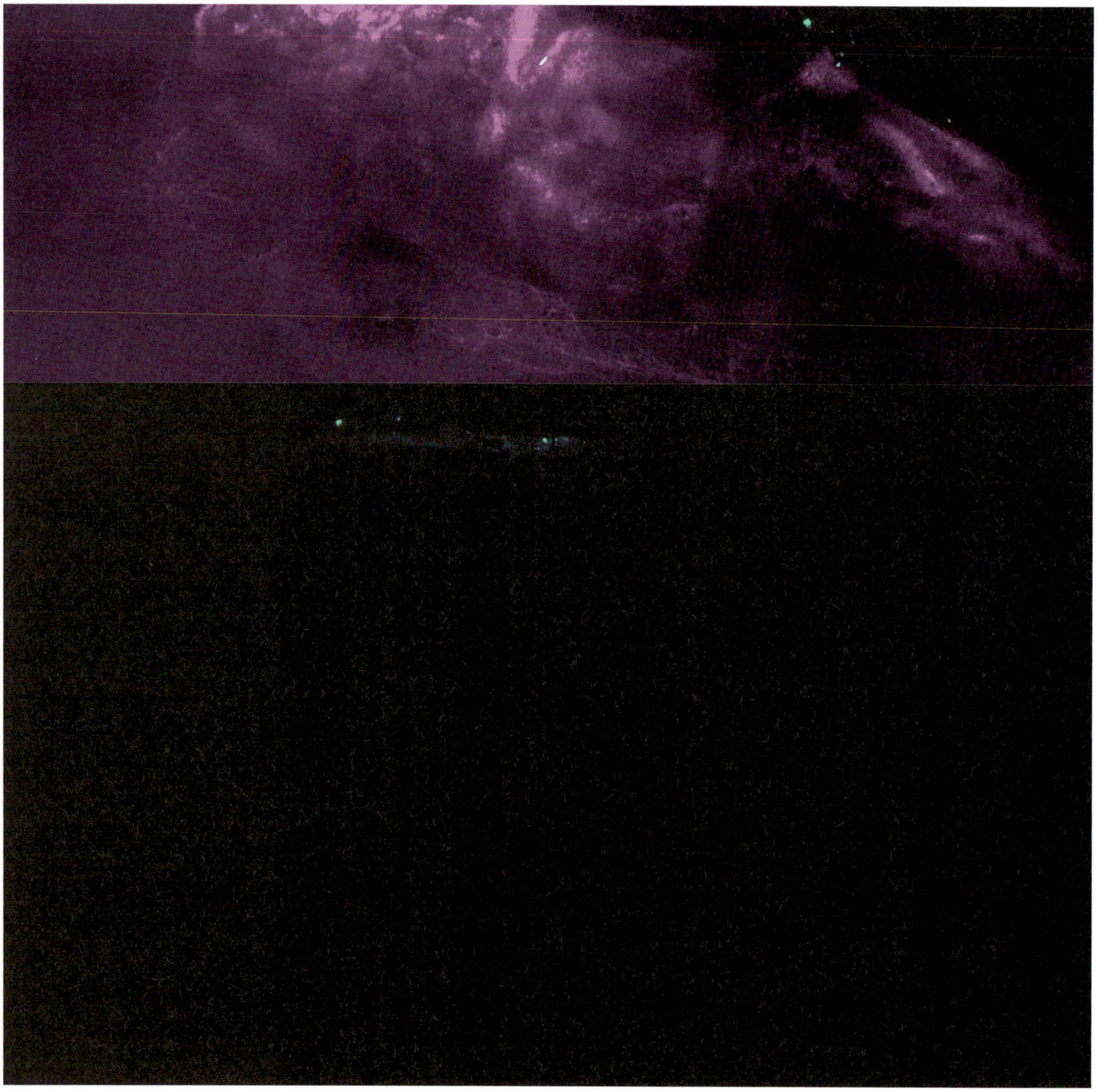

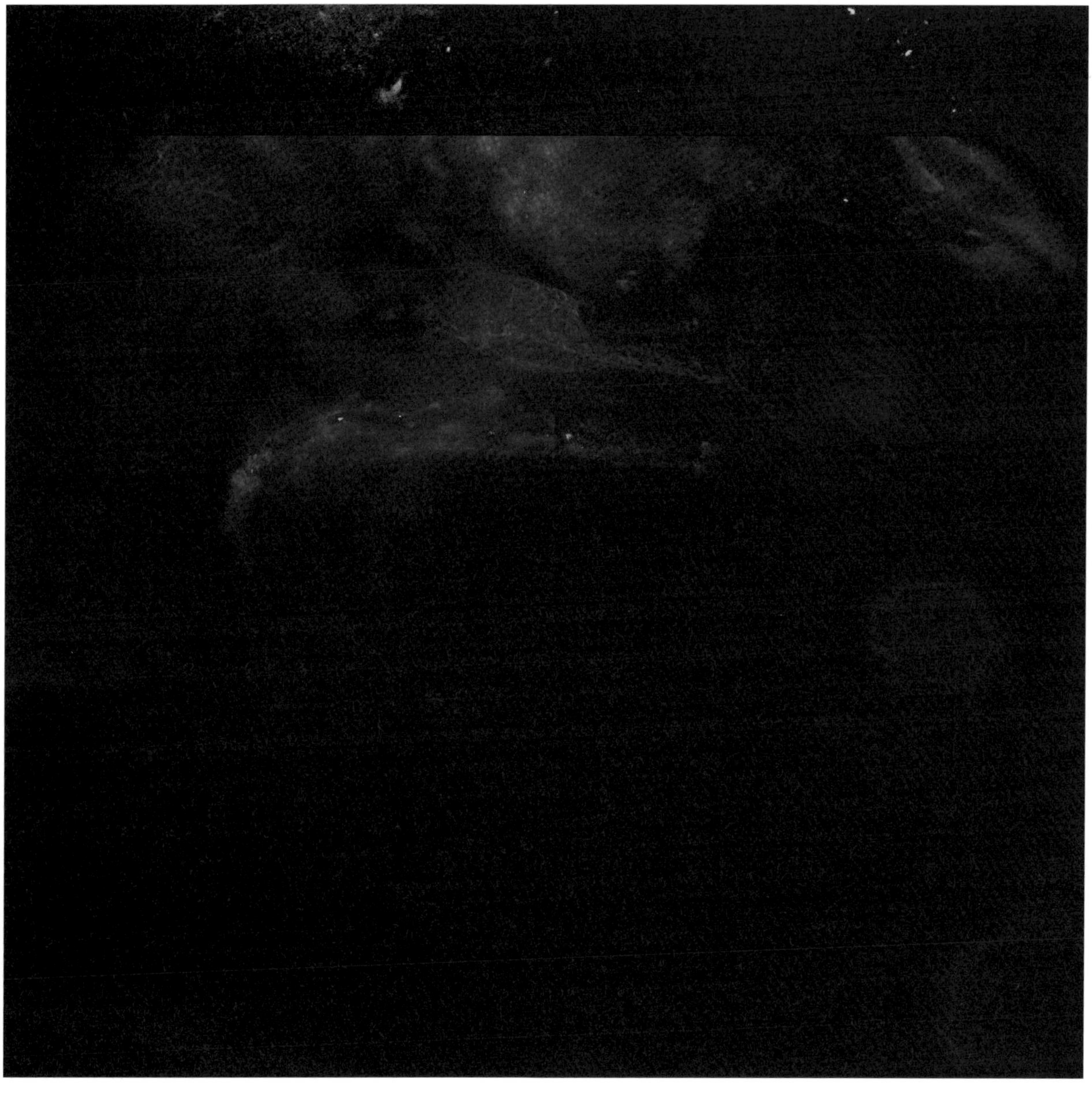

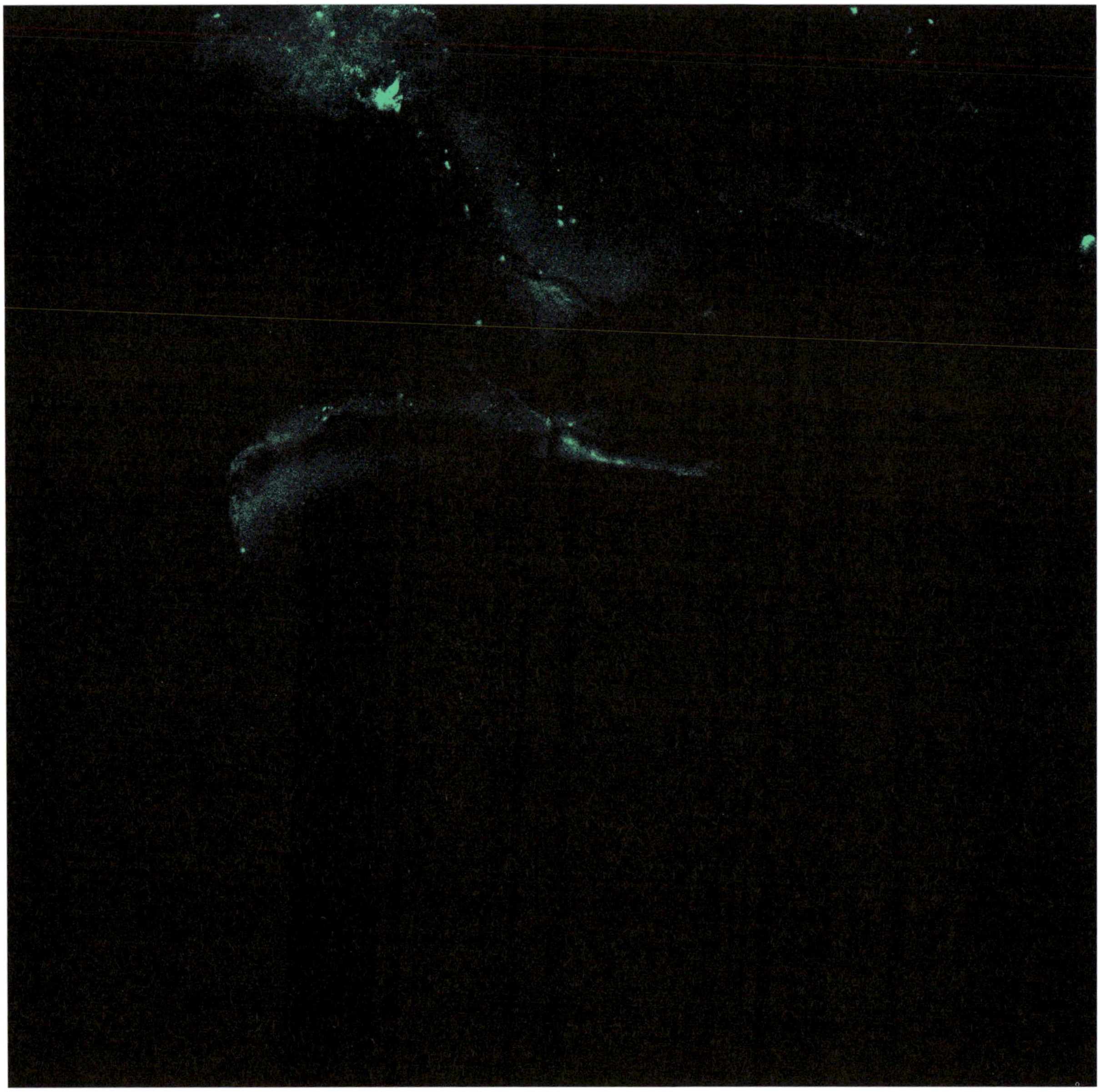

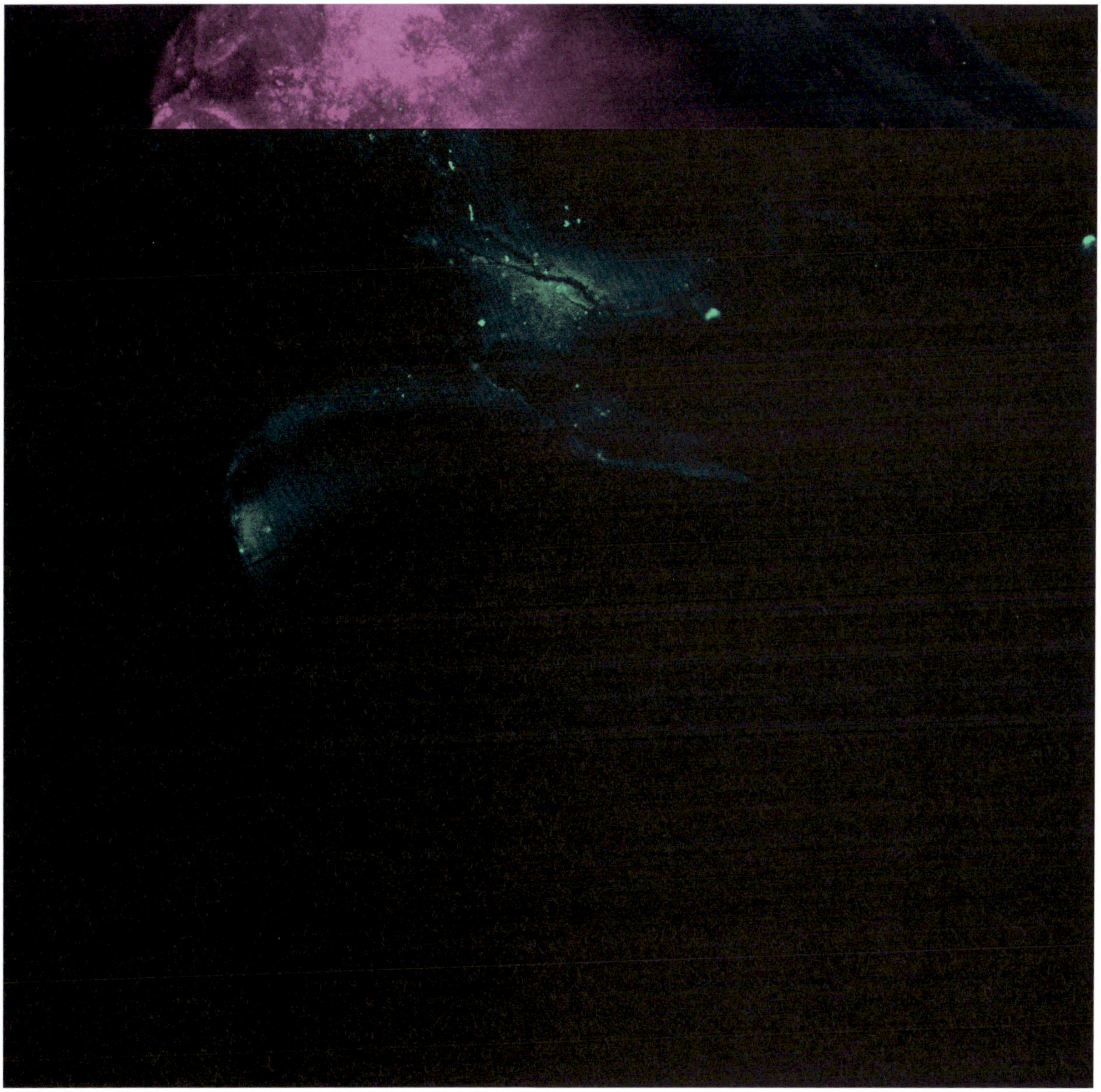

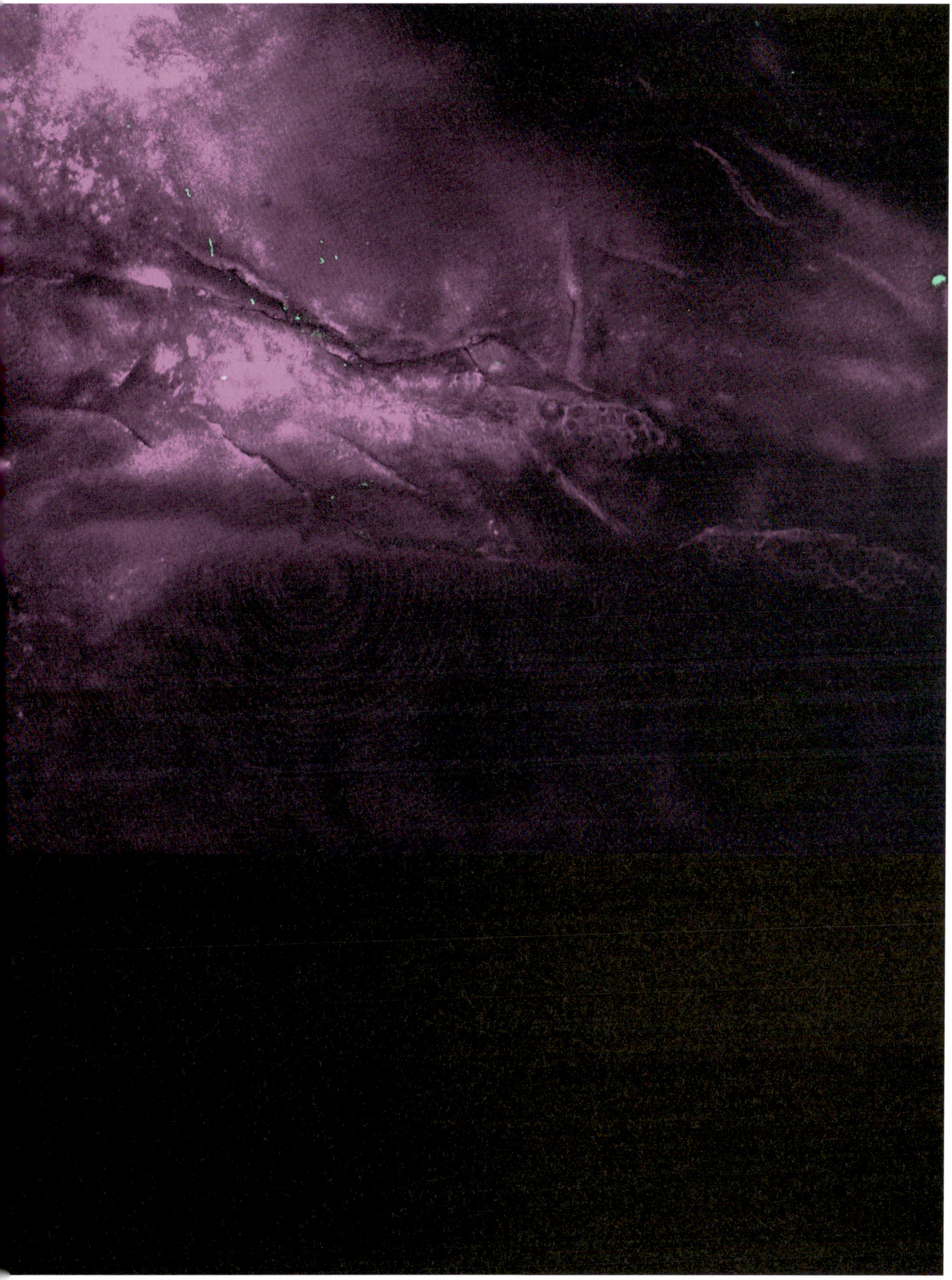

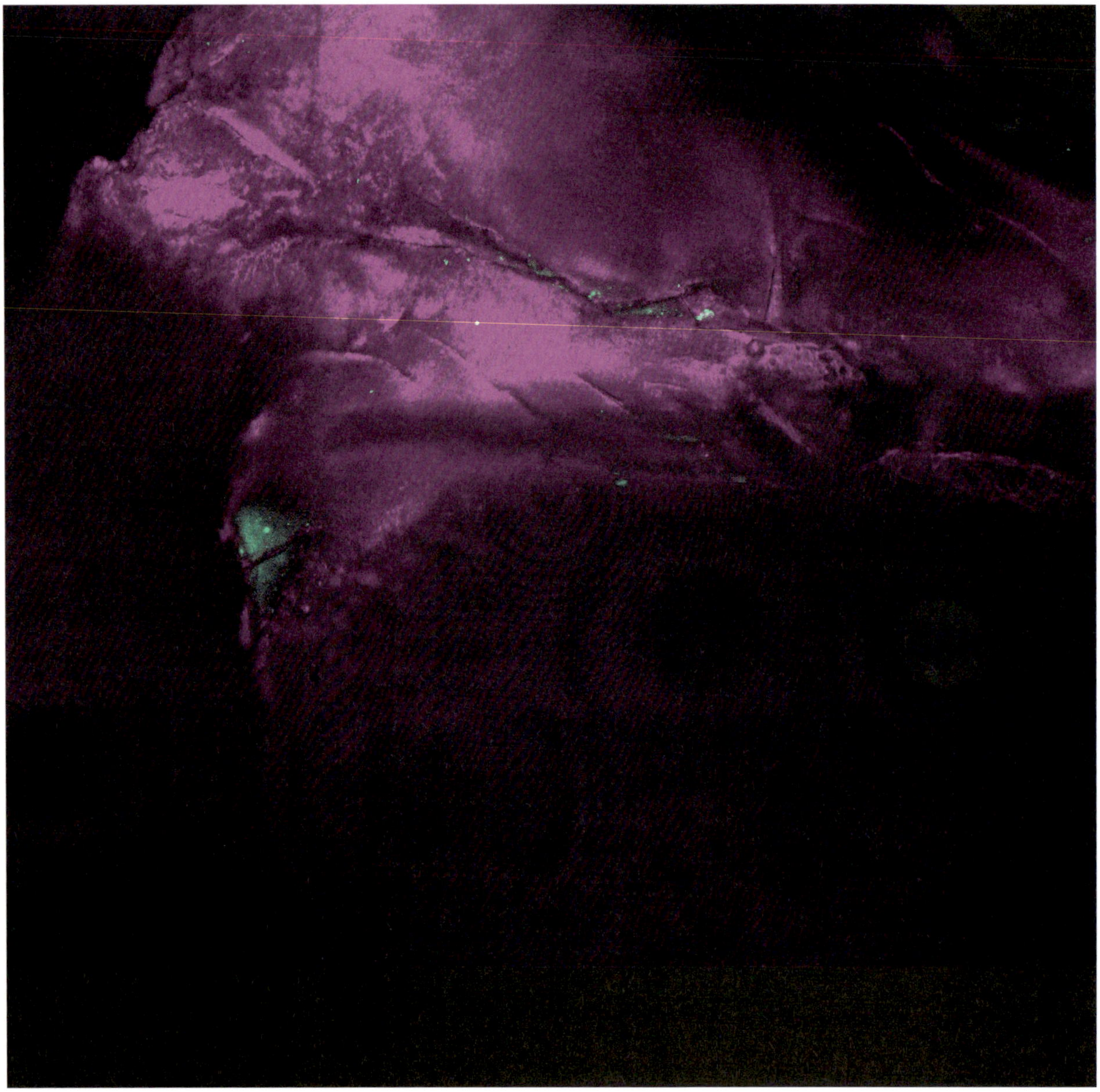

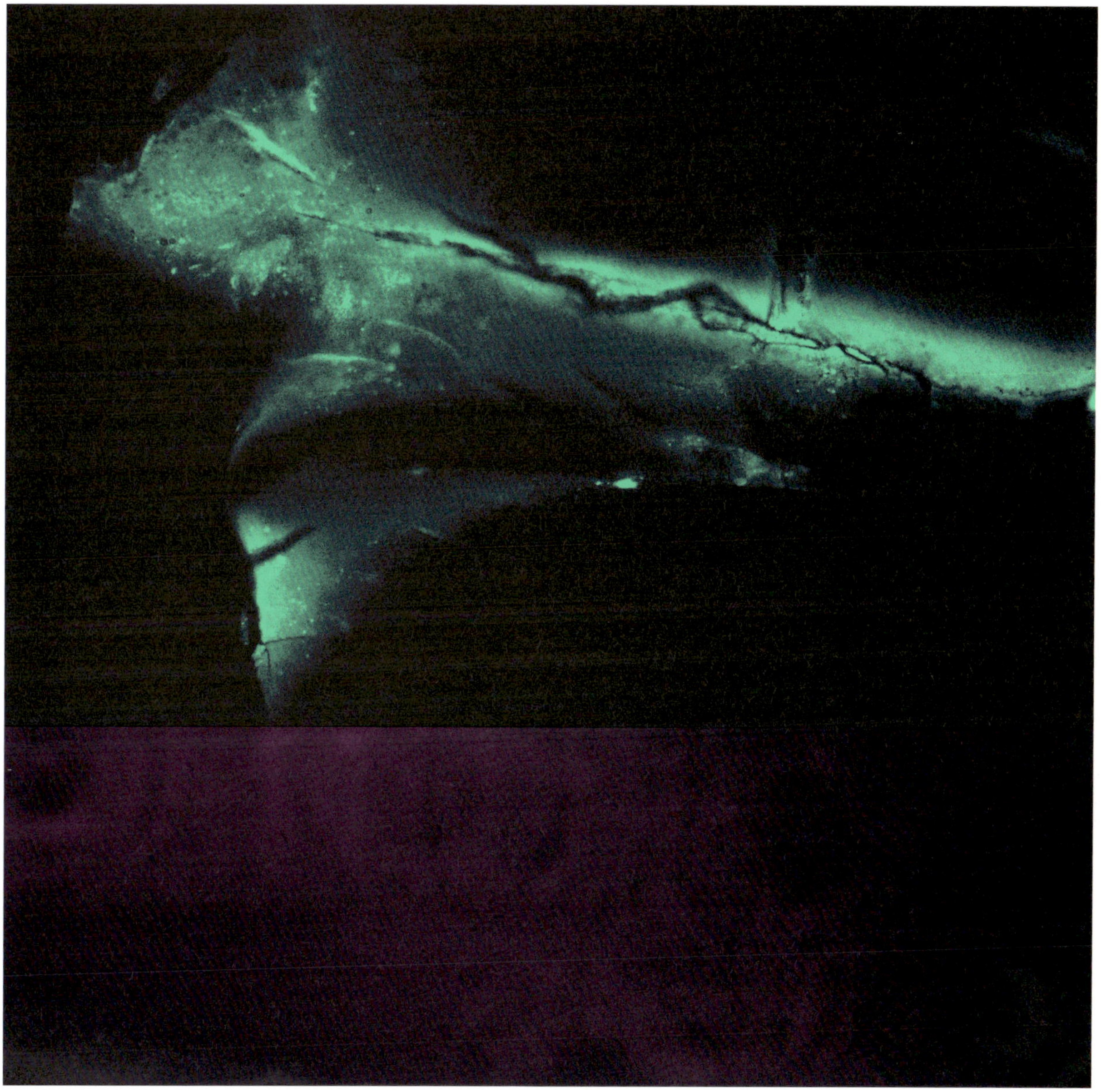

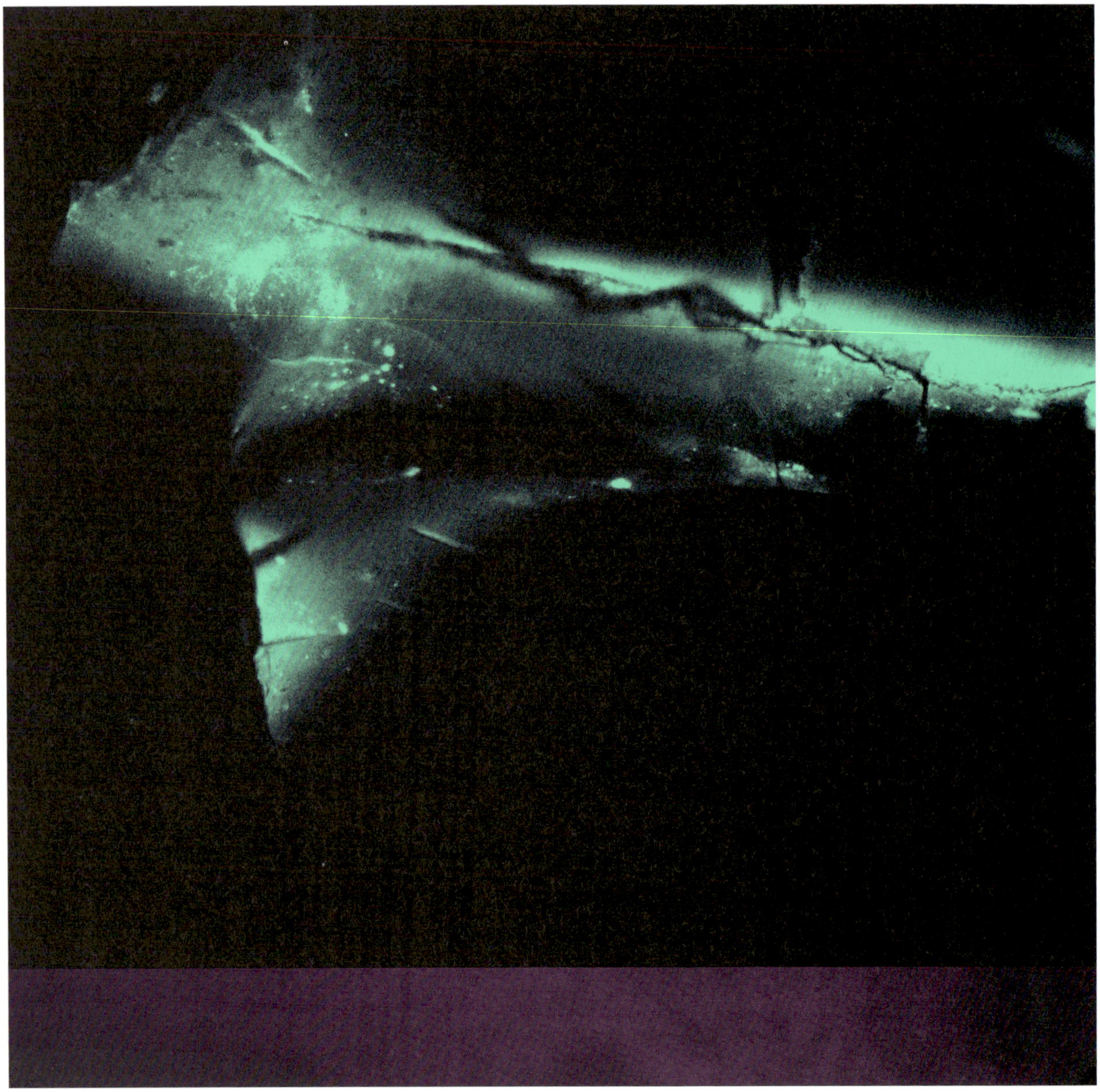

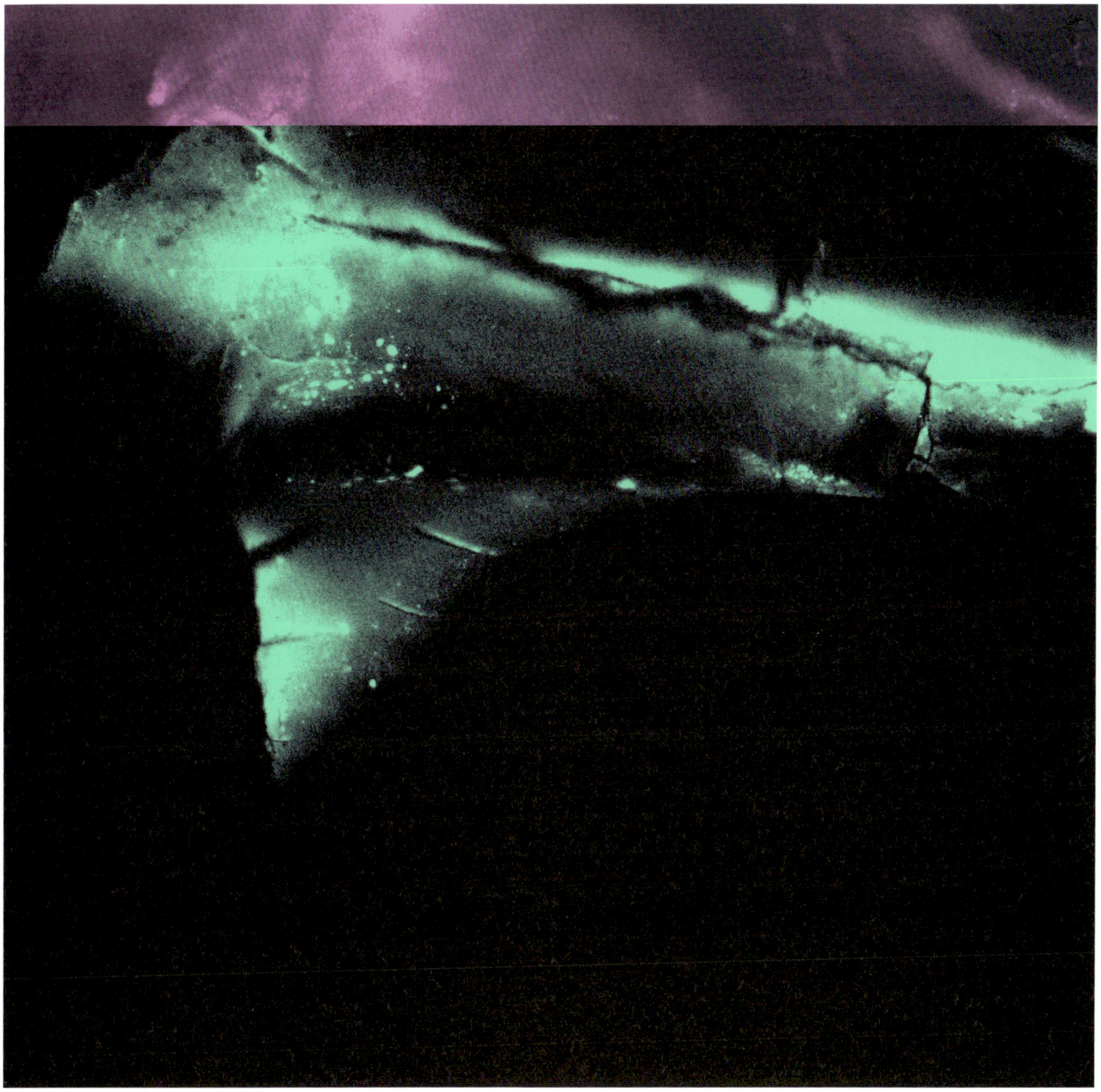

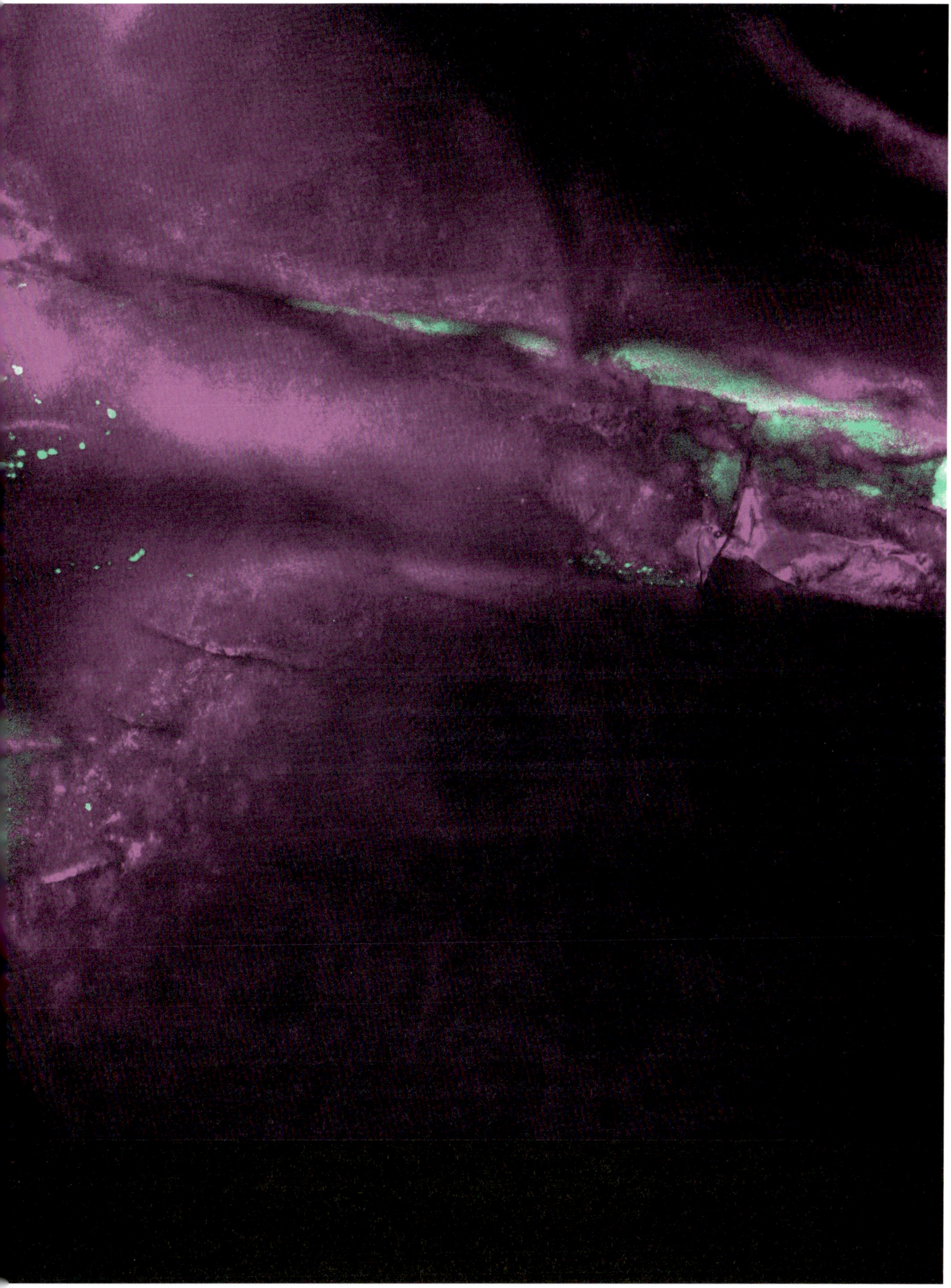

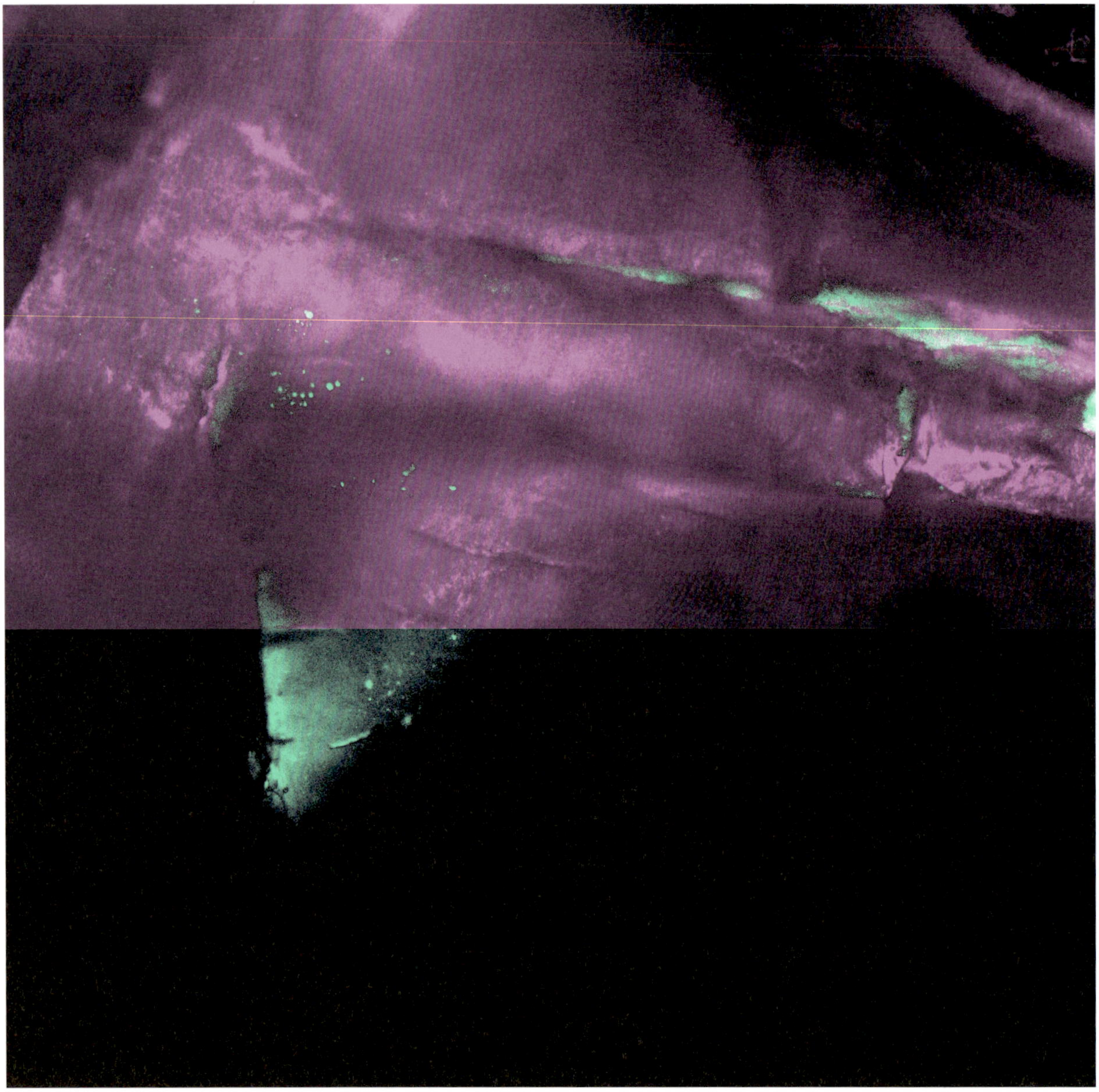

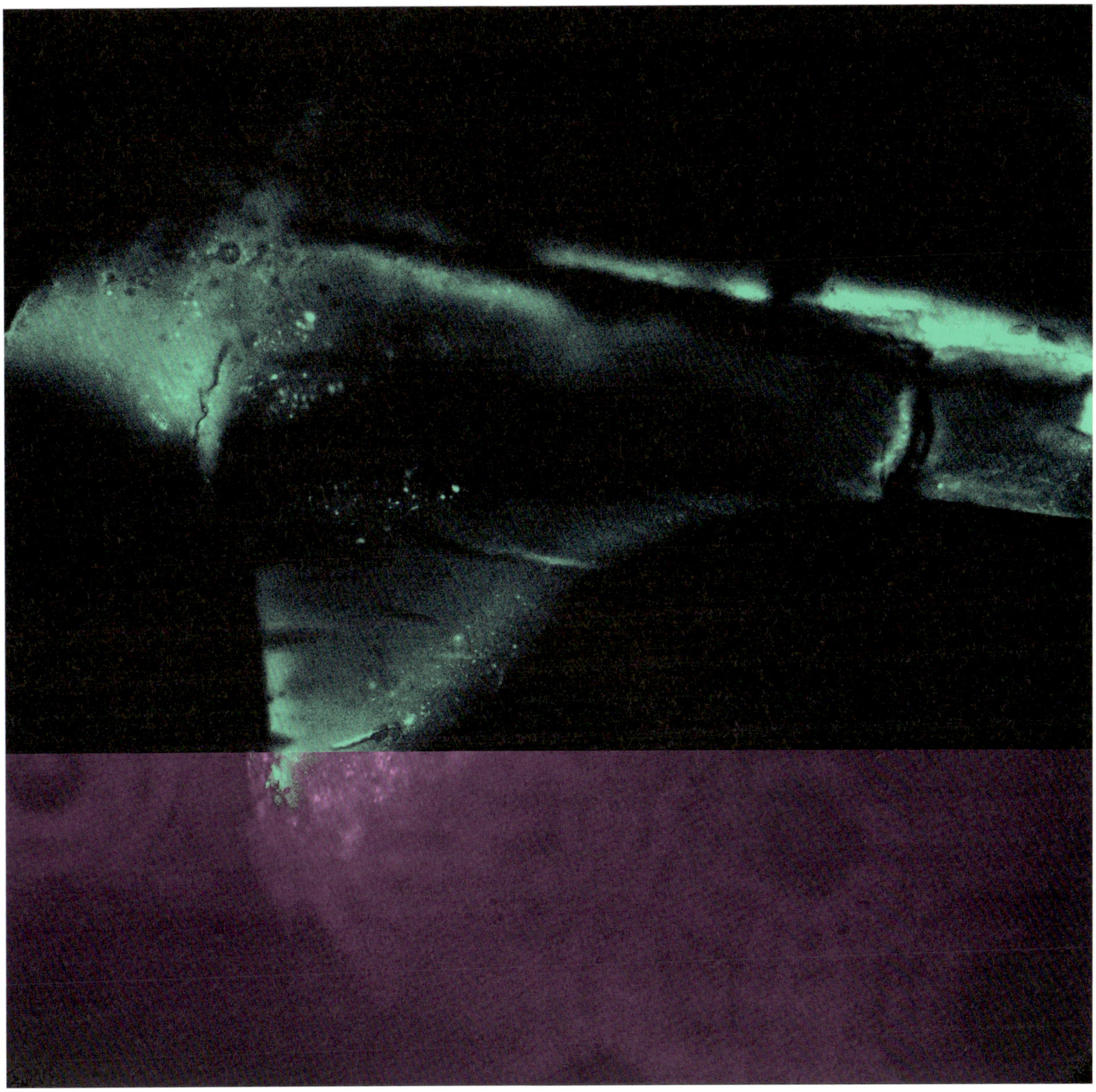

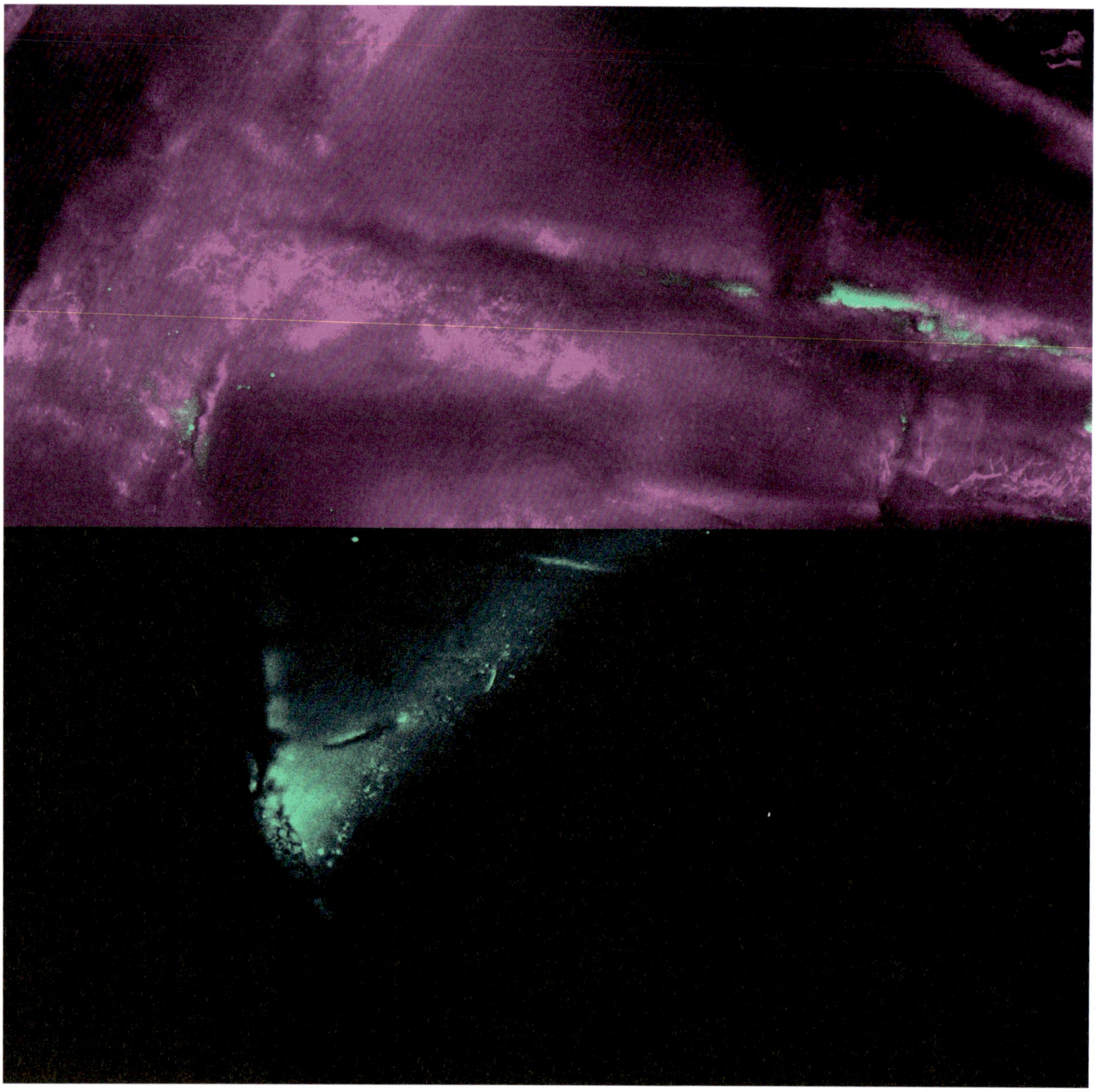

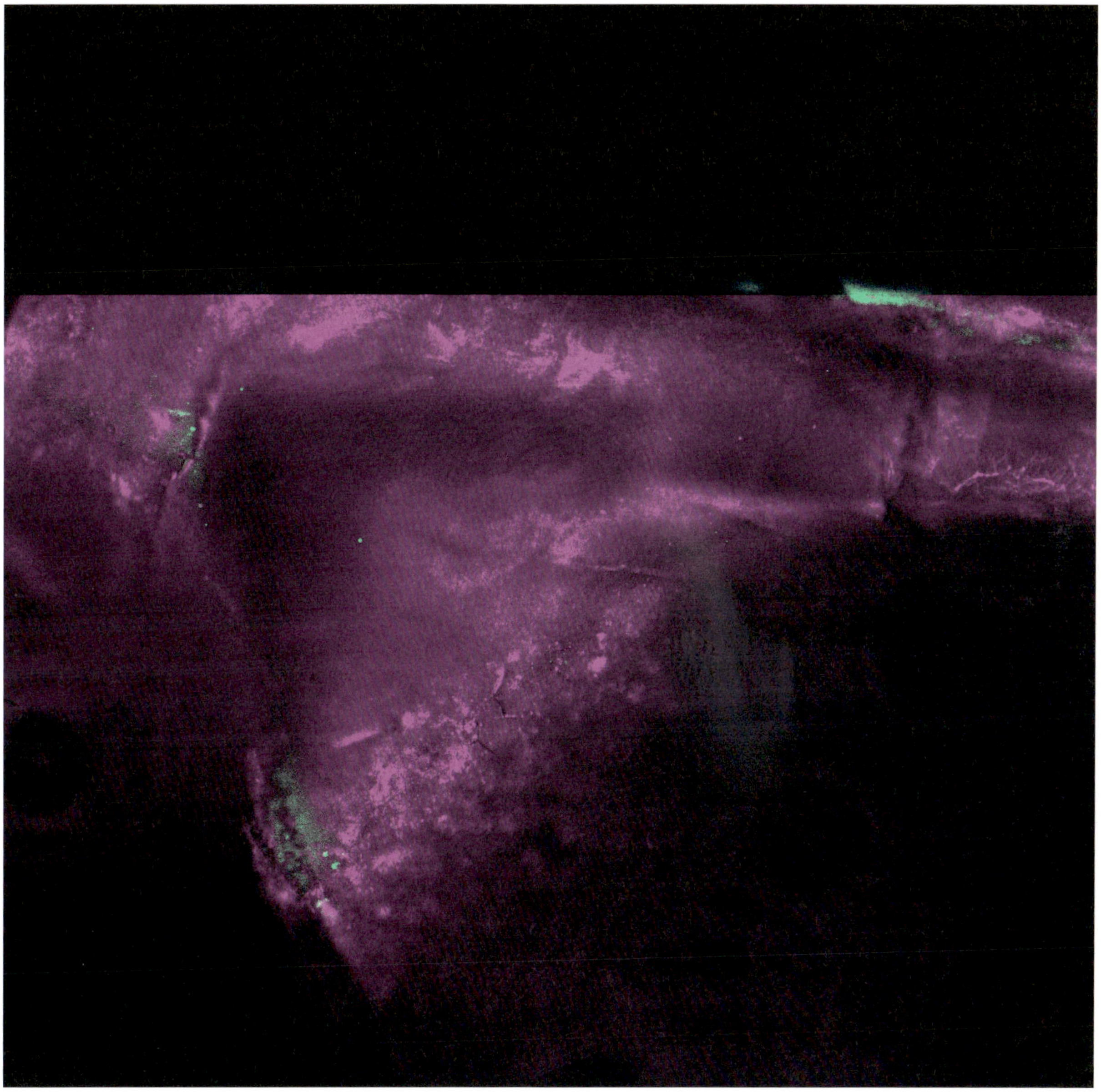

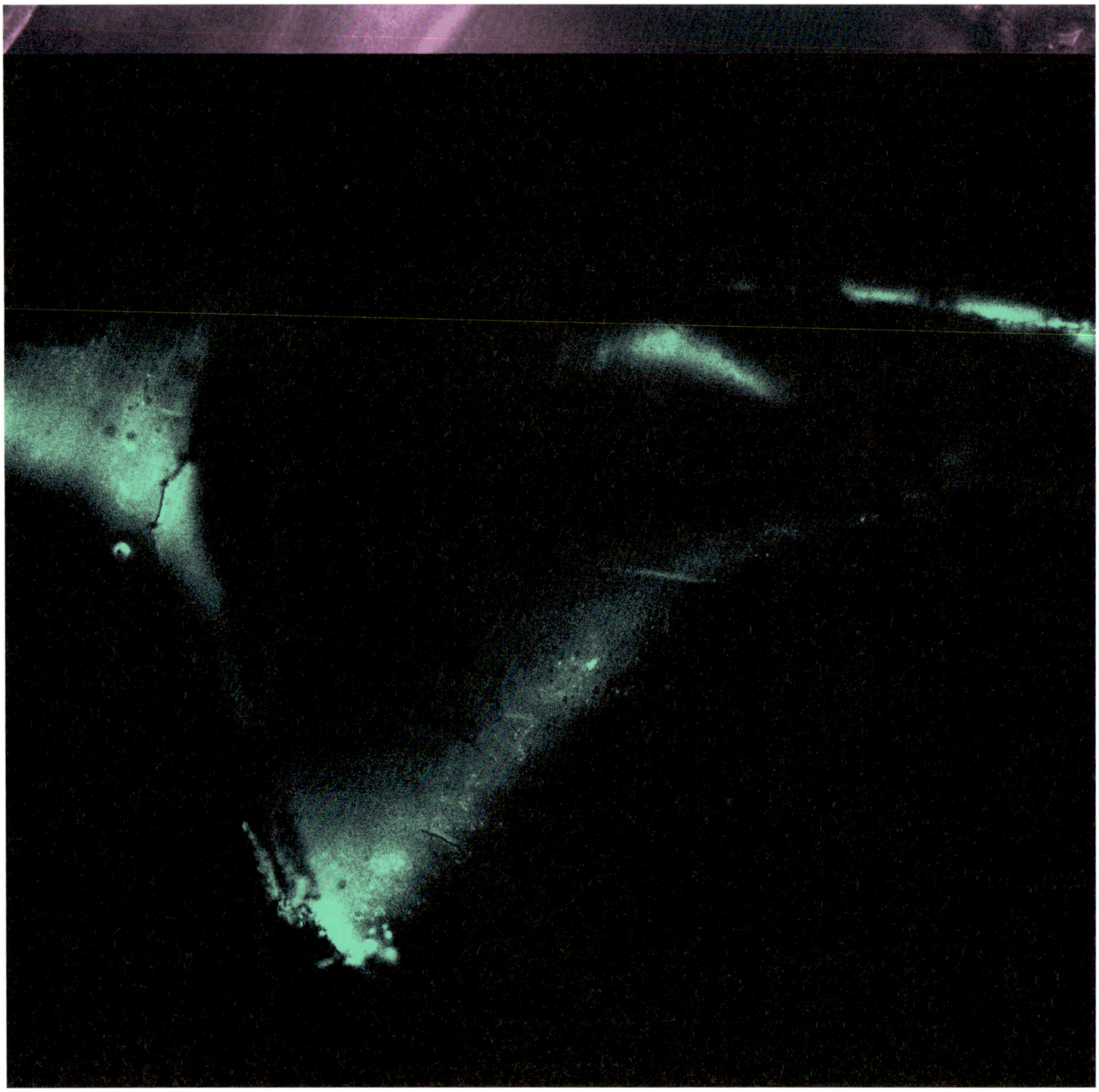

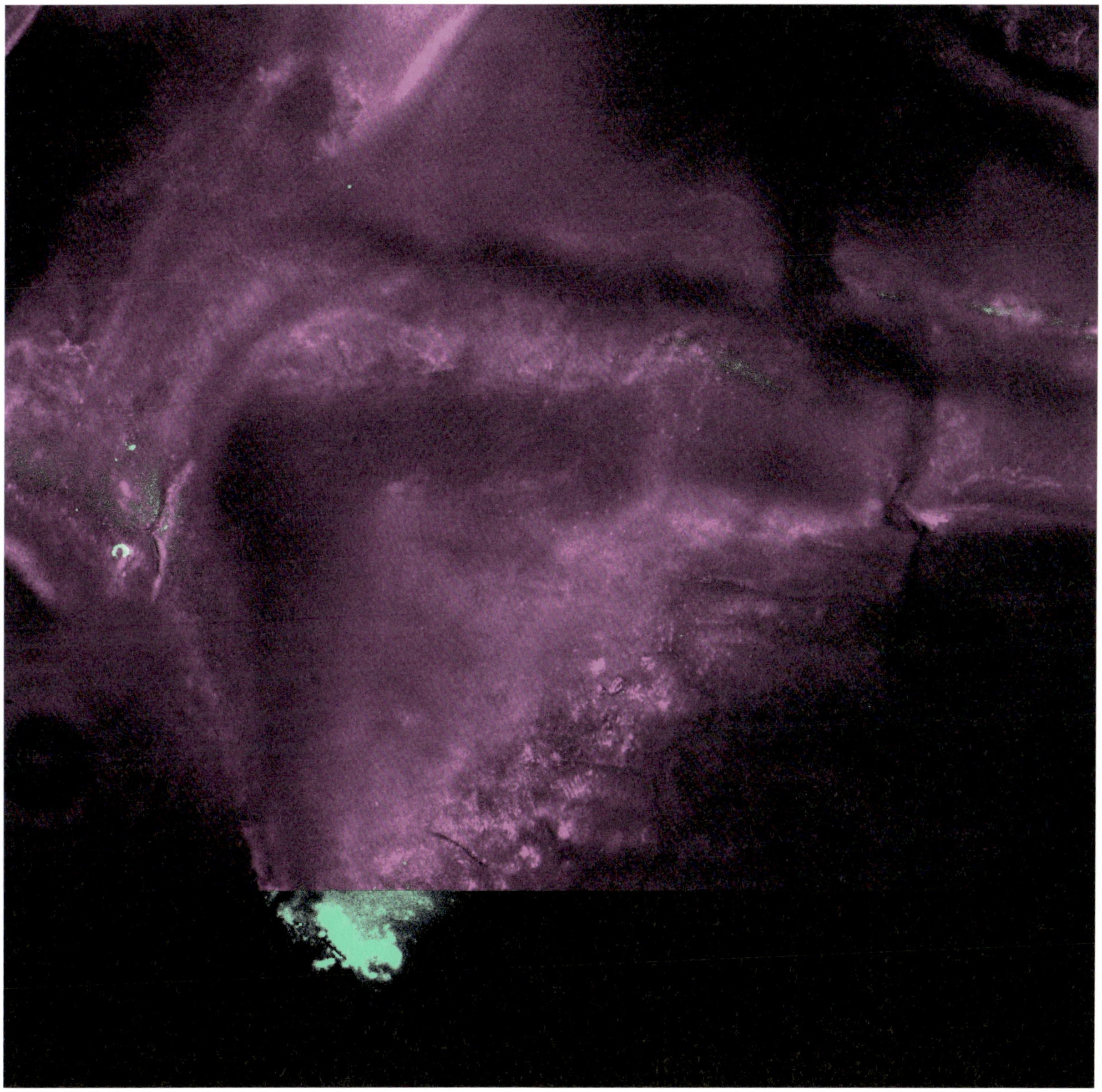

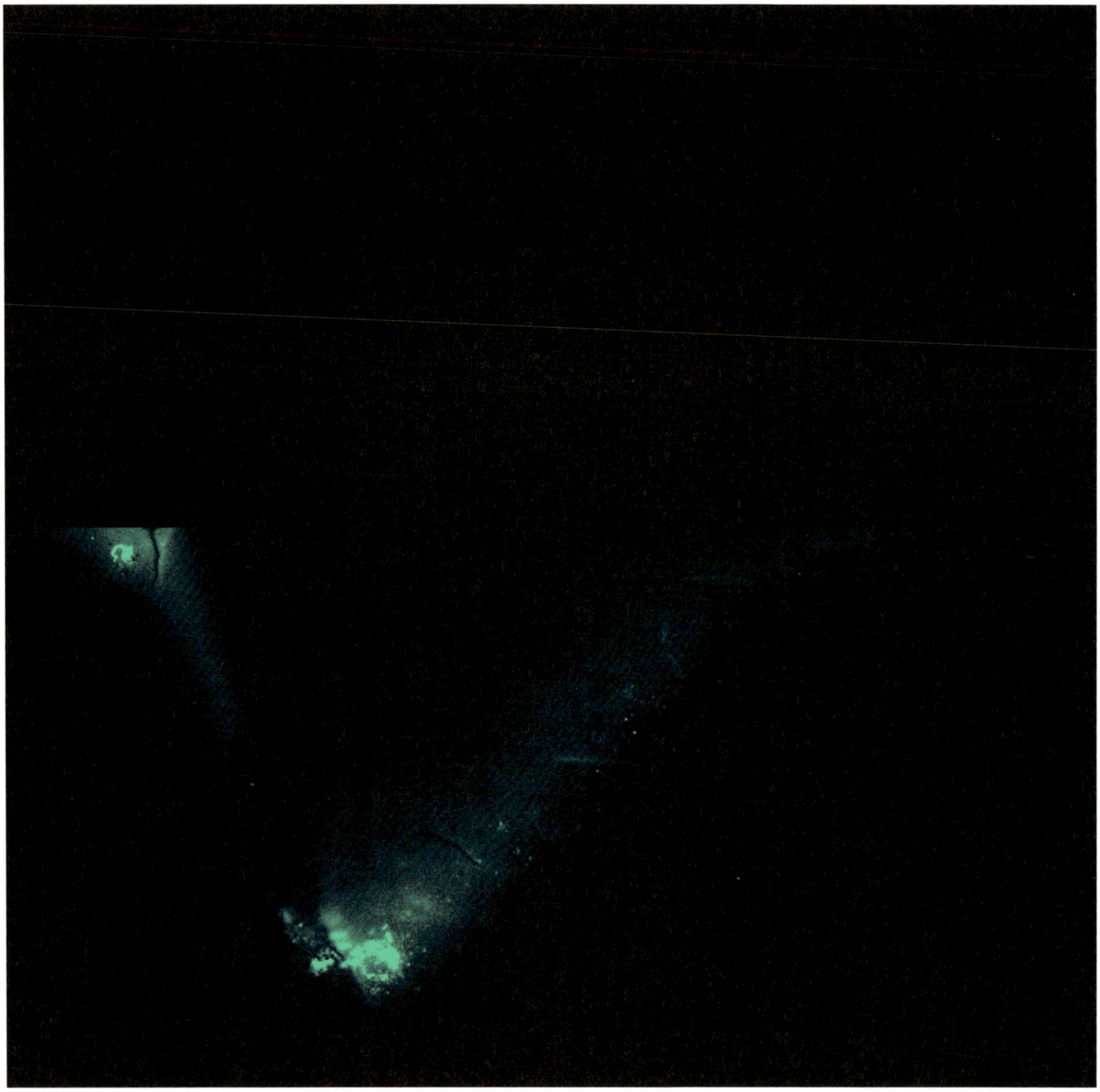

CONTENT

LEARNING TO SEE IN PITCH DARKNESS
ISABELLA RJEILLE

To the Huni Kuin people, chants and shamanic rituals involving the ingestion of *nixi pae* [1] were learned after the first human being, Dua Busen, came into contact with the Anaconda people, and this knowledge has been handed down from generation to generation. The myth describes the fascination and fear Dua Busen felt on sighting an anaconda-woman while hunting, and the process of his own transformation into *Yube*: an anaconda-person. A summary of that narrative, collected and translated by anthropologist Els Lagrou, tells how:

> *When hunting, Dua Busen saw something strange happening. He saw some animals walking around wearing earrings. Then he saw an anaconda woman coming out of the lake. She was covered in design and beautiful. Tapir had called her, throwing genipa fruits in the lake. After tapir made love to anaconda woman she went back into the lake. A few days later, unable to forget, Busen goes back, throws the genipa fruits in the water, and the snake woman appears. He jumps on her, thus frightening her. The anaconda woman transforms into an anaconda and wraps herself around him, threatening him with her tongue in his face. Now he is afraid of being eaten and begs her to come back to her human form. She agrees and makes him explain his intentions. He promises to accompany her to the lake. They make love and, before she takes him on her back to jump into the lake, she uses a "perspectival leaf" to change his perception. Underwater he sees the anaconda people as people.* [2]

1. Psychoactive drink, also known as *Ayahuasca*, produced from a vine and used in ritual ceremonies by some Amerindian peoples of the Amazon region.
2. Els Lagrou. *Anaconda-becoming: Huni Kuin image-songs, an Amerindian relational aesthetics. Horizontes Antropológicos* [Online], 51 | 2018, 2022. URL: http://journals.openedition.org/horizontes/2102.

Dua Busen's fascination for the anaconda-woman led him to the depths of the river and provided him with knowledge that would change the history of his people forever. However, to be able to see what once frightened him as an equal, Dua Busen had to have his outlook altered by the 'perspectival leaf'. His turning into an anaconda-person and going to live underwater — where he came to see anacondas as his fellows — interrupted the process that set them apart and thus dissolved the standpoints of the threat and the threatened. In the narrative, that shift in perspective is essential to the transmission of knowledge, namely the ingestion of *nixi pae,* that would in turn become central to the Huni Kuin culture.

Different ways of knowing the world are central to the work of Marie Kølbæk Iversen, whose research traverses science, technology, mythology and oral traditions in order to understand how human and non-human beings coexist and interrelate. In the video installation, *Rovhistorier|Histories of Predation*, she investigates the possible forms of agency that exist between humans, animals and machines — three characters that, in different contexts, may occupy the role of predator. Akin to the situation experienced by Dua Busen in the Huni Kuin narrative, Kølbæk Iversen questions how shifting one's perspective may interrupt the process that establishes, separates and determines creatures as being 'prey' and 'predators'. Her work deploys the instruments of modern science and research methods to set up an interplay of mirrors to scrutinise the Western idea of what is 'human' along with its tools for conceptualising the world.

This work began in 2020, after Kølbæk Iversen happened upon the longest-living vertebrate animal known to humankind: the gurry shark, known as a merman (*havkal*) in her native Danish, as in Icelandic and Faroese (respectively, *hákarl* and *havkallur*), but as a mermaid in Norwegian and Swedish (respectively, *håkjerringa* and *håkäring*). By human standards, this animal has all the features of a mythological creature: its estimated lifespan is from 272 to 512 years, which reduces our human perception of time to its rightly limited proportions.

In the balance of years, the successions of colonial kidnappings, pillaging and invasions that have taken place in Atlantic over the past 500 years — and which have shaped the capitalist system and the Western world as we know it today — can be measured against this animal's lifespan. Although the gurry shark lives only in the very cold, deep waters of the North Atlantic, sharks in general inhabit the imaginary of colonial terror perpetrated by the traffic of enslaved people through the Middle Passage: the portion of the Atlantic spanning the ocean between Africa, America and Europe. Some shark species living off the west coast of the African continent, accustomed to warmer waters and capable of adapting to the varying temperatures of the mid-Atlantic, altered their routes to follow the European enslavers and feed on the people thrown overboard or trying to escape, either by suicide or swimming, from the horrors of slavery in the Americas. [3] In the dark of the ocean, and by virtue of its extreme longevity, the gurry shark may thus be seen as a potential 'eyewitness' to this past playing out across North Atlantic waters.

As the gurry shark is an entirely cartilaginous fish, the only part of its body to continue intact from the embryonic stage are its eye lens nuclei. This is what has enabled the shark's age to be determined by carbon-14 dating. With the aid of a microscope, Kølbæk Iversen conducts us through the various layers of this shark's eye lenses across the microscopic images that constitute the video-installation *Rovhistorier|Histories of Predation*. In this way, the work triangulates between observer, observed, and — as the triangle's third point — a reflection on the relative positions of power implicit in those different perspectives. To look at the relations that Western societies establish with animals through science — othering and dissecting them — also means seeing something of how those same societies understand their concept of 'humanity'.

With the Industrial Revolution, animals became a vanishing presence in urbanised Western life, until they returned as commodities in post-industrial societies — a fate which the gurry shark, despite its slow existence, trolling the waters of the North Atlantic, was unable to escape. The shark thus fed Nordic societies' drive to accelerate, as the process of industrialisation surged in the eighteenth and nineteenth centuries. This animal was fished primarily to extract oil from its liver, which was then used to keep trains moving, to lubricate machinery, and as lamp oil, [4] converting an animal that swims slowly in the darkest depths of the ocean into fuel to speed up machines and produce light on the world's urbanised surface. To John Berger, in his essay *Why Look at Animals?*, the process by which post-industrial societies reduce animals to commodities to be processed and manufactured as foods or products "(...) is part of the same process as that by which men have been reduced to isolated productive and consuming units." [5] Similarly, he relates this process to animals' role in modern science, which treats them exclusively as objects to be

[3] See Marcus Rediker, *History from below the water line: Sharks and the Atlantic slave trade*, 2008, Atlantic Studies, 5:2, 285-297. Available at: http://dx.doi.org/10.1080/14788810802149758.

[4] Fishing of this kind decreased with the invention of synthetic oil in 1948 and in 1960 was prohibited. See Camilla Bøgeskov, *Det danske fiskeri af grønlandshajen: En undersøgelse af det historiske fiskeri af grønlandshajen ved Grønland med fokus på dets udvikling samt det gensidige forhold mellem menneske og natur* (MA-thesis), 2021, Aalborg Universitet, p. 11.

[5] John Berger, *Why look at animals?*. London: Penguin Books, 2009, p. 23.

observed, thereby denying their agency and the relevance of their gaze as they return ours. Through the eyes of animals, we are seen as just another animal. Through the eyes of humans, 'we' distinguish ourselves from 'them'.[6] This modern separation between Nature and Culture fosters a process that has led to what is now known as the 'Anthropocene': a new geological era that acknowledges the centrality of human agency to the changes to life on Earth. The climatic, social, economic and cultural impacts of the Anthropocene, allied to the advance of capitalism, have accelerated a process of extinction that posits what we call 'humanity' as a predator of itself and of all living beings.

In response to these developments, *Rovhistorier|Histories of Predation* offers a dissection and interrelation of three ways of seeing: the human gaze, limited to the need for light to form images and process them in our brains; the gaze of the shark, dissected and observed; and the microscope, a technological device designed to expand sight into realms that humans, through our eyes alone, are unable to perceive. Yet light is another essential element of this triangulation. It traverses the lenses of all the optical apparatus involved: emitted by the microscope, its waves transit both the layers of the shark's eye and the lenses of the microscope, finally reaching — through the light of the projector in the exhibition space — the lenses of our eyes. Also, light and its symbolism have run through some 300 years of history in this animal's lifetime, with the Enlightenment and its impact on science and modern colonial thinking. However, the images drawn from the shark's eye lenses do not enlighten or reveal; instead, they are like points of light in pitch darkness that merely outline the geography of some unknown terrain. Light is diffused in the shark's eye lenses and reaches our retina, which is as human as it is limited against such a long-living animal. To learn to perceive from the perspective of this animal, we are brought to learn to see underwater to escape the excessive, blinding light at the surface. Learning to see in the absence of light also entails a process of activating other senses and other kinds of knowledge, dismantling the hierarchy established by sight and the light-mediated imagery it generates.

Accordingly, to understand the present and create possible futures amidst the imminent extinction announced by the Anthropocene, it is fundamental to salvage other kinds of knowledge. In a work parallel to *Rovhistorier|Histories of Predation*, Kølbæk Iversen reaches back to her ancestors — to her great-great-great-great-grandmother, Johanne Tygesdatter, who lived on the West Jutland heathlands — for the pagan knowledge that was passed on in song, recorded by the

6 John Berger, *op. cit.*, p. 13

ethnomusicologist and folklorist Evald Tang Kristensen in 1873. Those songs tell of conflicts over the cultural homogenisation of diverse native peoples in a process of nationalisation and consolidation of the Danish state. In order to address the predatory effects of that process, the songs often refer to hybrid mythological beings, part animal, part human (such as mermen and mermaids), who are alien to nations and borders drawn by humans. Titled *Donnimaar*, this music and performance project was launched at the autumn equinox, which in the Northern hemisphere marks the transition into winter, when nights grow longer and darkness descends. Kølbæk Iversen regards this work as a way of celebrating "the power of dreaming to unsettle the fabric of reality by rendering strange and contingent the waking life of our troubled modernity." [7]

Dreaming, as a device for understanding waking life, is an absolute necessity for mammals' survival, but has been losing centrality in the life of Western societies in tandem with the latter's modernisation process. However, when the lights are out and reason is relegated to secondary importance, dreaming is the way to navigate the world. As Jung wrote, the dream "prepares the dreamer for the events of the following day," [8] and *Rovhistorier|Histories of Predation* may thus be understood as an attempt to incorporate the gurry shark's perspective: to learn how to see in the pitch darkness so as to prospect possible ways of *delaying the end of the world*. [9]

For the Huni Kuin, healing and knowledge come from the sights afforded by *nixi pae*: when it is ingested, one is also ingested by it. In that process, one becomes one with *Yube* and learns with him to see the world through the eyes of the anaconda. Placing a shark's eyes under the microscope is also a means of analysing our own way of seeing — questioning the scientific method, which says understanding requires looking more closely. In the case of the shark eye, however, the closer you get, the more diffuse the images become. Under the microscope, we encounter the raw structure of the anatomy of an eye, but never the images captured by it. What is needed then is to disengage the eye that sees only in bright light, that is, to learn to see the infinity that exists in darkness, in night, and in dreams.

[7] https://donnimaar.bandcamp.com/releases.

[8] C. G. Jung, "Two Kinds of Thinking," in: *The Collected Works of C. G. Jung, Volume 5: Symbols of Transformation*. Princeton: Princeton University Press Bollingen Series, 1967.

[9] Indigenous thinker and leader Ailton Krenak argues that Indigenous peoples have experienced several 'ends of the world' since the onset of colonisation. In his book *Ideias para adiar o fim do mundo* ['Ideas to Delay the End of the World], he asks whether non-Indigenous people will be able to survive the end of the world. Ailton Krenak. *Ideias para adiar o fim do mundo*. São Paulo: Companhia das Letras, 2020.

THE TRANSFORMATION
YANN CHATEIGNÉ TYTELMAN

When the genuine myth rises into consciousness, that is always its message. You must change your life. Ursula K. Le Guin

On 22 September 2017 in London, Marie Kølbæk Iversen gave her premiere performance of the project that would grow to become *Donnimaar*. The event took place at LUX on the evening of the autumn equinox. Accompanied by the artist and composer Diana Policarpo, she sang a repertoire of traditional songs, some of which were attributed to her great-great-great-great-grandmother Johanne Tygesdatter. At sunset, at the precise moment that marks the vanishing daylight and our definitive march towards winter, Marie's clear, luminous voice was cast upwards into the celestial vault. The lyrics were sung in the dialect of West Jutland, the region where Marie grew up and where her family comes from. One of the songs was titled 'Forvandlingen', or 'The Transformation'. Its protagonist is Donnimaar, a young woman in love, seductive and cunning, highly magically capable, and boasting of her powers. The story takes place in an enchanted Nordic landscape inhabited by elves and little people who dance on burial mounds surrounding heath valleys laden with dew and rime. Donnimaar is enamoured of the handsome Knight of the Rose Garden, but her father does not approve of their union. To render her lover invisible to the father, she offers to transform him, first into a pair of shoes, which the knight refuses, then, into a pair of gloves, which he also refuses, and finally, into a thread of golden flax that she may braid into her hair. To this he consents. But when Donnimaar and the knight, the latter now hidden in her hair, go to her father, he sees through the deceit and cuts off his daughter's hair and chops it into little bits, but her protean lover nevertheless manages to escape. *The Transformation* is thus an animist tale of metamorphosis, filiation and emancipation.

Inherent to folksongs is their uncertain origins. They are the product of a long process of oral and gestural transmissions and observations, migrations, variations, mixings and incarnations. Jacques Rancière notes that the term 'lore', as in the word 'folklore', is "an old English word that refers to the fabric of traditional knowledge and stories that people transmit." Perhaps it is not by chance then that Donnimaar turns the knight into a flax thread and that her father uses a knife to cut off her braid, i.e., the blend of her own making: The young woman was on the cusp of forming her own lore, weaving her own 'matrix of knowledge', to use Rancière's terms, by connecting to another source that lay outside the 'folk,' i.e., the people constituting the dominant group in this case and embodied by the patriarchal figure of her father.

Marie did not so much recite 'The Transformation' as *revive* it. By bringing it into the present, as if on the crest of a wave, she let the song change. This yields an interesting analogy between the composition and the subject. The song's evolving structure is based on precise moments in the story where Donnimaar proposes to use her magical powers to transform the knight into a series of apparently inanimate objects:

> *I will turn you into a little pair of shoes*
> *I will wear you on my two feet*

Later on she says:

> *I will turn you into a beautiful pair of gloves*
> *I will wear you on my little hands*

And she ends with:

> *I will turn you into a thread of golden flax*
> *I will braid you close to my rosy cheek*

The form of 'The Transformation' is itself subject to a constant modification and a spiralling, repetitive motion.

Gilles Deleuze and Félix Guattari saw the refrain — which they preferred to call *ritornello* — as a motif, a form that reveals the link between the vital, fluid impulse of our existence and the playing of music, as well as the organic bond it creates with elements, beings and things. In *A Thousand Plateaus*, they wrote: "... becoming-woman, becoming-child; becoming-animal, -vegetable, or -mineral; becoming-molecular of all kinds, becoming-particles. (...) Singing or composing, painting and writing have no other aim: to unleash these becomings." They also write, "Fibers lead us from one to the other, transform into the other, as they pass through doors and across thresholds." The golden thread — or link — into which the knight is transformed is certainly the alchemical mark of Donnimaar's status as a sorceress, but it also alludes to matter in motion, to flows and to the life that courses through all things across the landscape of history. The young woman's blushing 'rose-coloured' cheek is more than just an image to describe the effects of the icy air or a lover's desire. It expresses affect and shows how a substance — here, the Knight of the Rose Garden — impregnates and alters Donnimaar's body, which hosts him. Deleuze and Guattari go on to say that it is especially in music that these becomings are the most operative. Yet, importantly, musical becomings are not a way to imitate something or to identify with someone. Rather, Marie herself *becomes* something or someone else through this project, sharing particles with Johanne. Figures align and overlap through spiralling repetition, and Deleuze and Guattari conclude by saying that music is not the privilege of human beings, since "the universe, the cosmos is made of refrains."

On the vinyl recording featuring the first songs that Marie assigned to the character of Donnimaar, her interpretation of 'The Transformation' is quite revealing. The somewhat slow, delicate, airy, almost solemn way that her vocal melody glides over Katinka Fogh Vindelev's arrangements creates floating, distilled and restrained layers of voices. The suspended, almost monotone and hypnotic gentleness of the composition feels as if it came straight out of the night on which the song was sung for the first time in public. Mirroring its premiere, the *Donnimaar* record was released on 20 March 2022, the date of the spring equinox.

Back in 2017, on the threshold of winter, 'The Transformation' seemed like an incantation to accompany the coming of the night, a change in the cycle that transformed the atmosphere. The words half-sung, half-spoken, were a way of welcoming, of immersing oneself in a particular enveloping state, a sound environment that acted as a threshold, a passage to another *mode*. In the motion of the song, we hear a slow, rhythmic, pendular pulsation, evoking the movement of a body swaying, as if in a cradle, as if to descend gently into the world of sleep and dreams. "'The Transformation' was the first song I worked on," Marie explains. "The melody came to me one night. I was alone at home with my child. The moon was full. I was unable to sleep and started singing in a low voice to avoid awakening my son. The melody came to me just like that, in that peculiar state, a kind of trance." Five years later, listening to the recording of the artist's crystal-clear voice lifts the songs from their initial darkness. In the transitional space of the stellar composition, I no longer need to open my eyes to see — or rather to *feel* — another bright, moon-lit night somewhere between dreaming and history where this music takes me: The presence of the figures of Marie, Johanne and Donnimaar,

a flax thread, a frozen brook, rime-covered hills.
Initially, the song about Donnimaar did not have a title. It was the Danish folklorist Evald Tang Kristensen who attributed the title 'Forvandlingen', 'The Transformation,' to the song when, in the late-nineteenth century, he was drawing up a repertory of Johanne's songs on one of his field trips. Like many of his European peers at the time, Tang Kristensen was driven by the national-romantic urge to catalogue his country's age-old myths and traditional songs. These practices, disappearing under the brunt of modernisation, had remained alive in the heath regions of West Jutland, where the population had until then remained largely insulated from the rest of Denmark. When Marie consulted the archives of the Danish Folklore Collection, she read that Tang Kristensen had visited Johanne in December 1873 in the isolated Sammelsted By settlement, which was located on Ørre Heath. There, Tang Kristensen recorded thirteen songs from her, one of which would become 'The Transformation'. This song intrigued him in particular: "This highly strange old magical song has so far only been found in the memory of one single old woman in Sammelsted By, Ørre Parish. No other old or new recording of it is known, neither from Denmark nor other countries," he wrote. In her practice-based artistic doctoral thesis which she defended in 2023, Marie produced a biography of 'The Transformation', which the intrigued folklorist sent to his superior, who — on congratulating Tang Kristensen for his "first-class find" of this "truly strange" song — encouraged him to "squeeze as much as possible out of this Johanne." Ethnomusicological study was thus also a colonialist enterprise. In fact, concomitantly with the undertaking of preserving folklore, nineteenth-century Denmark was in the grip of a political process of cultural homogenisation, particularly in the western part of the Jutland peninsula — with its low population density and historical-cultural separation from the islands of Funen and Zealand — which had fostered ways of living that differed greatly from those that the budding Danish nation-state was promoting to unify the country.

Denmark's unification was based on marginalising internal and external 'foreigners', admitting 'morally deviant' women and men to specialist asylums, and erasing any 'aberrant' linguistic and cultural traits to be found within the population, such as those embodied by the so-called *Kjeltrings*. While the word 'Kjeltring' is an exonym, it was used by the authorities to describe and declass different groups of wandering and semi-sedentary peoples, who formed part of the heaths' intricate commons-based ecologies. What we may then characterise as the heathlands' 'colonisation' was based on the targeted destruction of their cultures and of the networks of exchange that enabled life in pre-industrial West Jutland; it was based on the state's subjugation of these 'people of the night,' who were independent and non-Christian, and for whom gender roles were not clearly defined. The state's enclosure of the heath commons eclipsed their way of living: They were required to speak the national language; their rituals were ridiculed or prohibited; they were christened by force; children were separated from their parents to be assimilated, and able-bodied adolescents and adults were distributed among the peasants as labour force and to be 'educated'.

We do not know whether Johanne was a Kjeltring, but we do know that, in 1873, Tang Kristensen visited her twice on two consecutive days. The first day, he wrote down the lyrics of her songs. But when he returned the following day to record her melodies, one of her sons forbade him from entering: a missionary, he considered these songs the devil's work. Today the peoples designated as 'Kjeltrings' are all but forgotten; what remains is a crude parodic outline of a debased class of people at the bottom of society. Apart from Tang Kristensen's transcriptions, almost nothing tangible is left of the knowledge and traditions of Johanne and her community. The collection remains incomplete, consisting of mere fragments of myths and suppositions to suggest how they might have been more and other than merely poor and crooked. I imagine Marie gazing eyes wide open at this destruction, staring into the void, into its darkness.

Singing is an exercise in breath and breathing. Looking at a photograph of Ørre Heath, I think of Donnimaar, and I tell myself that the song came into being while listening to that silence, to the elements. I sense the connection between these open landscapes, these horizons along which Johanne's songs took shape, and the ethereal vocal melodies that Marie composed. Even after a culture has been assassinated, an invisible, lingering residue most likely resonates in our aural world. *Donnimaar's* vast sound environments allude to what remains in the air of such places. The beauty of Marie's project lies in the fact that it consists almost entirely of the human voice, of her voice and of those accompanying her. The laying of voices over voices to reclaim and revive those of Johanne and her peers that were twice muted.

Reflecting on the destruction of cultures of the Global South by imperialist forces, Boaventura de Sousa Santos explains how — even before breaking the cultural structures of colonised lands — thinkers and anthropologists would begin talking about 'the Other' so as to reduce people to objects, bereaving them of a voice of their own. This is the first step towards epistemicide, the eradication of a cultural environment, and towards linguicide, the killing of a local language. And this is structurally similar to what happened on the West Jutlandic heathlands: The same forces that strove to change, industrialise and exploit the natural environment, to displace, constrain and even annihilate bodies also managed to kill off a culture and a language.

The power of the *Donnimaar* project thus lies in making these voices touch one another, those present and those absent, in a space that is itself composed of a breath; semi-real, almost ungraspable.

This is an act of extraordinary delicacy and force, which might begin as follows: Johanne takes a breath. Facing this man who has come to write down the things she remembers, she inhales and begins to sing. At the other end of the story, Marie observes, monitoring the traces of his appropriation. She exhales and Donnimaar appears.

In 1942, when the Nazis' occupation of France was in full swing, Simone Weil took refuge in Marseille, where, in reading through the pages of the magazine *Les Cahiers du Sud*, she discovered medieval Occitan poetry. Occitania is a cultural zone of loosely defined borders that extends across the southern third of France, Monaco and parts of Italy and Spain. People have spoken Occitan here since Antiquity, and in the eleventh century, the region was the birthplace of the troubadour movement.

Unlike their Parisian counterparts, *Les Cahiers du Sud* focused on regional cultures and Pan-Mediterranean exchanges; it looked at marginalised cultural forms in search of alternative modes of resistance, especially decentralised ones. Occitania was also the region where Cathar mysticism developed. Rapt with a lack of worldly goods and a sense of purity, this spiritual and political movement was crushed in the thirteenth century with a series of bloody crusades.

Weil's article 'What the Occitan Inspiration Consists Of' appeared in the Marseille-based magazine in 1943, and it focused on the revolutionary vision of singing about courtly love, known at the time as *fin'amor*. For the troubadours and their female counterparts, the trobairiz, love was *the opposite of force*. The poet Lisa Robertson, who translated Weil's piece into English, specified in an essay accompanying the translation that it was precisely this "cultivation of an intensely heretical vision of love," which for her was a form of resistance. "Greek civilisation, absolutely no adoration of force," Weil wrote. For Robertson, what makes Weil's analysis so powerful today is that, "using Plato's *Symposium* as her companion thinking, she describes love as a social practice of consensual relationship."

Further north, Donnimaar and her knight embody this very ideal when the young woman asks him, on obtaining his consent, what she can turn him into. Donnimaar uses a ruse, and not force, which is instead the purview of her father. Donnimaar is a figuration of power as agility, while her father embodies power as violence, as force. Robertson writes, "In our current political climate, we live in the midst of the refusal of love; force is normalised as a socio-economic value and as a practice of self."

Inspired by various cultural influences, the art of the troubadours drew no distinction between poetry and music. Like in Johanne's community in Midwestern Jutland, this art could be practised indiscriminately by men and women, but unfortunately the majority of their creations were destroyed by the Inquisition of the Catholic Church. And that is not the only connection to the songs of Marie Kølbæk Iversen's great-great-great-great-grandmother. In quoting an interview between Edouard Glissant and Alexandre Leupin, Lisa Robertson scrutinises the Cathar epistemicide within a broader context: For Glissant, the crusades of 1209–29 represent the start of the construction of "a walled-in, excluding, rationalist and racist" Europe. History begins at the end of this process. "Song was born, and was killed," wrote Jacques Roubaud, poet and historian of troubadour poetry.

The already colonial, intra-European destruction of local cultures, languages and individuals begun under the Occitan sun extended into the Jutlandic night, and remains ongoing within and beyond Europe's borders to this day. In Sammelsted By, songs were sung after nightfall in *Æ Bindstouw,* — 'the knitting room' — not itself a separate room, but the living room renamed after its nightly function during winter. Here, people took turns singing, with no distinction of gender or social hierarchy, as they would knit with wool cut from sheep grazing on the surrounding moors. The songs thus interlinked several dimensions: A link through one's voice to memory and song. A link through threads of wool to the landscape. And a link in the song about Donnimaar, of course, to flax and braiding, to knitting. The song as sung by Marie is itself a kind of conceptual braid, a thread for each world and each realm: One for the young woman, embodying myth and the imaginary. One for the ancestor, embodying history and lore. And one for the artist, her physical presence and biography. Woven together into a whole, these threads generate what Simone Weil understands to be a 'passive force': one that is ultimately a form of resistance against force as violence.

Our lives are made of tangled connections and the social bonds we weave between each other, between ourselves and other beings across the environments in which we evolve. As the anthropologist Tim Ingold reminds us, we are ourselves made of ties and connected threads, from muscular fibres to nervous systems. And we likewise connect to those who are now absent through lines, linkages and lineages. Ingold explains that the way we represent genealogical ties has itself changed over time. In the Middle Ages, it was drawn in the form of a tree with roots extending downwards. Later, this structure became upended so that the roots would instead point to the sky, towards progress. And later yet, it took the form of a diagram connecting people of the same line of descent on a 'point to point' basis, without any change between generations.

In the early-nineteenth century, Ingold writes, "the founder of modern biology, Jean-Baptiste Lamarck, had seen in the evolution (...) of organic forms the clearest evidence that creatures of every kind were working their way up the scale of nature, with each new generation taking up the cumulative achievements of its predecessors and passing them on enhanced by its own." Very interestingly, he called this process 'transformism'. It would be but a small step to proceed from that to describing the transformation of Donnimaar as a genealogical manifesto for consensual exchange across generations (rather than for the crude force with which hereditary traits in the populace were later sought to be controlled through the social-Darwinist measures of the State). Yet for Ingold, the passage of generations is mainly a matter of transportation. In quoting Bergson, he replaces the diagram and the connection-based model with one based on the notion of trajectory, of "a continual moving around, or coming and going." He goes on to say that in this case, once again citing Bergson, each generation "far from following the previous one in a connected sequence of synchronic 'slices' (...) leans over (...) and touches the next." The model he proposes shows "a series of interlaced trails," a way of passing on stories like so many 'relays': "The result is a braid of lines that continually extends as lives proceed." "The braid of life," he writes, rests on "a narrative interweaving of present and past lives" into a shared, legible form of time. It is this connection — the matrix, the shared essence of a multifaceted political symbol — which Donnimaar's father cuts in order to split the genealogical model of rootedness from that of trans-generational flow and exchange, and ultimately instill the power of the State to separate, parse and destroy heterodox traditions. Seeking to mend this patriarchal cut, Marie has reworked her foremother's songs with voices transparently laid over voices to allow for the past to extend into — and resonate with — the present anew.

And what if we envisioned the linkage of generations musically, in terms of variations, melodic transpositions and fluid lines that evolve like the melody of a song?

Songs are pathways and modes of connection, lines drawn on an invisible map that travel across history and soar over landscapes. Simone Weil talks of bridges: "We have inherited them, but we no longer know how to use them (...) We merely know that they are bridges, things to cross over." She calls them *metaxu*: "Things created [that] are by their nature intermediaries towards each other and without end," she writes in *Gravity and Grace*. The *metaxu* are the epitome of the in-between, the interval, the transformation and passage between two states, from one moment to another, between beings and between worlds.

"What would it be sacrilegious to destroy?", she writes. "The *metaxu* (...) no human being should be deprived of his or her *metaxu*, meaning his or her blend of relevant forms of heritage (...) which feed the soul and keep it warm, and without which human life is impossible, unless you are a saint."

Donnimaar's golden braid is a bridge. Johanne's songs are fabrics. Marie's work invokes an infinite choir of voices, which tell us that art, like songs, is not only made of sounds, words or images but also of knowledge.

— Marie Kølbæk Iversen, *Neo-worlds: Transformative Agency through Fright, Rite, and Myth* (dissertation), 2023.
— Marie Kølbæk Iversen, *Donnimaar. Vredens Børn*, Kunsthal Rønnebæksholm and MoBC Records, 2021.
— Gilles Deleuze and Félix Guattari, *A Thousand Plateaus* (translated by Brian Massumi), 1987, Minneapolis: University of Minnesota Press.
— Boaventura de Sousa Santos, *Epistemologies of the South*, 2014, New York: Routledge.
— Simone Weil, "En quoi consiste l'inspiration occitanienne?" ["What the Occitan Inspiration Consists Of"] in *Les Cahiers du Sud*, February 1943.
— Simone Weil, *Gravity and Grace* (translated by Emma Craufurd, New York: Routledge, 1963.
— Lisa Robertson, *Anemones: A Simone Weil Project*, 2021, Amsterdam: If I Can't Dance.
— Edouard Glissant with Alexandre Leupin, *The Baton Rouge Interviews* (translated by Kate Cooper), 2020, Liverpool: Liverpool University Press.
— Jacques Rancière, preface to William T. Lhamon Jr. *Peaux blanches, masques noirs. Performances du blackface, de Jim Crow au hip-hop Zones sensibles* (translated by Sophie Renault), Paris: Kargo/L'éclat.
— Tim Ingold, *Lines: A Brief History*, chapter "The Braid of Life," 2007, New York: Routledge.

MARIE KØLBÆK IVERSEN
SELECTED WORKS 2015-2023

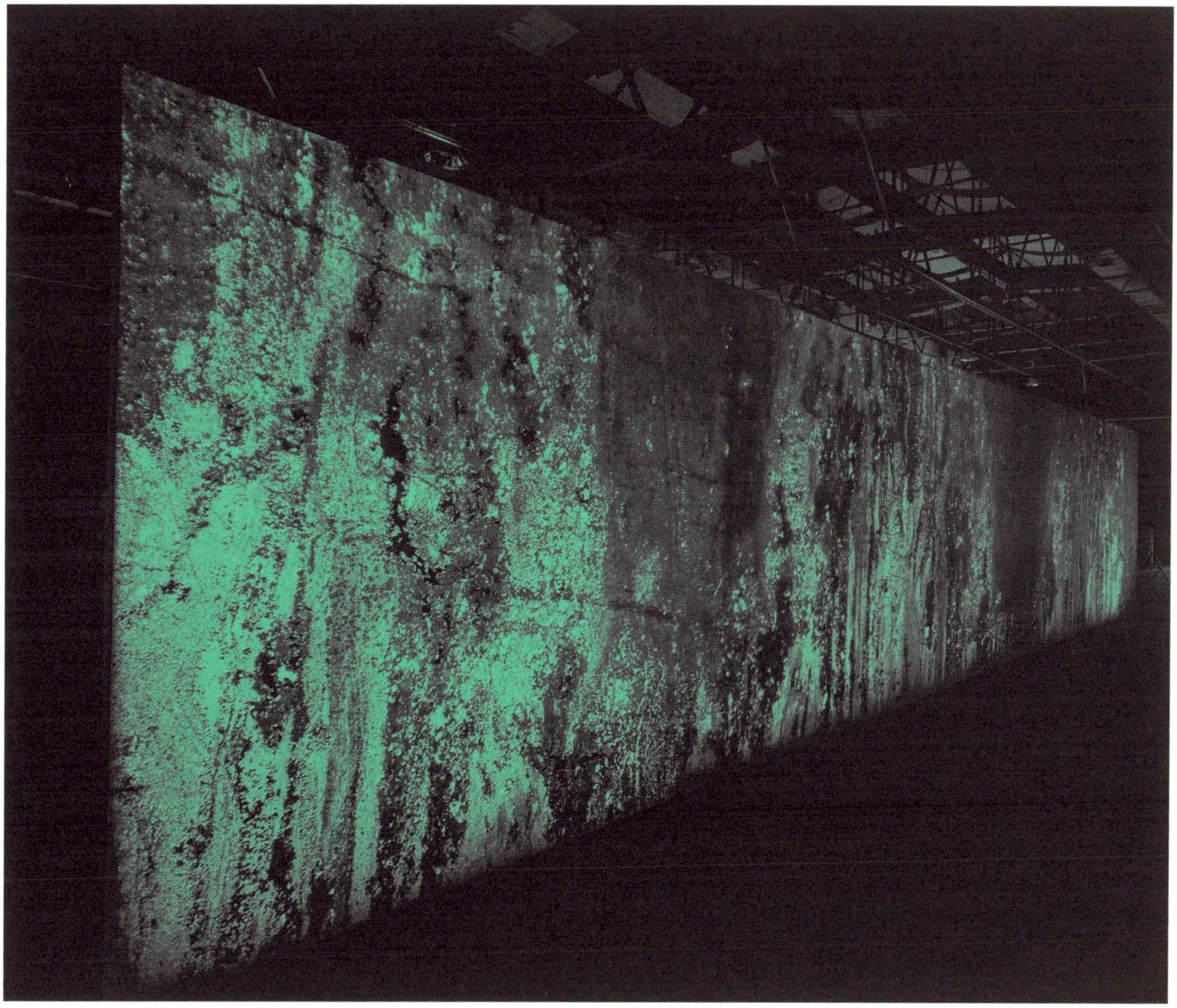

2015 In early 2015, I presented the installation *Mirror Therapy* in a solo exhibition at the Fotografisk Center in Copenhagen. The work consisted of five abutting slide projectors illuminating thinly polished slices of lapis lazuli, the source of ultramarine pigment that came to play a big role in Western art before the advent of chemical colours. The stones for my work had been extracted from the ground in Afghanistan, where Denmark was militarily engaged from 2001 to 2021 as a NATO ally. Applying the name of the body therapeutic treatment method 'mirror therapy' to my work, I propose a displacement of geographies and a cross-reading between human and mineral wounded bodies that inhabit the geopolitical and (art) historical spectrum between Western Europe and Central Asia.

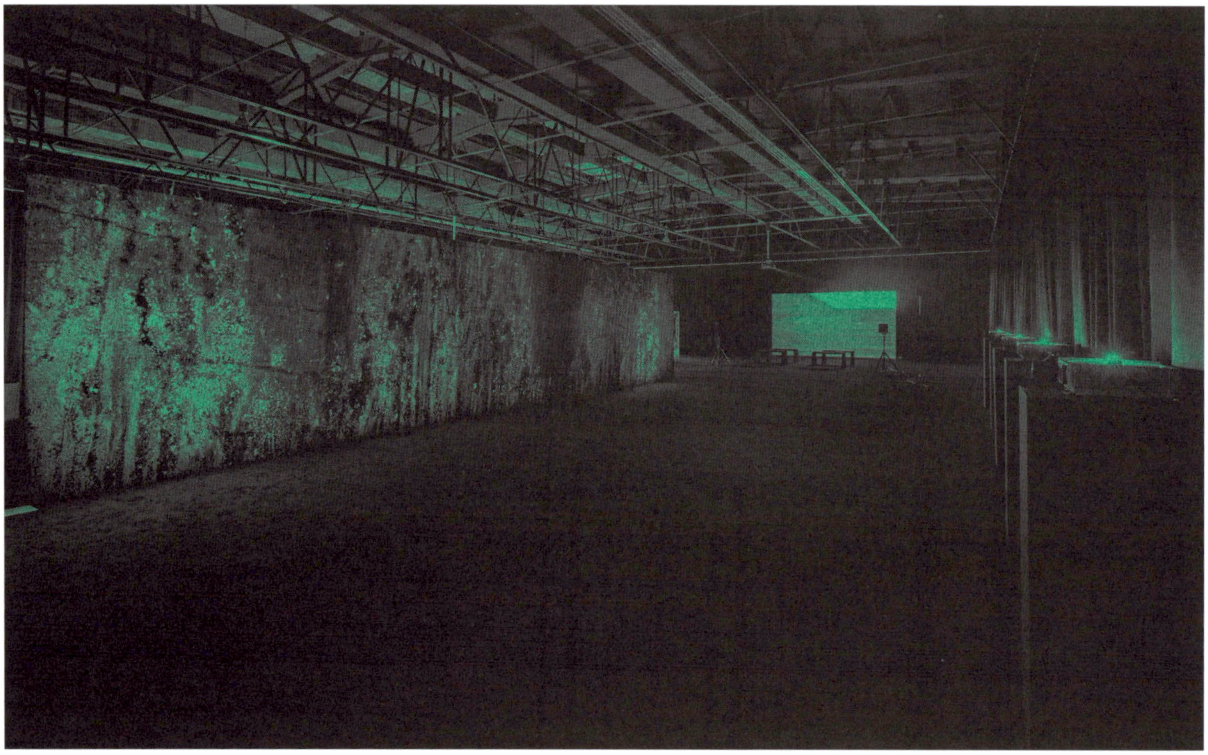

2015–2016 The treatment method 'mirror therapy' was developed by the American neuroscientist Vilayanur S. Ramachandran in the 1990s to alleviate phantom pain in amputated limbs. By placing a mirror along the body's vertical axis and mirroring the remaining limb in the place of the amputation, the amputee's mirror neurons are activated to fire across the disparate forms of their bodily asymmetry, thereby forging a connection between real and virtual body parts. In the context of how mirror therapy in the 2000s became applied in the treatment of wounded war veterans from the Western invasions of Iraq and Afghanistan, the work sets out to explore the transformative potentiality of virtual images between neuroscientific, therapeutic, geopolitical, artistic and imaginary realms. In 2016, *Mirror Therapy* was presented at the 11th Gwangju Biennial, *The Eighth Climate (What does art do?)*.

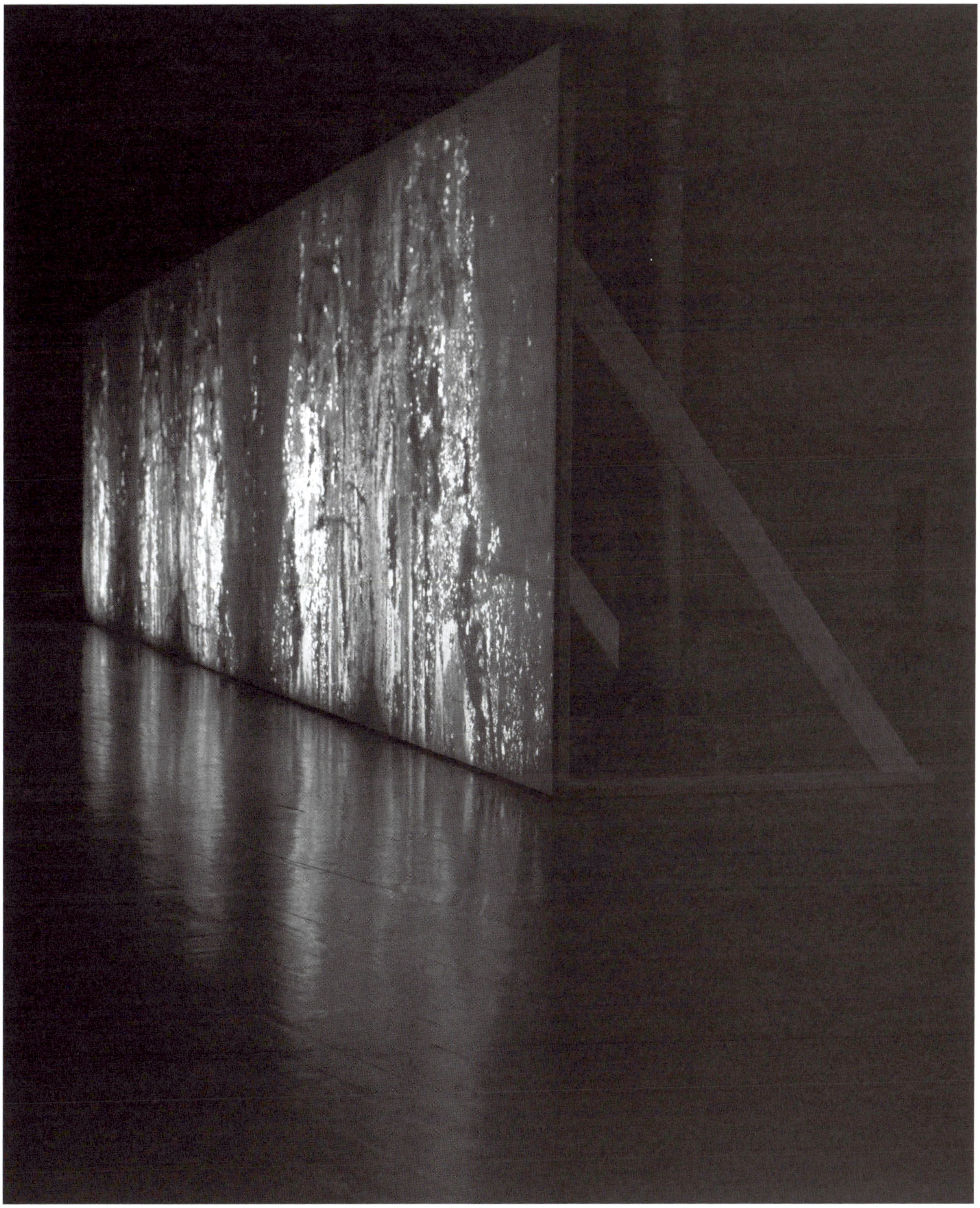

2016 The terms ‘phantom limb’ and ‘phantom pain’ indicate the perceived but non-existing limb as a ghost in the body: An exposure of the wounded soul, a virtual part of the self. Extrapolating the logic of the treatment method to describe how trauma is asymmetrically inflicted on real and social bodies of warring nations — between invader and the invaded — the work traced transformative capacities that, albeit weakened or wounded, would allow for empathic identification across disparate locations and remote-seeming pains. Not as a given, but as a future-oriented goal and effort (or hope, aspiration).

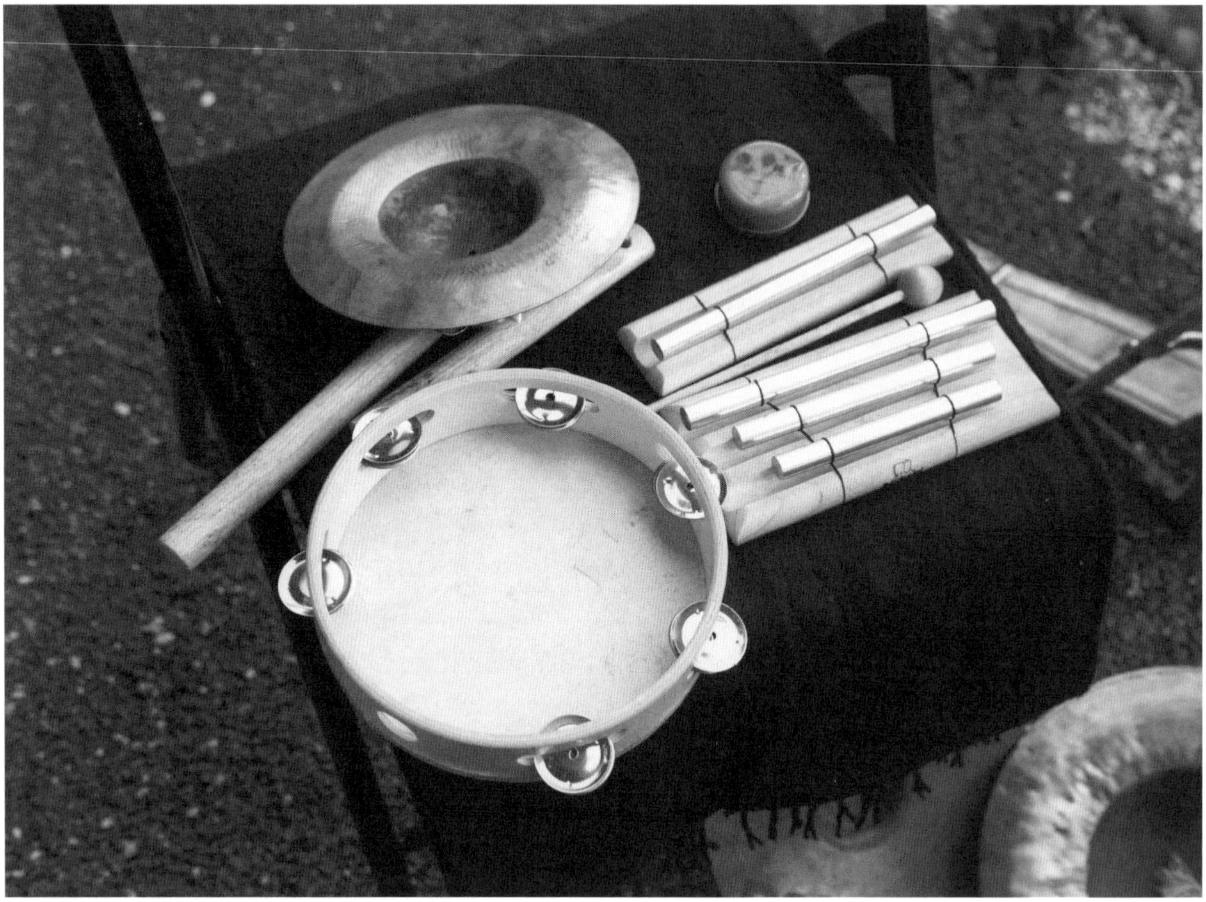

100

2017 For PS/Y's *Hysteria* at LUX in London, at the autumn equinox I performed magic songs handed down to me from my great-great-great-great-grandmother, a denizen of the West Jutland heathlands in provincial Denmark, who in 1873 was the ethnographic subject of folklore collector Evald Tang Kristensen. The songs spring from a very different cultural source than the Protestant Christianity dominant at the time of their collection: they tend — at times explicitly — towards the proto-feminist, the apocalyptic, the anti-Christian and the anti-Danish.

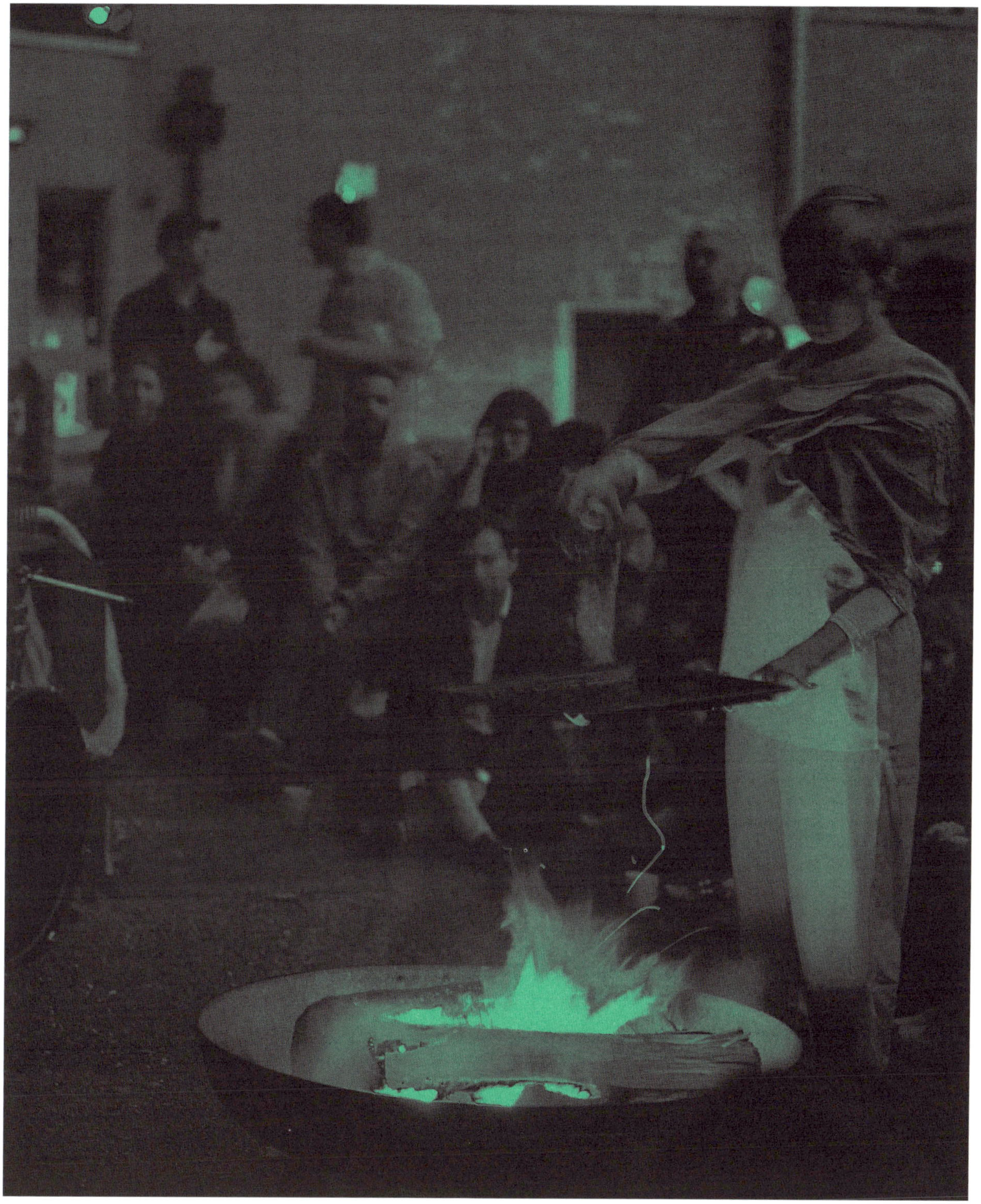

In the Northern hemisphere, the autumn equinox marks the threshold of winter darkness, and extends symbolically into the dreams of an extended night. It is a celebration of the power of dreaming to unsettle the fabric of reality by rendering strange and contingent the waking life of our troubled modernity.

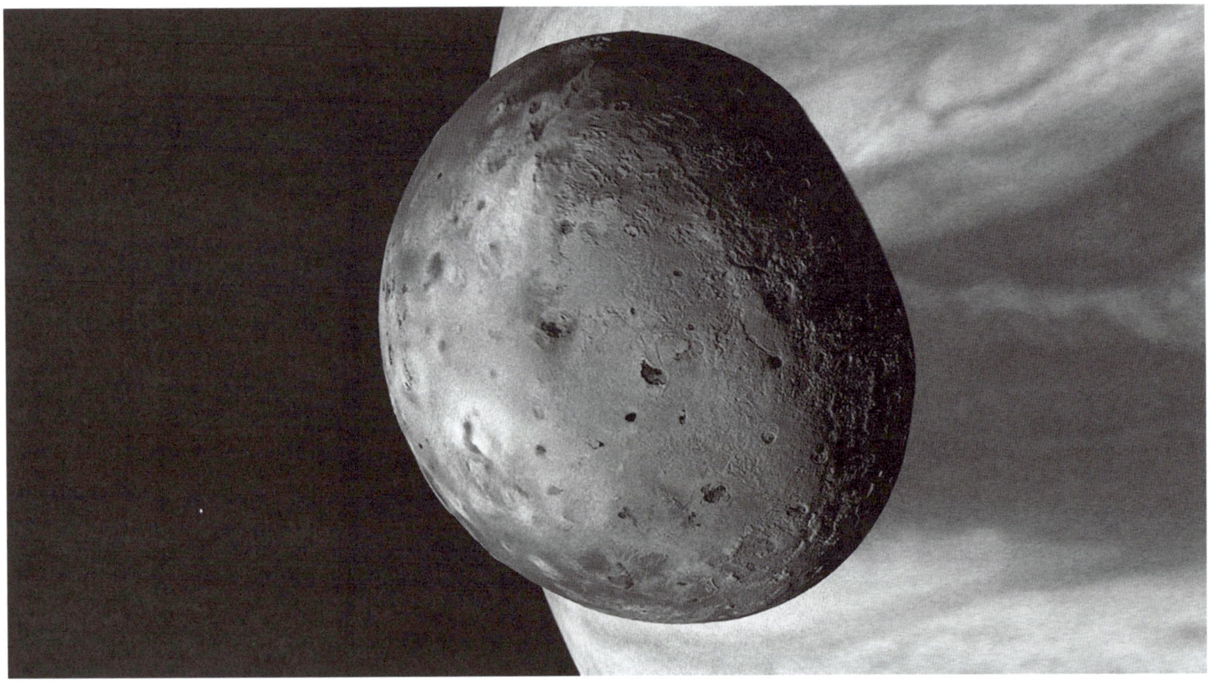

2017 Shifting my exploration of matrilinearity in relation to cultural memory and mythic storytelling from the ultra-local to the pan-Western, I turned towards Jupiter's innermost moon Io — the most volcanically active body in our solar system, a burning world in constant eruption. Io was discovered by Galileo Galilei and Simon Marius during the same days of January in 1610. While Galilei was first to present his discovery of the Jovian moons, it is Marius's names that have been used by posterity for these moons: Io, Europa, Ganymede and Callisto — names drawn from Greek-Roman mythology, where they reference the female victims of Jupiter's "insatiable lust," according to Marius.

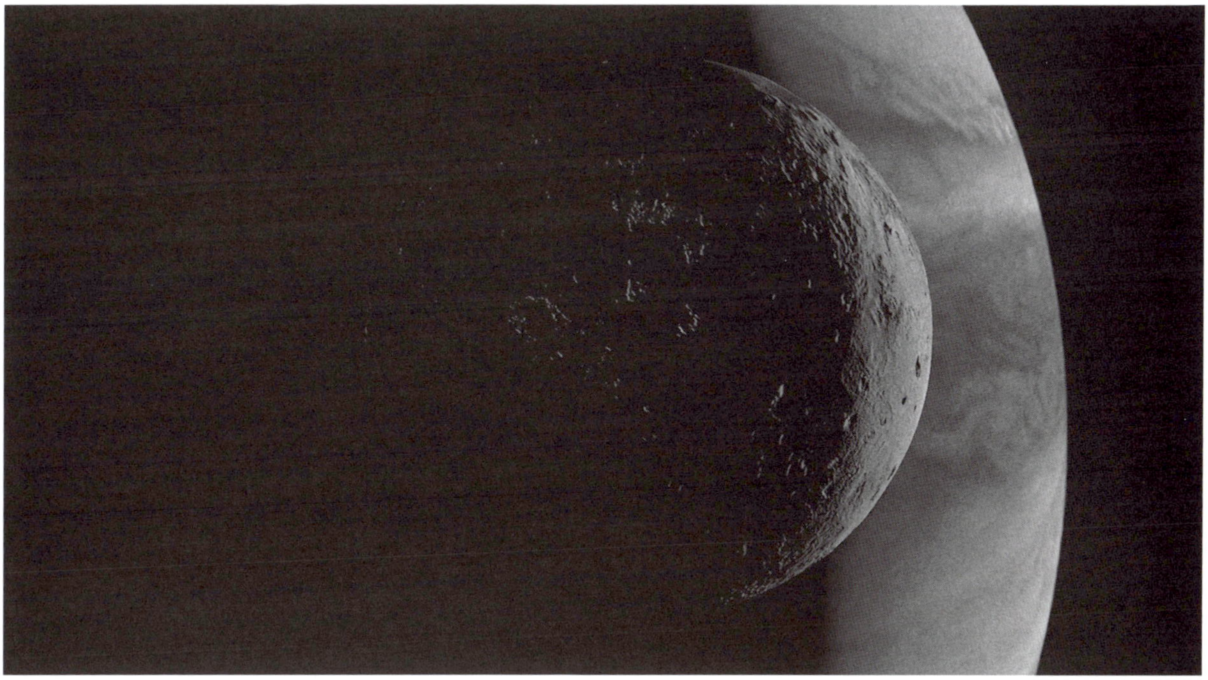

2017 In the myth, the young girl Io was dispelled from her father's house at the command of Jupiter, who — in the shape of a cloud — went on to rape her. Jupiter's wife Juno however noticed the heavy amassment of clouds over the Mediterranean, and came down to confront her husband. Seeing her coming, Jupiter transformed Io into a white heifer, but Juno saw through the deceit and sent a gadfly to bite Io every time she stopped to rest. In this way Io roamed the Earth, restless, transfigured and in pain. At last, she arrived in Egypt where she gave birth to her son and regained her maiden form. Horns however remained on her forehead, mythologically fusing her with the Egyptian mother goddess Isis, an epitome of female authority, she who has gained her insight through pain.

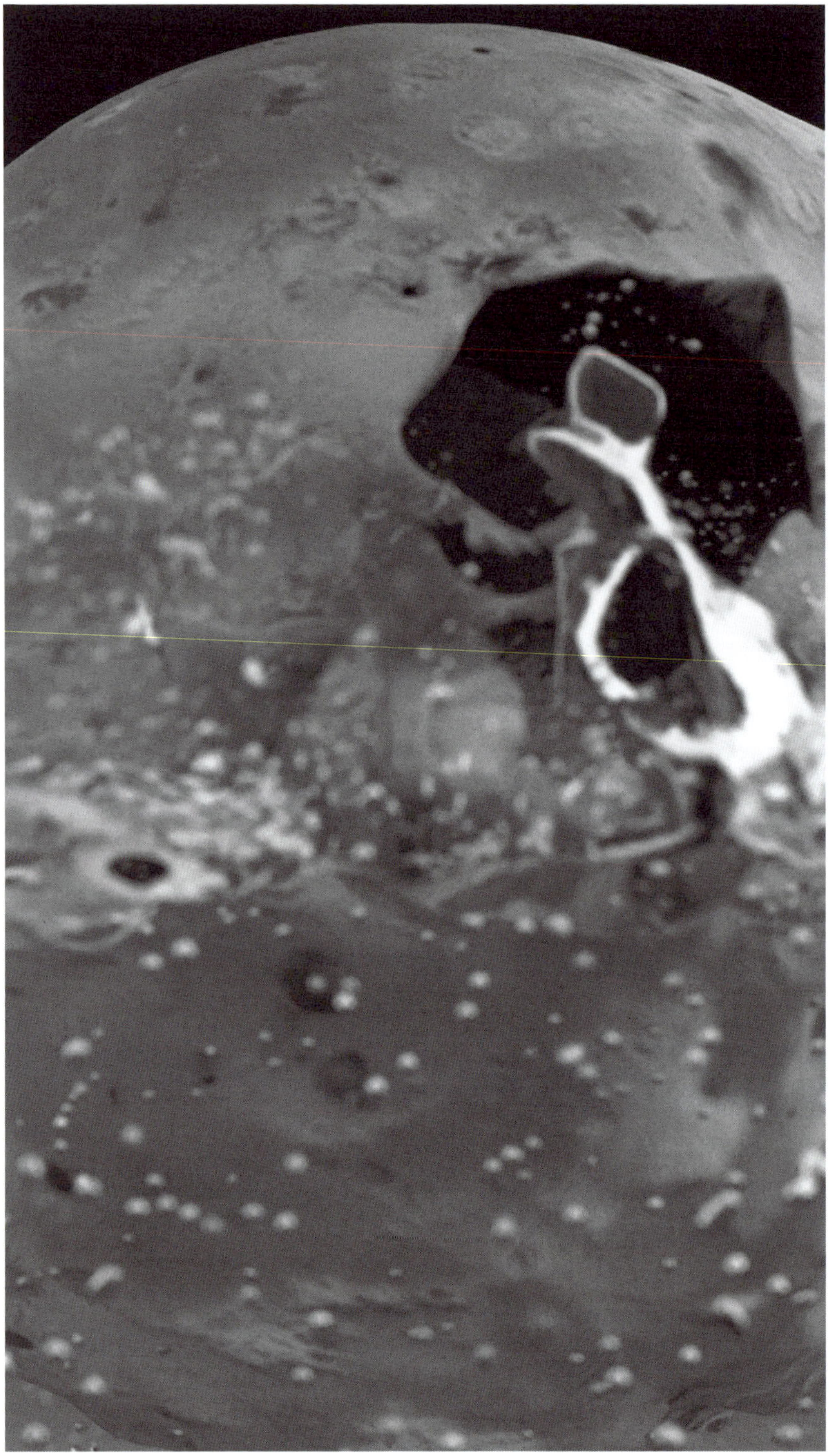

2018–2019 My work series *Io/I* traces the gendered plight of childbearing and birth through mythology, astronomy and cosmography across deep time and outer space. "I have come here to the prints of ancient feet, my mother's," the Danaïds plead in Aeschylus' play *The Suppliants:* "Look benignly upon the women's cause, look upon our race ancient in story, and recall (…) our ancestress [Io], the woman of your love. Show that you remember all, you who laid your hand upon Io." The work was shown at the exhibition *The Moon* at Louisiana Museum of Modern Art in Denmark in 2018 and at the Henie Onstad Art Centre in Norway in 2019, including the opera *Moonologue* which I produced in collaboration with composer and soprano Katinka Fogh Vindelev.

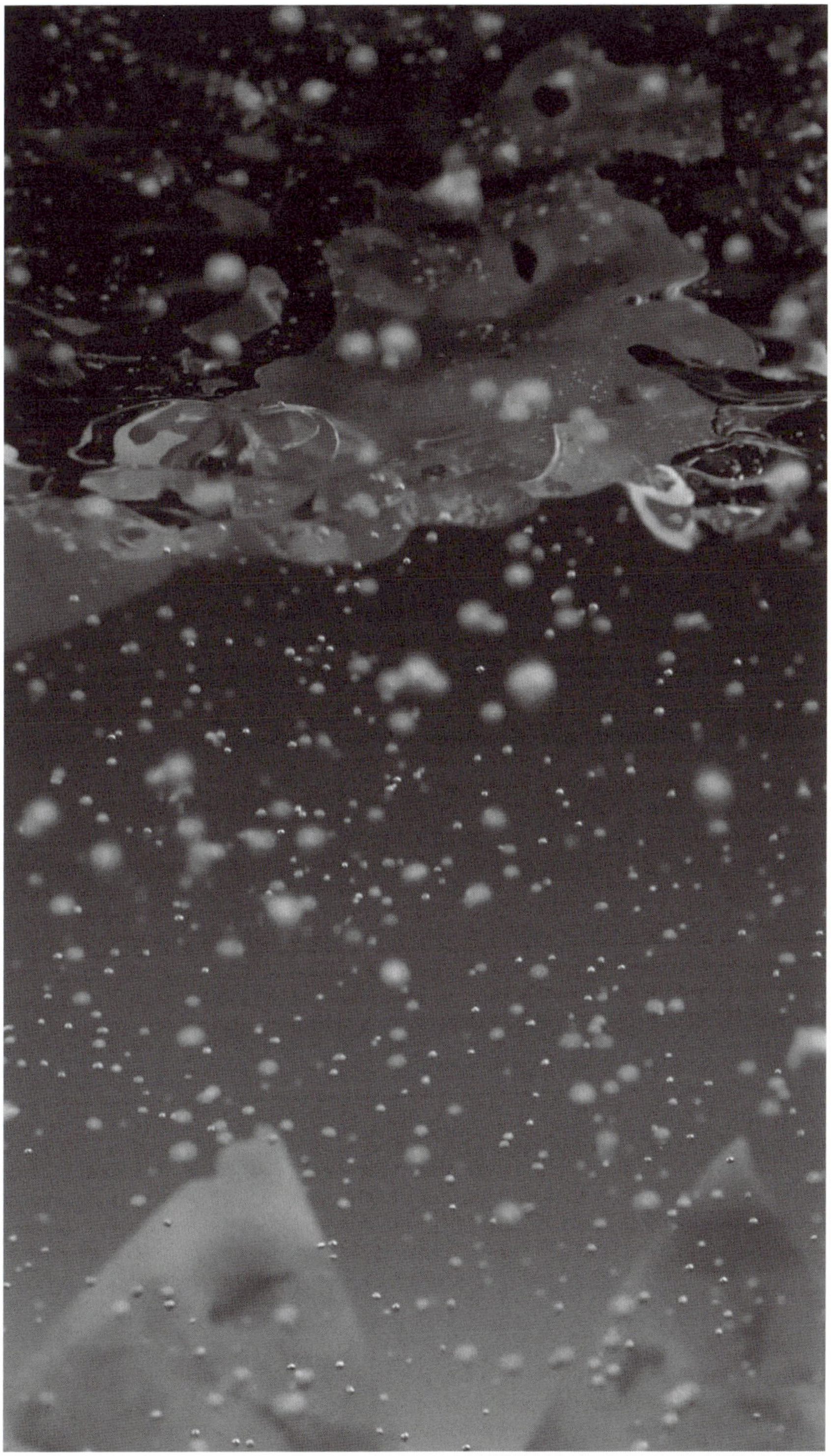

2019 Mistranslating 'Io' from Galileo's native Italian into the English first-person pronoun 'I', my work synthesised Io's different manifestations into a composite and collective, human and more-than-human self: The mythological maiden, the astronomical satellite, the white roaming heifer, Galileo, me, you-as-me and me-as-you, thereby insisting that Io's pain is shareable beyond the threshold of any of her specific abstractions.

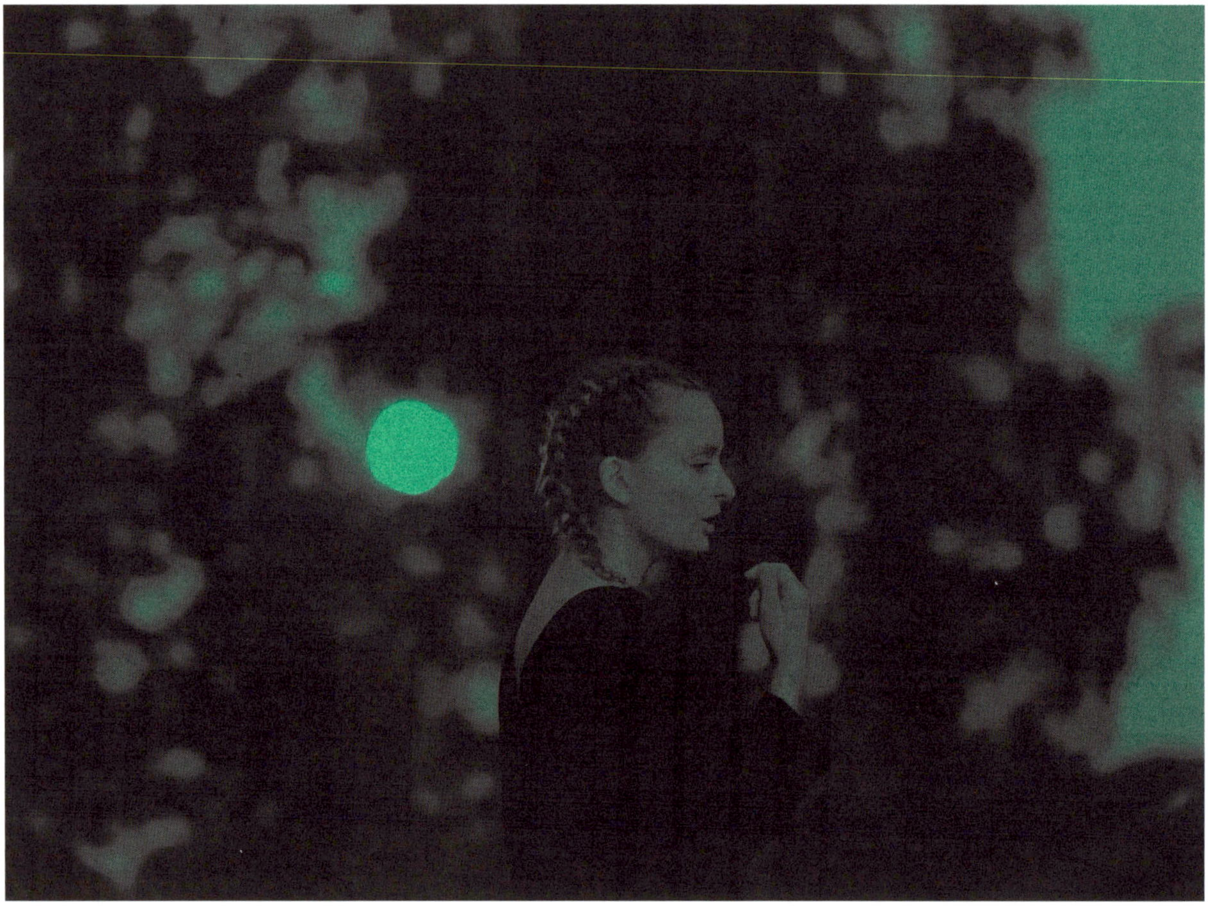

2021 For the exhibition *Soil. Sickness. Society* at Rønnebæksholm, Næstved 2021, I launched my first album as Donnimaar, titled *Donnimaar. Vredens Børn* ('Children of Wrath' in Danish). The album title synthesises the name of the heroine Daughter Donnimaar from my foremother Johanne Tygesdatter's song 'Æ Fåwanleng' (i.e., 'The Transformation') with the title of Jutlandic writer, socialist and regionalist activist Jeppe Aakjær's novel *Vredens Børn* (1904). The album revolves around the magic songs and folktales collected by Evald Tang Kristensen from Tygesdatter and her peers in the 1870s. In different ways, each of the songs thematises the conflict and controversy surrounding the East-Danish co-optation and agricultural development of the West Jutlandic heath commons from 1866 onwards.

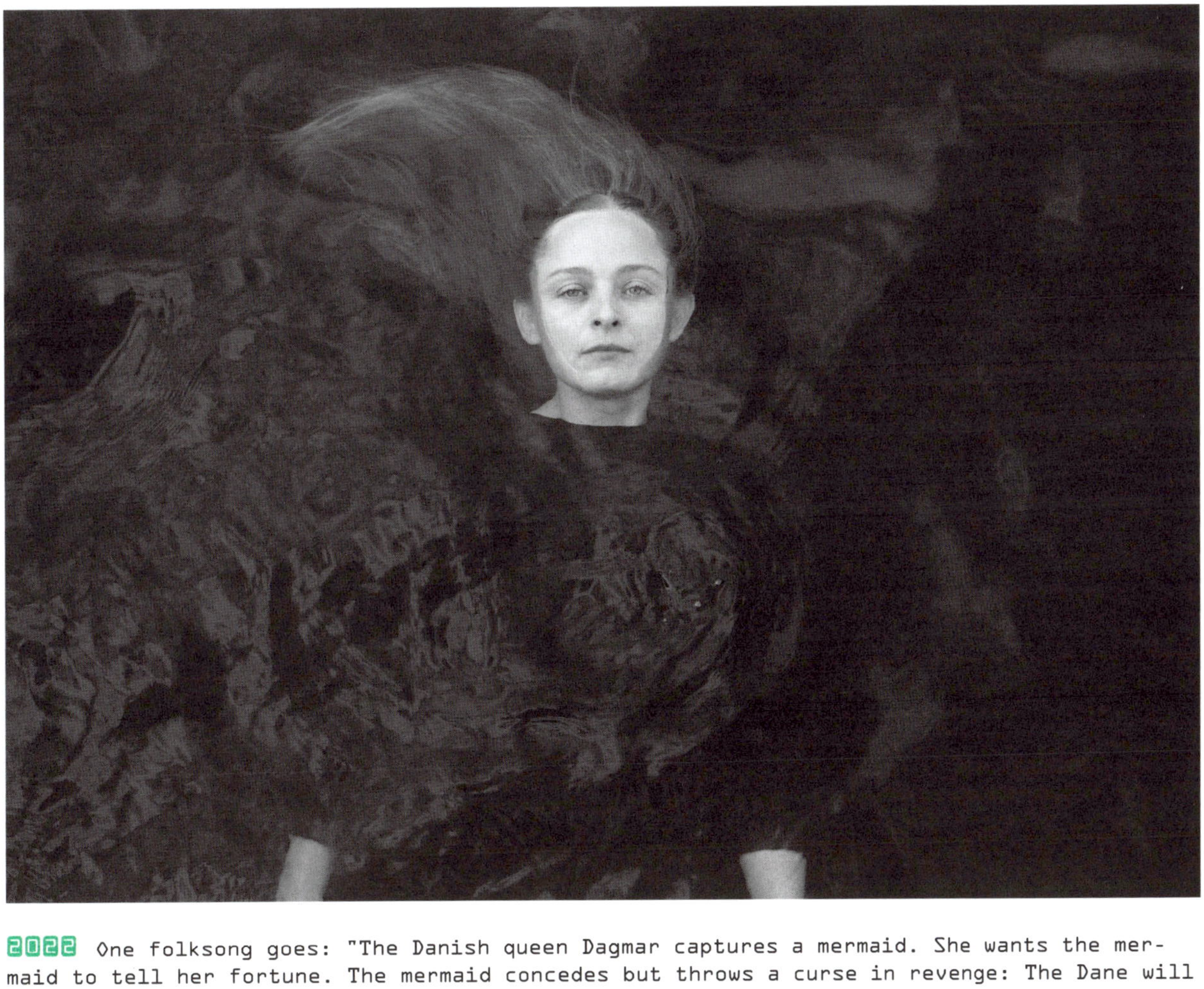

2022 One folksong goes: "The Danish queen Dagmar captures a mermaid. She wants the mermaid to tell her fortune. The mermaid concedes but throws a curse in revenge: The Dane will mother three sons but will soon die for them. The first will be the Danish king, the second wears a crown. The third becomes the wisest man, receiving news from distant towns. Now Dagmar begs the Danish king to let the mermaid live. But he rejects her plea: 'She has sunk my seven ships!' Dagmar faints, the king gives in. They return her to the sea. The mermaid sits atop a wave, the queen is crying woefully. The mermaid says: 'Don't cry for me. I have opened heaven's gates for thee. The bells of heaven are ringing for thee, and my little children are longing for me. The angels of heaven are longing for thee, and the depths of the sea are open for me.'"

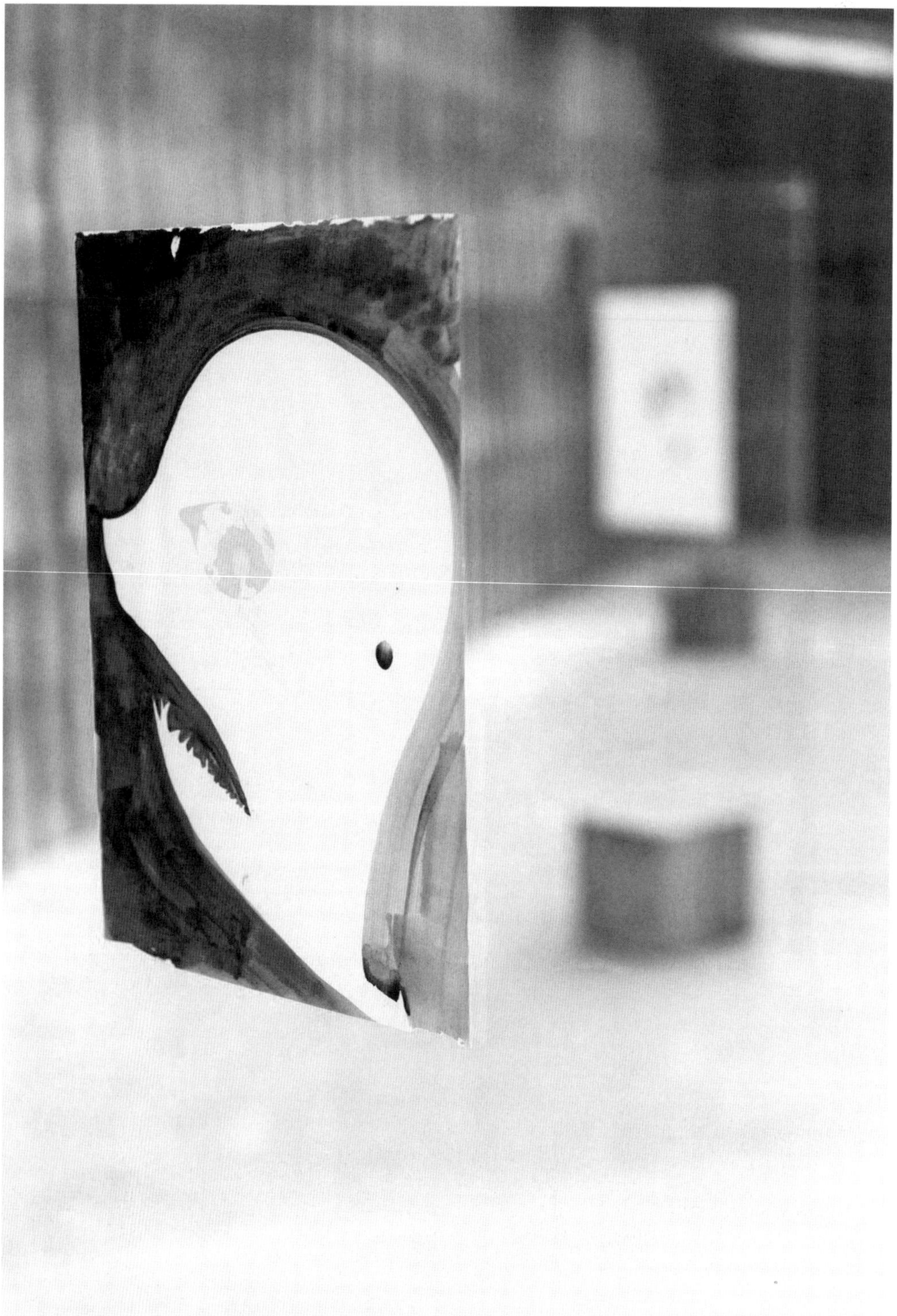

2022 For my solo exhibition *Ø Tilli* ('On the Floor' in West Jutlandic) at the Ebeltoft Kunsthal in late 2022, I engaged with the idea of merpeople as humanity's others: mythical dwellers of those natural environments underwater, underground, uninhabitable to humans, and ciphers of cultures and peoples that have been barred from entering the modernised present. Merpeople represent the spirits of the physically or culturally 'dead' who continue to haunt the living in their desire for revenge or justice.

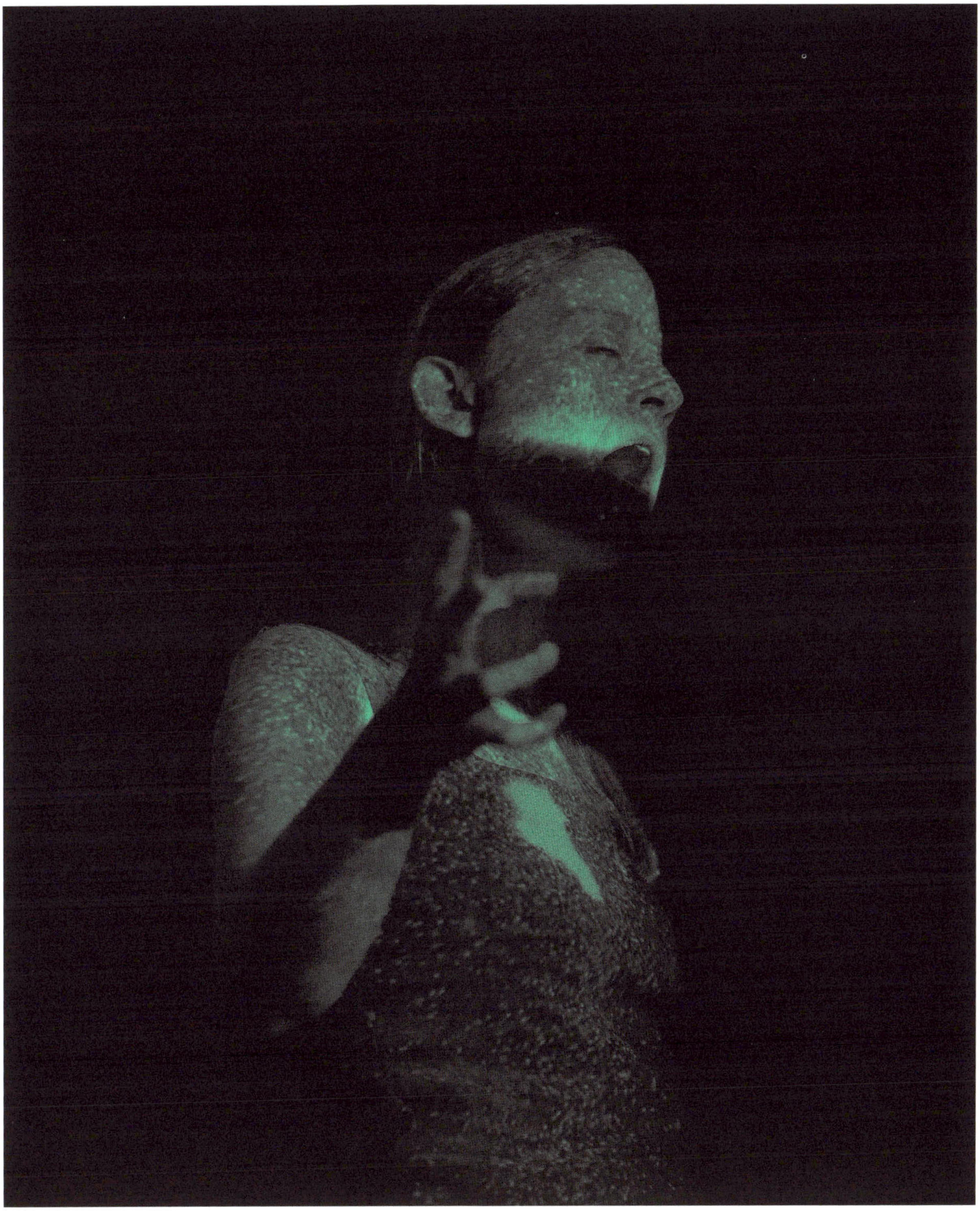

2022 My solo exhibition *Rovhistorier* ('Histories of Predation' in Danish) at O—Overgaden, Copenhagen 2022, traversed time, borders and cultures by travelling into the eye lens nuclei of the gurry shark, an extremely long-living deep-sea fish also known as the Greenland shark. Across the Nordic-Germanic languages, the gurry shark has historically been referred to as 'havkal' or 'håkjerringa'—that is: merman or mermaid—endowing the shark with mythological and anthropomorphic features. As a contextual framework for *Rovhistorier*, and as part of my music project *Donnimaar*, I sang folksongs about merpeople from my East Atlantic home region in Western Jutland in the exhibition.

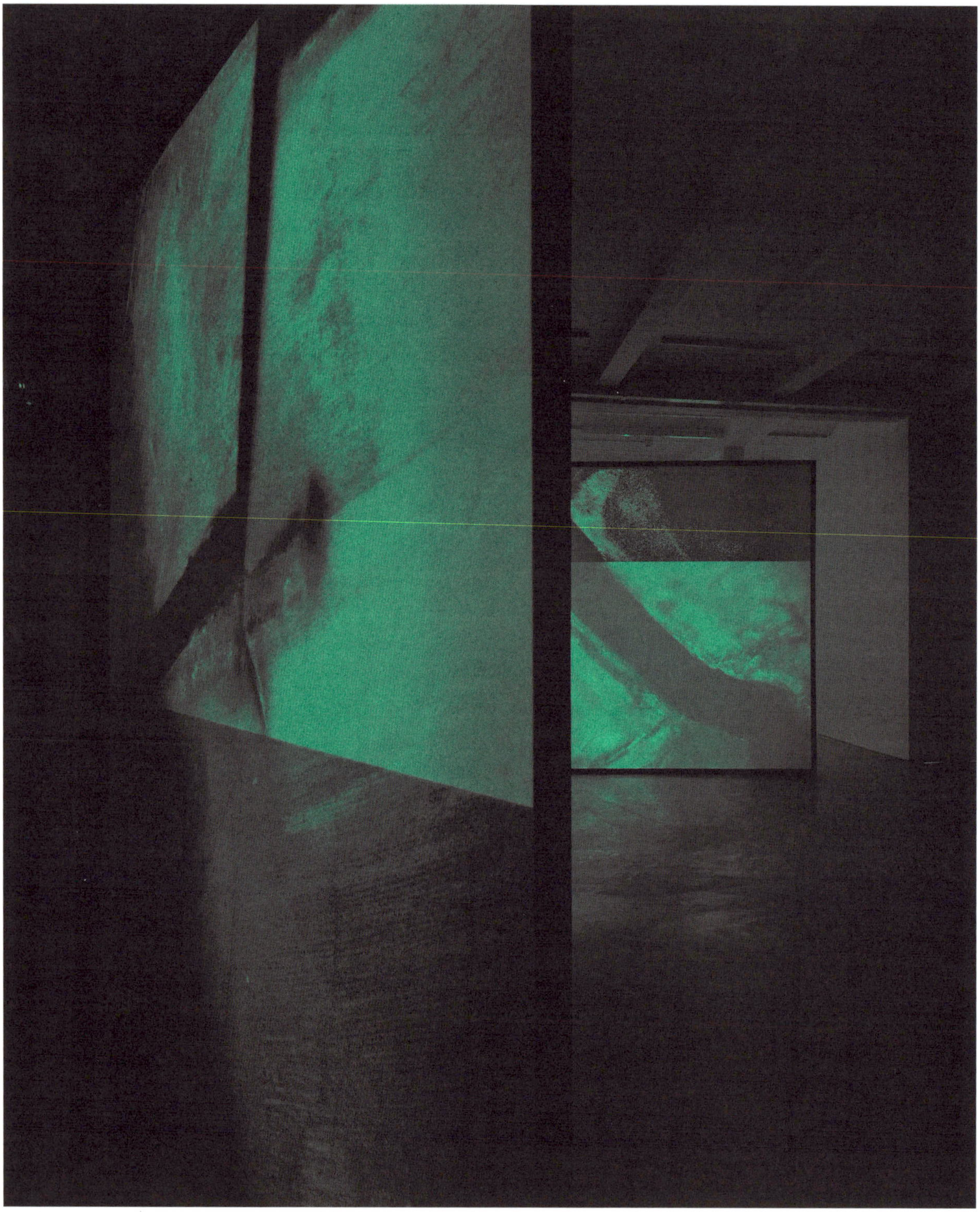

2022 Via carbon-14 dating of the nuclei of the animal's eye lenses, marine biologists have recently estimated the longevity of the gurry shark to be potentially more than 500 years. This makes the gurry shark the longest-living known vertebrate in the world, with contemporary specimens potentially having lived through the centuries that witnessed the European colonial expansion across the Atlantic Sea. Interweaving folklore and science, the exhibition reflected on half a millennium of imperialistic and environmental struggles in the North Atlantic region. With the shark's eye as its crux, it invited viewers to consider their own stakes in the predatorial dynamics that have fuelled the advance of capitalist modernity since the fifteenth century.

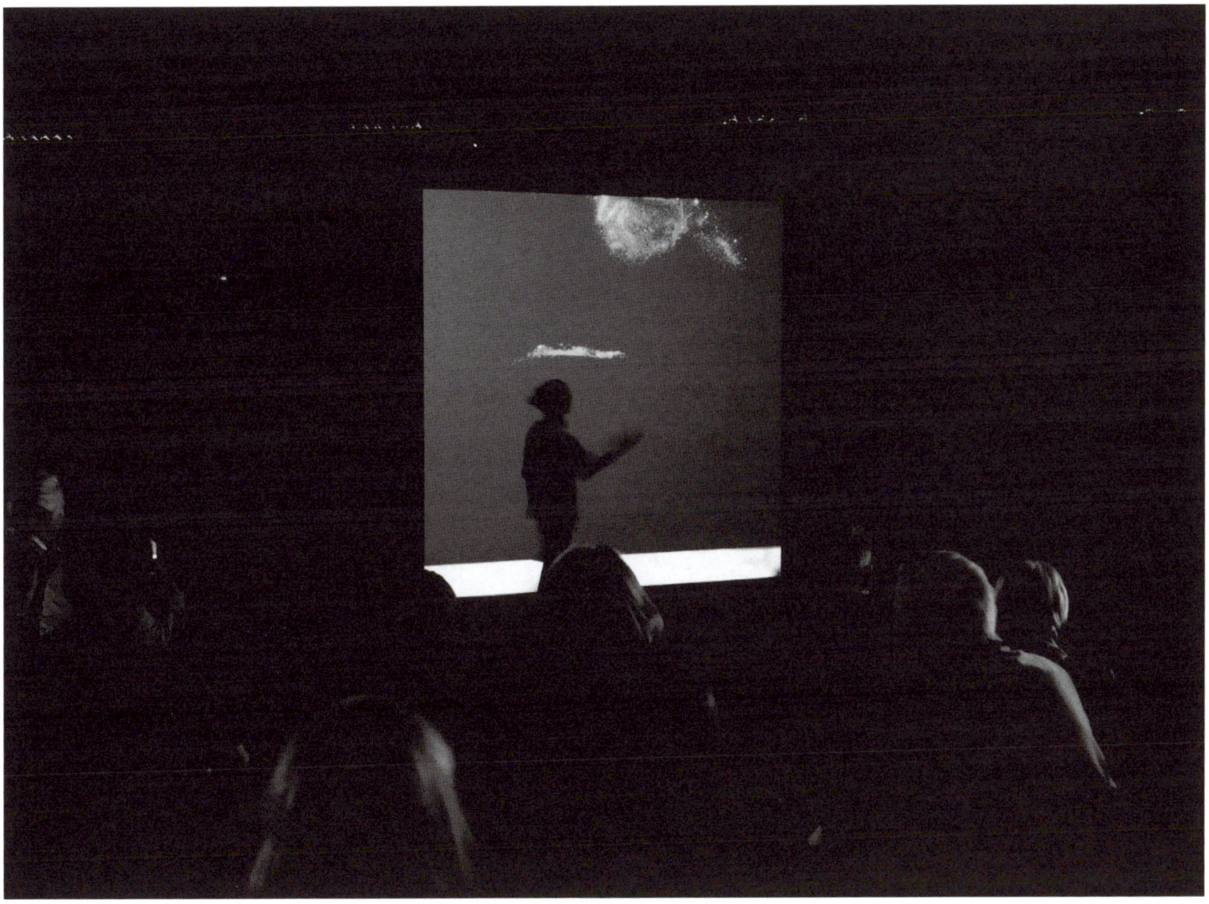

111

2023 Three monumental projection screens show hypnotic and brightly coloured images in shades of pink and green: Microscopic recordings of the thousands of stratified fibres created inside the gurry shark's eye lenses over the course of its centuries-long life. In its simultaneously abstract and ultra-concrete appearance, the work is a filmic time travel through the 'historical' gaze of the predator, including the shark whose eye is under scrutiny, but equally — or even more so — contemporary techno-scientific humanity as represented by the confocal microscope which enabled the production of the imagery for the work. Installation view from the 2023-exhibition of the work at SMK Thy, Doverodde, DK.

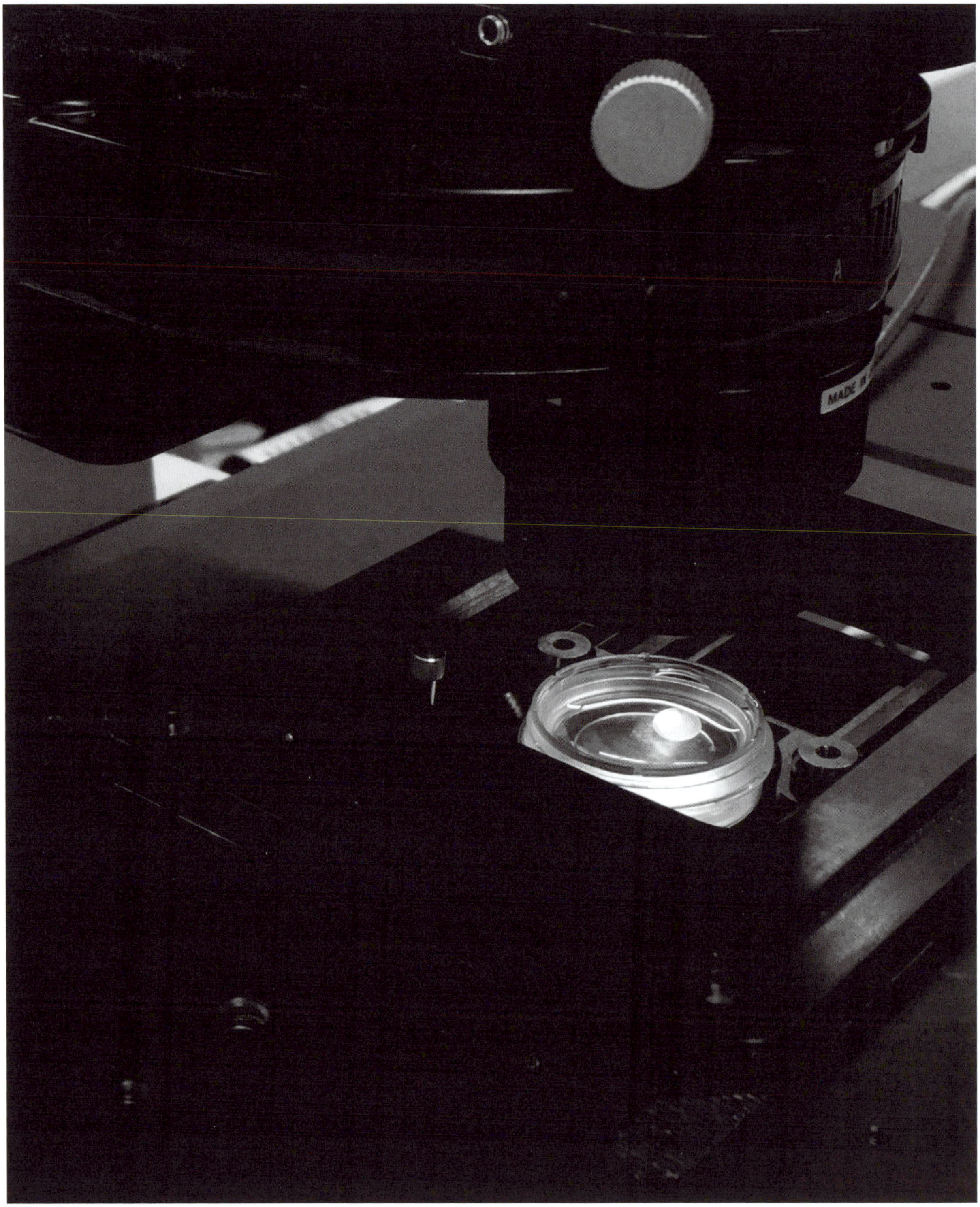

2020 In 2020, I obtained a pair of gurry shark eyes from marine biologist Julius Nielsen, who in 2016 determined the longevity of the shark via carbon-14 analysis of the nuclei of its eye lenses. Nielsen's research indicates that it may live to between 272 and 512 years of age. Then working at the Greenland Institute of Natural Resources (GINR), Nielsen and his colleagues monitor potentially endangered species to protect them from over-fishing as commercial bycatch. The gurry shark eyes used for *Rovhistorier* came from a research specimen that had been caught as bycatch in a GINR scientific survey.

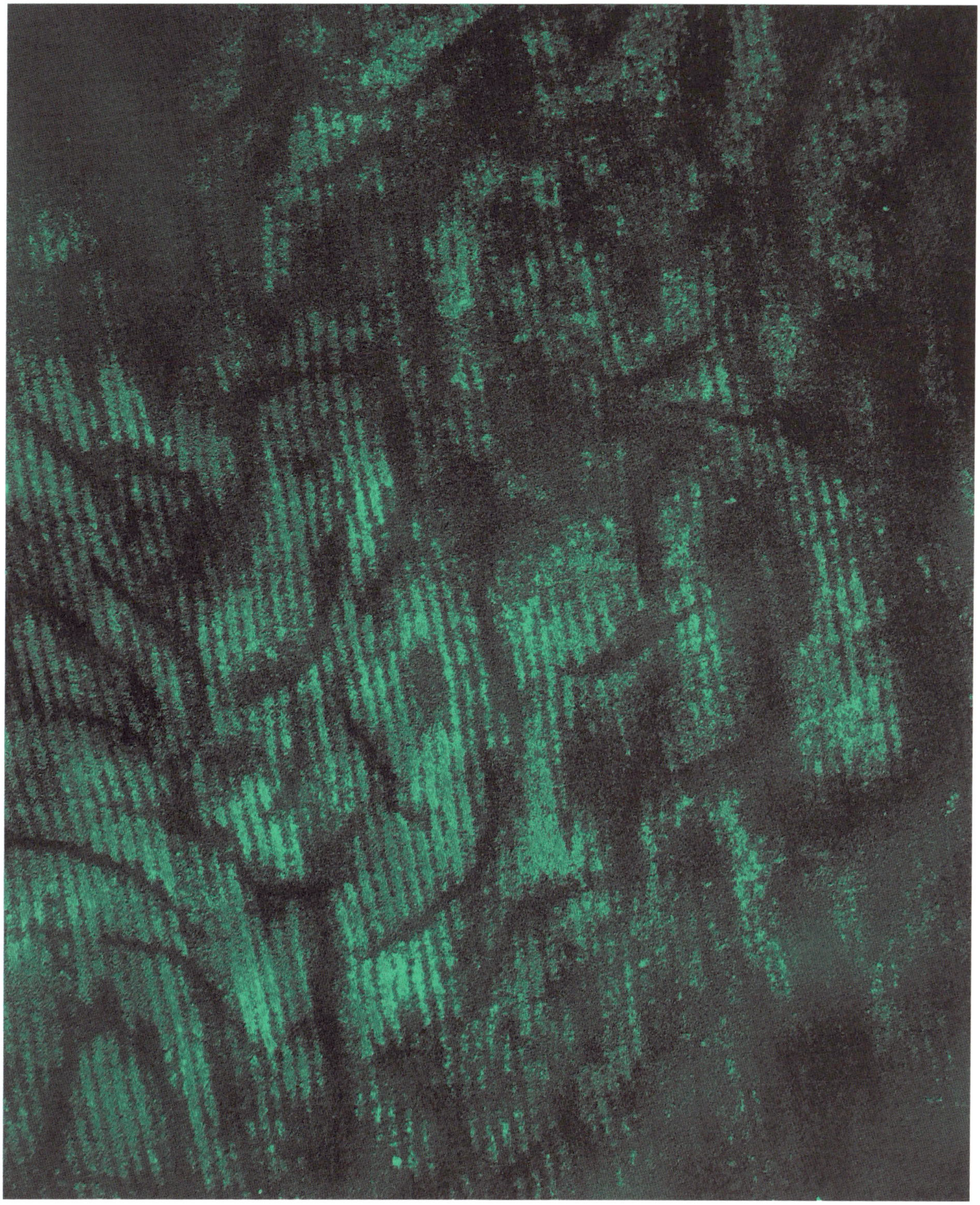

2020 Microscopic exploration of the shark's eye lens nuclei was carried out over a two-year period between 2020 and 2022 in collaboration with associate professor Jonathan Brewer and post-doctoral researcher Line Lauritsen, both from the Danish Molecular Biomedical Imaging Center (DaMBIC) at the University of Southern Denmark (SDU) in Odense, Denmark. The ensuing process of compressing the microscopic data into a standard 4K video format through the open-source bio-imaging application FIJI was done in collaboration with visual artist Silas Emmery and senior data engineer Søren Kølbæk Iversen.

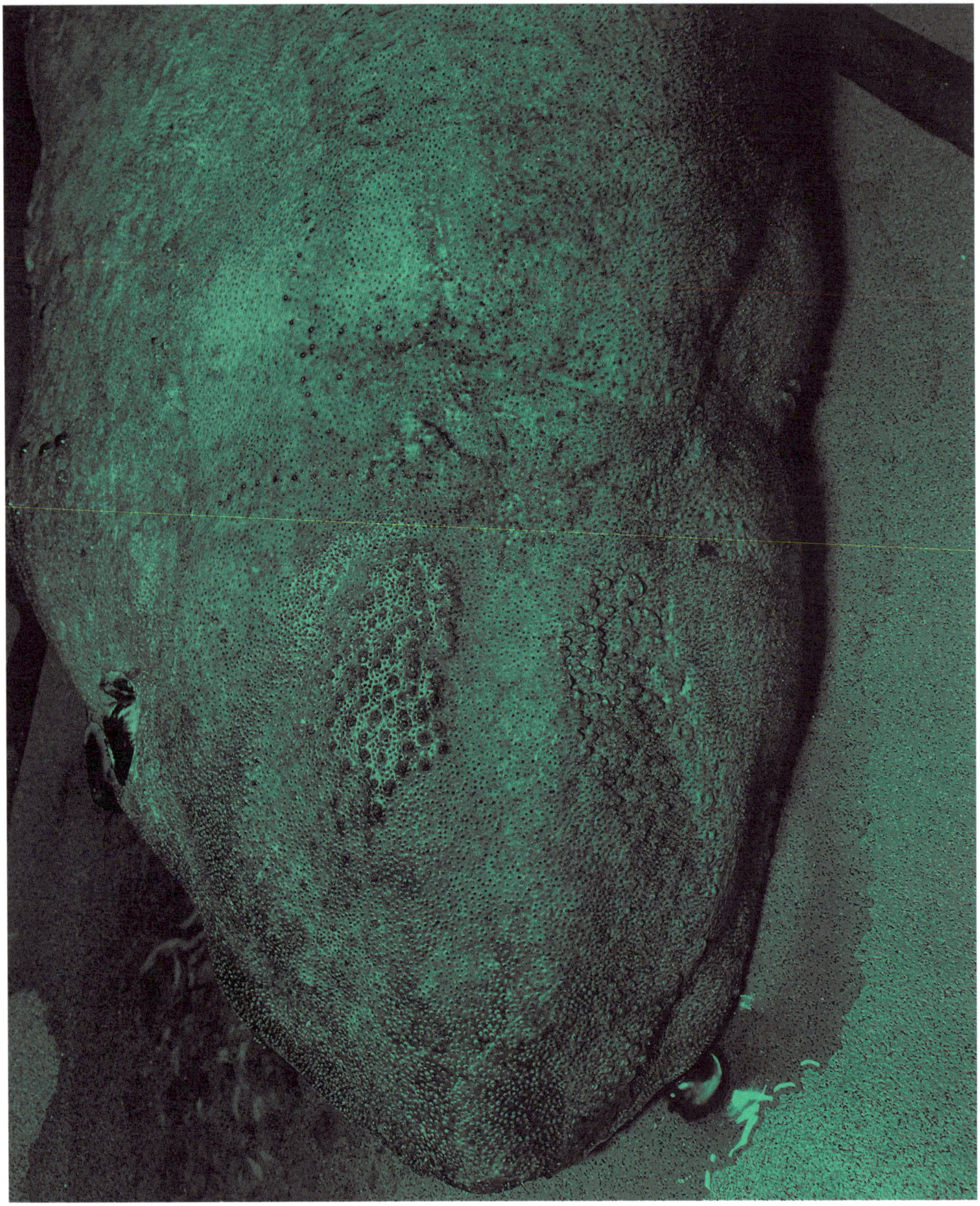

2021 Attempting to trace the commercial and scientific circuits that mediate contemporary human engagements with the gurry shark, in a laboratory in Nuuk in late 2021 I was brought face to face with an individual that had died as bycatch. The shark had subsequently been donated to the Greenland Institute of Natural Resources (GINR) for research purposes. Even though she had not died for my sake, her dead presence on the laboratory floor still haunts me and reminds me of my own structurally predatory agency in the world as a citizen and consumer. So does the knowledge that deaths like hers are mere trivialities from a commercial point of view: Gurry sharks are among the most commonly bycaught fish in the Northern North Atlantic, and a big nuisance to fishermen, who complain that they ruin their nets and crush the catch.

A WORLD YOU WOULD WANT TO LIVE IN? ADAM KHALIL AND MARIE KØLBÆK IVERSEN

This conversation between artists Adam Khalil and Marie Kølbæk Iversen took place in Copenhagen in June 2022. A shorter edit of the conversation was published on the occasion of Kølbæk Iversen's 2022 solo exhibition, *Rovhistorier,* at O—Overgaden in Copenhagen.

Adam Khalil, a member of the Ojibway tribe, is a filmmaker and artist from Sault Ste. Marie, Michigan, currently based between Brooklyn, New York and Copenhagen, Denmark. His work centres Indigenous narratives in the present, and looks towards the future, through the use of innovative fiction and nonfiction forms that subvert traditional forms of image-making through humour, relation, and transgression. A core contributor to New Red Order and a co-founder of COUSINS Collective, Khalil posits collaboration and exchange at the centre of his artistic methodology.

From their different backgrounds, Khalil and Kølbæk Iversen set out to explore the implications of tracing their respective heritages into the present, in order to consider how colonialism has signified for different minoritised people in different places across Europe and the Americas. In this way, their exchange also probes the potentialities of working across racialised divides to test the ground for potential 'under-common coalitions' — as Stefano Harney and Fred Moten put it [1] — pointing beyond the suffocating constitution of the present, with a view to conjuring a 'we' across disparate struggles and troubles. This is done in order to find ways in which crafting coalitions — solidary complicities — may sound a much louder call for ending "the world that created those particular troubles as the ones that must be opposed," as Jack Halberstam puts it. [2]

1 Stefano Harney and Fred Moten: *The Undercommons: Fugitive Planning & Black Study* (Brooklyn: Autonomedia, 2013).

2 Jack Halberstam: "The Wild Beyond: With and For the Undercommons" in Harney and Moten, Ibid. p. 9.

Marie Kølbæk Iversen (MKI) First of all, thank you so much, Adam, for agreeing to having this conversation with me. I have been really inspired by our exchanges so far, not least on the occasion of *TEDtalks on Acid* that you organised as part of New Red Order's (NRO) show *One if by Land, Two if by Sea* at the Kunsthal Charlottenborg earlier this year. I am curious to share some of my thoughts leading up to the exhibition at O—Overgaden with you, since — like in many of your projects — my project engages subjugated knowledges at the intersection of modernity and science to attempt formulating alternative perspectives of futurity and becoming, beyond the gridlock of capitalist modernity.

In my video-work *Rovhistorier|Histories of Predation* I am speculatively appropriating the historical gaze of a specific type of shark, the Greenland shark or gurry shark, which across the Nordic Germanic languages is called either merman or mermaid — i.e. the old Danish name for the shark is *havkal*, that is 'merman.'

New marine biological research shows that this 'merman' — the shark — may live to become as old as from 272 to 512 years. Additionally, it transits the whole of the northern North Atlantic Sea, which makes it an interesting imaginary interlocutor or 'eyewitness' with whom to reflect on the historical developments across the North Atlantic Sea, and to consider alternative views leading into the future.

As a Dane, I represent a colonial presence in Greenland, where the shark I have been working with was caught. But the project also seeks to reflect on how I came to become a Dane in the first place, as it were.

Adam Khalil (AK) The temporal scope of the gurry shark is a pretty juicy hook, and it got my brain buzzing! I'm not sure it's a 100% line-up, but I have been reading this essay by Lou Cornum about Indigenous futurism, which feels kind of relevant in terms of world-building:

> *'Indigenous Futurism' is part of a tradition that represents an alternative to Western sci-fi, which tends to be structured by the tension between utopia and dystopia. The temporality of Indigenous existence exceeds these terms: there is no pre-apocalypse or post-apocalypse, only perpetual revelation. Indigenous Futurism then, is about the struggle for a different future as well as a distinctly different idea of 'future'—one that goes beyond the conflict between tradition and progress, and asks us to inhabit the present.* [3]

[3] Lou Cornum: "Who Belongs to the Land?" on *Triple Canopy*, March 17, 2022 (canopycanopycanopy.com/contents/who-belongs-to-the-land — last accessed 15 February 2023), pp. 31–32.

Also, on my way over here, I was thinking about this — maybe it is a little stony baloney — but things like merpeople or dragons; like dragons emerged in Europe and Asia, but simultaneously. So they must be real, right?

MKI That's a good point. Generally it's interesting to consider how cultures and cultural narratives have exchanged historically, and continue to exchange, converging at minoritarian rather than majoritarian levels. In the conception of this project, another point of reference was Linebaugh and Rediker's *The Many-Headed Hydra* from 2000, which is lying here on the table in front of me. In the book, they unfold a historical account of the Atlantic under-commons, which took the shape of a motley crew proletariat originating in Europe, Africa and America:

> *It included clowns, or cloons (i.e., country people). It was without genealogical unity. It was* vulgar. *It spoke its own speech, with a distinctive pronunciation, lexicon, and grammar made up of slang, cant, jargon, and pidgin—talk from work, the street, the prison, the gang, and the dock. It was* planetary, *in its origins, its motions, and its consciousness. Finally, the proletariat was* self-active, creative*; it was—and is—alive; it is onamove.*
>
> *What does the experience of this proletariat have to offer us today?*[4]

This in many ways reflects the other vantage point for my project: the West Jutland heathlands, which is where my family originates and where I grew up, and where my great-great-great-great-grandmother Johanne Tygesdatter was one of Evald Tang Kristensen's informants in 1873. Trying to think from the perspective of the nineteenth-century heathlands, I attempt to pick up the bastardising linguistic logic and cultural outlook of my forbearers, which was precisely as proletarian and hybridising as Linebaugh and Rediker describe, including the various Jutlandic dialects mixing Scottish, English, German, Frisian, Danish, Swedish and Norwegian — influences from overseas.

If we are to trust the songs that Johanne sang to Tang Kristensen as valid testimony of their original culture, they questioned governmental efforts to promote agricultural development, nationalisation and homogenisation, as well as concepts of land-ownership and the authority of certain people over others. Which makes sense, because life on the heath was largely commons-based, meaning that it couldn't

4 Peter Linebaugh and Marcus Rediker: "Tyger! Tyger!" in *the Many-Headed Hydra* (Boston: Beacon Press, 2000), p. 333.

have felt like anything but a loss during the nineteenth century to see the heath being fenced off, and for the locals to lose access to the land they had long relied on for their livelihood.

In response to these developments, many of the songs seem to reflect on the ethics and premises of cross-cultural alliance and exchange through fictionalised figures such as, for example, the merperson. As such, the song about Adeluds — a sort of mermaid living in a hill or mountain — relates how she is seduced and deceived by one of the Danish king's men, who says he wants to marry her, when in actual fact he is only out to subjugate her and use her offspring as labour. But before the deceit is revealed, he approaches her accompanied by a young boy, and Adeluds is so happy at the thought of her upcoming marriage that she dons a gilded dress and teaches the boy to control the weather and the waves, to write magic runes, to twist and turn the winds and settle them again; to stir up waves so high that all ships will sink. When they then reach the ship, the captain snatches her by the arm and says she will not be allowed home until she has given birth to a son who can row and a daughter who can sow. But she escapes the ship and even though the captain is sailing while Adeluds is swimming, she reaches the shore far ahead of him. Once ashore, she tells him her son will never row, and her daughter will never sow — and had it not been for the young boy, she would have drowned them all.

So, the young boy stands in a tricky position because he is between cultures, between struggles, between contrasting interests. But to me that also speaks to the potentiality of the child as a representative of the future, to bridge deadly conflict and ontological opposition. And I think of the figure of the merperson — maid or man — along similar lines: that they may be interesting for us to think with today, because they reside in the fluid spaces between national demarcations and specifically do not belong to any state or people.

You have also worked with merpeople in the context of NRO, right? In relation to Lemuria, was it?

AK Well, we were kind of investigating Lemuria with a little bit of a critical eye, because it is part of this new-age movement where people believe there are these seven-foot tall Viking-looking people who live underneath volcano tunnels. I guess there is Atlantis and Lemuria, and they were kind of competing. Atlantis disappeared but Lemuria persisted as a fantasy because of the volcano tunnels. And there's this place in Northern California, Mount Shasta, where people say they see Lemurians all the time.

We have been working with them as a way to explore this idea of 'being there first', or some kind of strange new-age claim to being part of the land in relation to Indigenous concerns. When we were in Hawaii we learnt that there's a lot of Native Hawaiian mythology around Lemurians too. Not enough that I know about to go into, but it's interesting how such a figure travels.

MKI So Lemurians are not merpeople?

AK There are different reports. I mean, it's tough to get a full composite sketch of them. Sometimes they're referred to as merpeople. Sometimes they're referred to as beams of light that exist somehow. That's maybe the more new-age version, which is the most prevalent today.

Sean Connolly — a Hawaiian artist-architect who was also in the exhibition at Kunsthal Charlottenborg — has been researching how continents and bodies of water have shifted, and how back in the days, travelling from a place like Oceania to Africa was much easier. Or how thinking about different migrations that could happen if you go up and over the world or down under, as opposed to around. To think about how there exists all of these weird confluences and convergences of different cultures around the globe as a result of them actually meeting much before what we think of as being possible. That dives into ideas of people popping up in multiple places, like this idea underlying Lemurian mythology of the lava tunnels or underground tubes that connect the world. Where I grew up, there are a lot of Bigfoot sightings. Sasquatch. And where I'm from, they're called root travellers.

MKI Root travellers?

AK Yes. And part of the idea behind why they can't be seen or known about is because every time someone notices them, they jump into the hole of a tree and then they can travel the root system like a subway network. So they'll show up 600 kilometres away in a matter of seconds through this root system underground. I guess I'm thinking about it because I went snorkelling for the first time last year and just seeing underwater, I was like, "Oh, my god." You know, I feel like I've travelled around the world and know my geography, and then seeing that 70% of this Earth is water is something I'd never encountered before. So humbling. Especially with merpeople exploring around all of those depths; of course we don't know about them, you know? They have no particular interest in exposing themselves to us.

MKI I remember reading this text by archaeologist Neil Price where he draws on the ideas of Hawaiian historians Sir Peter Buck/Te Rangi Hīroa and Herb Kawainui Kāne to attempt to read and understand historical Oceanic and Viking seafaring cultures through each other in order to fill the gaps of their respective historisations. It's an interesting collapse of how these two seemingly different cultures from radically distant locations on the Earth may be thought of as having something in common anyhow, and how they may inform a general understanding of sea- as opposed to land-based cultures.

AK Meeting or encountering the sea? Because it's something that they can never do, you know. They're actually living *on* the sea, not *in* it. This is essentially living *on*.

MKI You're right. But perhaps it could be seen as yet another facet of community-building enabled by the sea — albeit not *in* the sea — that speaks to the potentiality of transcultural exchange and becoming through its in-between-ness... Across the world, there are so many accounts of people living commons-based lives on ships, and how people that we have been taught to perceive as pirates were — are? — in fact commoners. Linebaugh and Rediker call them 'hydrarchies.'

AK Although the flipside of that is someone like Ayn Rand, who is a conservative ideologue from the '60s and '70s. She wrote this book called *Atlas Shrugged* that became foundational to anti-government libertarian philosophies. Her book is really big in Silicon Valley right now. In *Atlas Shrugged*, she kind of says that people smart and skilled enough, and good enough for capitalism, should form their own island off the coast of the country so they don't have to deal with government regulation. But if we think that's also a kind of colonisation of the sea, is it still on the people's premises then?

Anyway, it's interesting to think about that book in relation to ideas of commons and commoners too, because it's like this distrust of government or national commons, that once you're under a nation, to then go forge one on your own. I mean, there's this kind of anarcho-libertarian dream to it that's kind of appealing, even though it's also so demented. Or like an Atlantis, you know?

I worked on this film, *Nosferasta*, which is thinking about Christopher Columbus and 1492 as bigger than interplanetary space travel or maybe equivalent to. But also thinking about this conflation of the ocean and outer space and how before that moment, they were kind of the same thing. And again, maybe that's not true, because we've just been talking about Oceanic Vikings and of prehistory in terms of our own understanding of what we're taught in school, about where those people travel to and how. But it gets trippy.

MKI It gets trippy. Still, I think that maybe that point where it gets trippy is also where new things become possible.
I read about this battle that took place in Alken Enge around the year 0, after which the bones of the slain were collected and submerged

into the water of a nearby lake. One can only try to imagine the stench rising from this lake and how poisonous it must have become with all these bodies decomposing, and how — combined with the traumatic history of the battle — this turned it into a dangerous but also a sacred territory. Archaeological finds suggest that it did in fact become a site of sacrifice, since people would return for several hundred years after the battle — up until 500 years later — to make offerings.

I think it must have to do with some belief that the spirits of the slain still reside in and around the lake — which is now dried out — and this makes it ritually and magically potent, but also very dangerous, because they are just as adversarial in death as they were in life.

If you follow this line of thought — that the spirits of the dead are still in the water, envious and antagonistic of the type of human life that emerged around it — it completely changes the imagined agency of merpeople and water spirits: to think that they are present-day extensions of cultures and people that were annihilated (by us), and that they continue to haunt the living in their longing for revenge.

AK Yeah, yeah, yeah. Well, it's also interesting to think about the weird slippage between history, narrative and spirituality, and how those things have been isolated or separated. Thinking creatively or making stuff up, or just this idea of conflating things. It's taboo now where there has to be a rational, logical answer to everything. But then again, something I carry with me is this idea that history should be a narrative at the service of the present: that these mythological beings or creatures are actually some kind of conflation of a spiritual belief that merges with history in a pretty seamless way, maybe so seamlessly that it's unbelievable. Like Drexciya.

MKI Drexciya?

AK Drexciya was a group that was part of the Detroit techno movement operating from the perspective of Afro-pessimistic futurism, I guess you could say. They were a very secretive techno group, and the mythology that they arose out of is that pregnant mothers who didn't survive the Middle Passage, their unborn babies were born underwater and started a kind of Black Atlantis called Drexciya. And that's where their music comes from and that's where they're from. And I was like, "Whoa!" In a similar way, it suggests how terrible pain or suffering, or the sight of so much trauma, can also bring about the birth of an alternate narrative in order to understand or create a world that you'd want to live in.

MKI That's a very potent vantage point, and heart-breaking. A complete subversion of the rendition of merpeople as these ahistorical fantastical creatures. In fact, some of the merpeople tales from...

AK No pun intended?

MKI What?

AK No pun intended? Merpeople tales? Merpeople tails?

MKI Oh, no. No. No pun intended at all, actually, because in West Jutland merpeople didn't have tails. They just had legs, so you didn't know when you found a dead body on the shore whether it was human or a merperson. The only way you could know was if a terrible noise and weather followed the burial of such a person, and if they were sucking their thumb when you dug them from their grave. In that case, it was a merperson and you had to deliver them back to the sea as soon as possible. So the saying goes.

Fishermen might also encounter merpeople on the sea, and there they would be, sitting high atop a wave, shifting a sock from one foot to the other. If you gave them another sock or a new pair, they would tell your fortune or help you in different ways. You could also give them a pair of gloves. I think that they — by being associated with the souls of the dead in the water — were related to the elves, who live in burial mounds on the heath. Because water runs underground between the sea and different springs and rivers, the water and the underground are connected, and so are the beings that reside there. There are several accounts of people claiming to have seen a woman — an elver or a mermaid — sitting in one of these mounds, combing her hair and flashing her gold.

And to me it's been inspiring to think of elves and merpeople as representing the relations between the water and the shore, humans and nature. And of merpeople as humans' ontological others that are at the same time fluid, in the same way that the ground beneath us is also fluid, just on a much longer time-scale. That all essentialisms and fixities are eventually up for change.

AK I've been coming across all of this writing recently about the power of belief and how the left has abandoned spiritual belief and now only believes in rationalism, science and democracy. Of course, it gets into this sticky territory — especially post-truth — and therefore I always feel a little hesitant to even bring up this stuff, but I also think it's really juicy if we can step back from it a bit. Not to question the fundamental pillars of Western democracy to propose something whack-a-doodle instead, but because it's important that we don't get too foolhardy in our own beliefs either, or sustain the idea that science fifty years ago was totally different from science now, and that that will continue to be the case. If we do that, we end up privileging our position in the present as some kind of all-knowing or most right.

The reason I'm bringing this up is because people are asking why Standing Rock was effective? Why Black Lives Matter is effective? Or even why the 'right' is effective? And it's because they're all still utilizing that power of belief. This made me think about the radical potential to reclaim belief, even if it's secular belief, to know what that looks like. And I think maybe it leads back into our talk about merpeople and various ways of understanding history in relation to place and mythology. About how history can be a narrative and service to the present — even if it is a little fantastical or a little unexpected. How those things could maybe shift the way we look at history in general.

MKI Yes. And whether art may be a place to experiment with the potentiality of spiritual beliefs or narratives in relation to political struggles; not to exit reality, but to find ways of upsetting the way it's narrated so as to open up alternative perspectives on the future?

AK In a secular, rational world, art does in many ways connote a moment with the sublime or the spiritual. There's this guy, Nathaniel Dorsey, who writes about cinema and how movie theatres are like churches: the screen is like stained glass with light moving through it as the day progresses. In this era where few people believe in religion, art becomes the place for it.

Thinking about the embrace of culture and art after the Soviet revolution, where they were trying to imbue secular cultural forms with the aura of the sacred in order to move past — or possibly propose a new — religion. I guess that's something I've been struggling with a lot recently, and it relates to something I heard when I was in Hawaii learning about the Mauna Kea protests, where scientists are basically trying to build a huge thirty-metre telescope on a sacred volcano on the Big Island. I met with some activists who are involved in the struggle against that project, and they have this slogan, "Pro Science. Pro Sacred." It's so simple but so effective and yet radical, and it opened my mind to the possibilities of being able to hold onto both things at the same time, as opposed to making them adversarial or pit them against each other to make this kind of false dialectic where you have to pick one or the other.

MKI Exactly.

AK I still haven't figured out where that goes or how. But it's been really helpful.

MKI Researching the relation between myth and ritual for my PhD, I have been reading Victor Turner's account of Ndembu rituality in north-western Zambia in his book *The Ritual Process*, where he describes how the passing of a woman or couple through an earth tunnel is prescribed by the Ndembu medicine man as a cure against infertility for example. Both Turner and his informants contrast such practices with Western medicine. But then, reading West Jutlandic historian H. P. Hansen's account of pre-industrial medicine and ritual practices in West Jutland, I find the same ritual motif appearing: the digging of a tunnel in the ground or through a sod for the sick to pass through to receive healing or relief.

I feel the effect of the wide dissemination of the Ndembu example through academic ethnography, and what seems to be the wilful forgetting of Northern European examples such as the latter, is that certain groups or ethnicities become wholesale associated with 'the irrational,' and others with 'the rational,' when in reality all societies have always been — and continue to be — characterised by both rational and irrational features.

AK I like this idea of ethnography as a kind of psychoanalysis for a European Enlightenment society, like "Oh yeah, we don't do that stuff over here, but check out what these folks are doing!..." "Oh yeah. We did use to do that though." To produce the racialised Other as Europe's Id.

MKI Ha ha. Yes. Indeed modern Europe seems to be permeated by this idea that to the extent we have ever engaged in 'irrational' ritual or spiritual practices, it was in prehistoric time. Yet, looking at H. P. Hansen's examples — some of which date from the early-twentieth century — people were engaged in quite elaborate ritual and magical activity up until very recently. And I don't think that's only a feature of West Jutland, where — in addition to earth rituality reminiscent of the Ndembus — healers might also for example burn and pulverise remains from the dead and dissolve their ashes into potions to consume or apply to one's skin. From an outside view, such practices are not far from what may be described as cannibalism.

AK Well, that's another example of how an observation without understanding the epistemology kind of misses the point. You know this artist, Juan Downey? No? He's wild. He was a New York/Chilean artist working in the '70s. He made this film called *The Laughing Alligator*, which was kind of a 'fuck you' to ethnography and anthropology. He and his wife and their two kids moved down to Brazil to live with the Yanomami for nine months, and they made a sort of family home movie all together, in which he oscillates between this official anthropological voice and something much more ridiculous, and you can never really get a handle on it. It's really one of my favourite films.

In the film, he talks about pulverising the ashes of deceased loved ones and blending them into banana soup as the ultimate funerary architecture and kind of presenting these things as very matter of fact and maybe actually connected. His background is Indigenous and white Chilean and he's kind of like "that isn't too far removed from either parts of my ancestry, yet I'm made to believe it's only from one aspect of it," and that kind of confluence.

MKI It goes hand in hand with the whole practice of 'they-ing.' I mean, is there a way to talk about the potentialities of minoritarian ritual practices without succumbing to divisive speech? "*They* do this, but *we* don't." Is there a way to acknowledge the potentiality and force of minoritarian ritual practices without othering or caricaturing each other?

AK Yeah, oh damn. Because it's also a question of perspective. It's like you can lay whatever into the other if you're speaking from the perspective that you have the authority. So it's also a question of destabilising that authority to become a part of all or something.

MKI Okay, so acknowledging the many essentialised and essentialising dynamics linked to this discussion, do you still feel there may be a kind of place, where coming from a background like yours is also an asset that allows you to imagine or project yourself into the future differently, against the present and Western majoritarian culture?

AK Yeah, I think, from my Ojibway perspective and because of how I think and feel about things, I'm always trying to imply things in a future perspective because there is so much emphasis on being placed in the past. But then it's interesting when people approach me about stuff like Native spirituality — I'm always encouraging them to explore their own ethnic identities' past. You know, and that's where it gets interesting or tricky in terms of projection, because people look towards Native cultures' past for their own.

 MKI Yeah, exactly.

AK Even though, especially from your research and work, there's such a rich wealth of culture and customs and resistance and histories within your own historical background to be looking towards and bring to the fore.

MKI But of course, one obvious obstruction to that work is the history of Nazism and how the Nazis actively appropriated heathen Nordic and Germanic heritages for their own ideological and eugenic purposes. I think that might be a reason why many left-leaning Northern Europeans feel weary of approaching the minoritarian customs and cultures of our own ethnic pasts, because they have been so heavily tainted by that history. This has also been a ghost in my own research, but the way I have been trying to tackle it is to stay really clear-eyed and stick to the actual wordings and accounts of my own family and other real people in the folklore archives. Not to dream of some kind of fantastical Viking utopia — which is a bit like thinking about Atlantis or Lemuria: it never did exist, but it's a strong and potent fantasy capable of making people succumb to unimaginable degrees of violence and othering in its name.

So I try to go about it from the bottom up; from the archival scraps I find, which I may fit together through my own embodied knowledge of growing up in Midwestern Jutland with all its unspoken codices — and then through art or imagination, or whatever, to dream of how they may form a spiritual or culturally dissident continuum against the nationalist or nationalising forces of the present. For one thing, what I read from the accounts and songs of my forbearers, they did not feel particularly keen on the Danish project. And so it would be very unethical to appropriate their mythic and spiritual heritages as part of a Danish or any kind of nation-building project.

So in trying to reach back for alternative tools to propel us forward, that's where I tend to go to folklore rather than these reverse-engineered mythical renditions of, say, the Norse pantheon. However, that said, the mythic narratives of my foremother's songs feature several recurring themes related to figures from the Norse pantheon, for example magically potent women dressed in blue capes and capable of transforming themselves into wolves and falcons, the latter invocative of the Vanir goddess Freja, who was the first master of Sejd magic and who travelled across worlds and time in falcon-guise. So the imaginary realm evoked by the songs is not unrelated to Viking mythology or Norse paganism, but it puts it together in a different way and for different ends than those of neo-pagan far-right nationalism. For example, the main motif of the song that mentions the heroine dressed as a falcon is the confrontation and killing of the Danish king, because he had subjugated the heroine's brother and tried to appease her with gold. To me, this seems to thrust a big fat stick in the wheel of any project that seeks to identify Danishness as a homogenous ethnic category to fuel a nationalist and racially exclusionary agenda.

AK Well, I totally agree with you. By extension, I think that's why I'm always trying to orientate any kind of background towards the future;

because I feel that by focusing on that past, not only is it like that double-edged sword of having to be authentic against an irretrievable past. But the other thing, related to what you're talking about, is that the over-identification with such pasts could in my case just lead to 'red supremacy,' and then we wouldn't have got any further.

MKI Right. I guess that's why I have steered clear of this for so long. But my foremother's songs don't go in that direction at all, and also she was not Viking — she was a woman living on the heath in the nineteenth century who held pagan knowledge. And that's another example of where her songs depart from a right-wing neo-pagan rendition of Norse mythology: the location of women in society. Where I come from, there was no division of labour or status between men and women. Everyone partook in all kinds of work — foraging, herding, butchering, knitting, singing — and equally it was as often women as men who were the locus of mythic narrative and transformative action. So for me, it is also a matter of employing my own concrete mythic and cultural heritage from the heathlands to subvert the way the Norse imaginary has been appropriated for nationalist and exclusionary purposes across the West.

As part of this work, I'm trying to think whether it's possible to conceive of a position where different Indigenous heritages may converge and cross-pollinate?

I mean, you and I, we're both moderns, living modern lives in a modern world. But that life is so heavily circumscribed by capitalist ideologies, and I wonder whether alternative points exist at which we might converge or join forces through our respective minoritarian heritages instead? I mean, right now I'm just singing, and what good does that do?...

AK Yes, but you're singing songs that are almost forgotten!

MKI Of course, but if I were to be self-critical, then how is that not just another instance of nostalgically over-engaging with past? Cultures change all the time; some things are bound to be lost, and maybe should be lost?...

 AK Someone I was talking to from where I'm from was talking about instead of seeking to revive things or resurrecting them or keeping them the way they were, to work from this idea that perpetual revelation of the culture is actually what's necessary and that things should be allowed to change. That it doesn't have to be this grappling with tradition. Tradition and culture have different qualities to them, and as long as the culture is being maintained, it's different than tradition being followed. So I think having these songs that are traditional but being performed and recorded using contemporary technologies is the perpetuation and recapitulation of the culture as opposed to trying to reproduce a facsimile of it. And I feel like that continuum — that chain of generations interconnected and touching at a certain moment — is where the heat is at.

But then there's also a weird double bind — especially when a culture is threatened or disappearing — that people get very uptight about how it's revitalised in terms of it having to be a certain way, and I guess that is where it gets slippery and scary too. You know, Hitler would consult Karl May's novels about Winnetou — this fictional Apache chief — because they were some of his favourite books. They said he would read those books the way one might read the Bible in a moment of crisis, and according to Gober, he even assigned it to a lot of the soldiers to read because it showed the valour and warrior principles of Indigenous people.

MKI Yes, I guess these pitfalls are ever-present, regardless of whether we talk about red or white or other kinds of Nativist supremacies. Such fantasies do a lot of damage and obscure the actual problems and pertinent struggles of precarised peoples today.

AK Yes, again, that's the slippery thing about focusing too much on the past or on tradition, because that leads to Native people starting to say "get rid of all the immigrants," which is the most hardline conservative far-right gesture possible.

MKI True. A Brazilian friend of mine is working as an anthropologist in the Amazon with this tribe that he says ensures its cultural continuity through perpetual transformation; transformations transforming transformations. I asked whether they might also transform to become moderns, and he responded "Yes, of course, but they always change back again," which left me a bit puzzled, thinking whether such transformative agency might also apply to me as a white descendent of a marginalised commons-based culture, or if it's an exclusively Amazonian capacity? I mean, I would like to transform...

AK That makes me think about the concept of the 'seven generations'. Where I'm from, there's this thinking that with your actions you're supposed to be keeping in mind seven generations into the past and seven generations into the future. And that's the temporal thinking for any kind of action or thought, even in order to perpetuate a culture or community forward. It's been really helpful and helped keep me sane in terms of political movements and thinking about things past our lifetime. This continuum of seven forward and seven backwards, which — when you do the maths, depending on life expectancy — gets pretty big. Like 150–200 years or so in one direction. Thinking seven generations both forwards and backwards opens a continuum of 350 years from the past to the future.

MKI I think Johanne is seven generations from me... My mother Margit's mother Maja's father Johannes's father Niels Kristian's father Niels's mother Johanne. Yes. Counting me in, Johanne and I are seven generations apart. Doubling that into the future, we have the average life-span of the gurry shark, the *havkal*.

AK Well, seven generations of the havkal. Now we're talking. That's like 1,500 years.

MKI Exactly. Seven generations of the shark. That's a perspective to consider.
Maybe that's a good place to end this conversation?

AK Yeah.

Det war æ kånng hans orlowsmæn’
—Æ dans dæn æ lirren.—
Å di kam sajlenn hær te æ lan’.
—Lyyr dero, hwo æ jåmfru te æ bjæær ble dåår(n)!—

Da di nu kam nææer te lan’,
Di høør æ frøkn Adeluds i æ bjææ’r, dæ sång.

Æ skipper han taaler te lirren smodræng:
”Å do ska go mæ te stålten Adeluds i løn’.”

Han pe’ket o æ daa’r med hans skin’:
”Vaagn åp, stålt’ Adeluds, du låå’ker mæ in’!

Hææer æ bue’r fra di fæsteman’,
I ska komm nier te ham ve stran’.”

”Håår du bue’r fra mi fæsteman’ kjææ’r,
Da søj mæ, hwa naw’n han monne mo bææer!”

”Niels Me’kelsen hie’r di fæsteman’,
Å do ska føøl(le) mæ mæ fra lan’.”

En selk’(e)særk hon føst drow’ o’,
En gullblo’met kjor’tel hon derøwwer slow’.

Hon drow Gul’ al’ øwer Gul’,
Brøst å Fen’ger dem sått’ hon ful’.

Frøken Adeluds tuk æ smådreng’ ve æ håå’n,
Å så gik di dær nier te æ stran’

Hon lææer ham æ væjle å steel o æ wan’,
Hon lææer ham rowner å skryw mæ æ håå’n.

Hon læær ham æ ven' å wrii å vææn,
Å hon læær ham åw å stæll'et igjæn.

Hon læær ham æ væ å rejs så stue'r,
Så all æ Skiw di sånk nie'r for æ fjue'r.

Stålt' Adeluds u(h)e i æ skiw da språng',
Æ skipper hin i æ arm da nam'.

"Ja, skam faa do, do skippertyw'!
Vill du så forråå mi ånng lyw'?"

"No ska do æ't komm o di fåå'r hans lan',
Før te du får en søn, dæ ka ta æ ruer i hans håå'n.

No ska do æ't komm o di mue'r hinne øø',
Før te du får en Dæ'ter, dæ ka skjæær å søj'."

Frøkn Adeluds u(h)e i æ haw' da språng',
Så svømme hun a hinne fåå'r hans lan'.

Æ skipper han sejlld, å æ jåmfru hon svømme,
Dog kam hon te lan' en stun' føø'r end ham.

"Når æ a ko'men o mi fåå'r hans lan':
Mi søn ka hwærken sejll hæller ta æ rue'r i hans håå'n.

No æ a o mi mue'r hinne øø':
Mi dæt'er hon ka hwærken skjæær heller søj'.

Men håj'et æ't wærn for di lirren smådræng',
—Æ dans dæn æ lirren.—
A sku ha drownet all æ kånng hans howmæn'."
—Ly'er dero, hwo æ jåmfru te æ bjæær ble dåårn!—

The king's men of war,
—The dance is slight—
Came sailing to this land.
—Listen to this, how the maiden of the mound was deceived!—

When they now approached the coast,
They heard Miss Adeluds in the mound singing.

The skipper spoke to the ship's boy
"You will come with me to proud Adeluds' chamber."

He knocked on the door with his skin:
"Wake up, proud Adeluds, and let me in!

I bring word from your husband,
You must meet him on the beach."

"Do you have word from my dear husband,
Then tell me what name he goes by."

"Your husband's name is Niels Mikkelsen,
And you will follow me from this land."

She dressed herself in a silk gown,
And thereover she wore a kirtle with gilded flowers.

She put gold on top of gold,
Breast and fingers were covered in full.

Miss Adeluds took the ship's boy by his hand,
And then they walked to the beach.

She taught him to calm the weather on the sea
And to write runes with his hand.

She taught him to twist and turn the wind,
And to settle it again.

She taught him to conjure a weather so mighty
That all ships would sink before the fjord.

Then proud Adeluds jumped aboard the ship,
Where the captain grabbed her by her arm.

"Shame on you, you skipper-thief!
Would you betray my young life like this?"

"You will not return to your father's land,
Before you have birthed a son who can steer the rudder.

You will not return to your mother's island,
Before you have birthed a daughter who can cut and sow."

Miss Adeluds jumped into the sea,
Then she swam to her father's land.

The skipper sailed, and the maiden swam,
Still, she reached the shore far ahead of him.

"Now I'm on my father's land:
My son knows neither how to sail nor steer the rudder.

Now I'm on my mother's island:
My daughter knows neither how to cut nor sow.

And hadn't it been for your little ship's boy,
—The dance is slight—
I would have drowned all the king's men."
—Listen to this, how the maiden of the mound was deceived!—

This book was published on the occasion of Marie Kølbæk Iversen: *Rovhistorier|Histories of Predation* at O—Overgaden (2022), the Danish National Gallery (2023) and Henie Onstad Kunstsenter (2024).

It is part of the Podere Trafonti Notebooks series following the artist's residency at Podere Trafonti (www.poderetrafonti.com) during the summer of 2022.

Led by Antonella Notari Vischer and Bernard Vischer, the Trafonti Art Residency welcomes an artist per year for two months and offers emerging to mid-career artists time and space to reflect on their work and deepen their practice. The residency is intended for visual artists who work with a variety of media including sculpture, digital technologies, sound, music, film, photography, painting, performance and writing.

The artist is selected in conversation with a jury of three renowned art advisers composed for the 2022 selection by Ariane Koek (independent curator, writer and art project manager based in London), Lucia Pietroiousti (independent curator, founder of the General Ecology project at Serpentine, London) and Yann Chateigné Tytelman (independent curator, editor and writer, Brussels).

Managing Editor
Bernard Vischer

Publishing Editor
Iliaria Bombelli

Publishing Concept
Yann Chateigné Tytelman
Marie Kølbæk Iversen

Texts
Marie Kølbæk Iversen
Adam Khalil
Isabella Rjelle
Yann Chateigné Tytelman

Graphic Design
Maximage

Translations
Peter Lenny
Gioia Guerzoni
Claudio Cambon

Proofreading
Bennett Bazalgette-Staples

Typefaces
Huma Regular, OCR-X Regular
maxitype.com

Images
All artworks, process images and stills are courtesy of © Marie Kølbæk Iversen

Image credits
Mirror Therapy, Fotografisk Center, 2015, photo © Marie Kølbæk Iversen
Mirror Therapy, Gwangju Biennial, 2016, photo © Doyun Kim
Autumn Equinox Celebration, PS/Y + LUX London, photo © Christa Holka
Io/I, Louisiana Museum of Modern Art, 2018, photo © Frida Gregersen
Io/I, Kai Art Centre and Tallinn Photomonth Biennial, 2019, photo © Hedi Jaansoo
Donnimaar, Rønnebæksholm, 2021, photo © Christian Brems
Donnimaar, photo © Martin Bubandt
O Tilli, Ebeltoft Kunsthal, 2022, photo © Kasper Palsnov
Donnimaar, O—Overgaden, 2022, photo © Christian Brems
Histories of Predation, O—Overgaden, 2022, photo © Laura Stamer
Histories of Predation, SMK Thy, 2023, © Martin Busborg

Printed in Italy by
Grafiche Veneziane, Venice

First edition: 2024

Acknowledgements
Marie Kølbæk Iversen would like to thank Antonella Notari Vischer and Bernard Vischer (Podere Trafonti), Tone Hansen (MUNCH), Julius Nielsen (Greenland Institute of Natural Resources), Line Lauritsen, Jonathan Brewer (Danish Molecular Biomedical Imaging Centre, University of Southern Denmark), Rhea Dall, Vera Østrup, Toke Martins, Maria Kamilla Larsen, Nanna Friis, Line Brædder (O—Overgaden), Aukje Lepoutre Ravn (Copenhagen Contemporary), Jon Holtze (Cineman), Emilia Nykjær Isaksson, Berit Anne Larsen (SMK Thy, Danish National Gallery), Mikkel Bogh (University of Copenhagen), Susanne Østby Sæther (Henie Onstad Kunstsenter), Berit Kiilerich (Lystbækgaard), Karen-Louise Smidth (Geopark Vestjylland and Nature Park Nissum Fjord), Adam Khalil, Isabella Rjeille, Yann Chateigné Tytelman, Emmy Laura Perez Fjalland, Aqqaluk Lynge, Mudi Kramer Berthelsen, Grethe Kramer Berthelsen, Ove Karl Berthelsen, Solveig Kramer, Richard Jensen, Jessie Kleeman, Camille Norment, Maria Lind, Line Dalsgård, Søren Andreasen, Mette Kjærgaard Præst, Diana Policarpo, Katinka Fogh Vindelev, Sophie Ziedoy, Michael Ejstrup, Christian Brems, Silas Emmery, Søren Kølbæk Iversen, Anne Kølbæk Iversen, Margit Kølbæk Iversen, Hans Iversen, Lars Jakob Bang Larsen, Viggo Napoleón Bang-Larsen Martínez, Louis Iver Kølbæk Larsen, Maja Johansen and Johanne Tygesdatter.

Special thanks are due to
The Shadow Foundation, Rolle (CH)
Henie Onstad Kunstsenter
O—Overgaden
SMK Thy, Danish National Gallery
Greenland Institute of Natural Resources
DaMBIC, Danish Molecular Biomedical Imaging Centre
KHiO, Oslo National Academy of the Arts
Aarhus University
Danish Folklore Collection, Royal Danish Library
Danish Arts Foundation

Published and distributed by
Mousse Publishing
Contrappunto s.r.l.
Via Pier Candido Decembrio 28
20137 Milan — Italy

Available through
Mousse Publishing, Milan
moussemagazine.it

DAP|Distributed Art Publishers, New York
artbook.com

Les presses du réel, Dijon
lespressesdureel.com

Antenne Books, London
antennebooks.com

Idea books, Amsterdam
ideabooks.nl

LibroCo, Firenze
libroco.it

ISBN 978-88-6749-598-6

€27/$30

IMPARARE A VEDERE AL BUIO
ISABELLA RJEILLE

Per il popolo Huni Kuin, i canti e i rituali sciamanici che prevedono l'ingestione di *nixi pae* [1] sono noti fin da quando il primo essere umano, Dua Busen, entrò in contatto con il popolo Anaconda, e questo sapere è stato tramandato di generazione in generazione. Il mito descrive lo stupore e la paura di Dua Busen quando vide una donna-anaconda durante la caccia, e il suo processo di trasformazione in *Yube*, una persona-anaconda. Una sintesi di questa narrazione è stata raccolta e tradotta dall'antropologo Els Lagrou:

> Durante la caccia, Dua Busen vede qualcosa di strano, animali che si aggirano con degli orecchini. Poi scorge una donna anaconda che esce dal lago, ricoperta di disegni, bellissima. Il tapiro era riuscito ad attirarla gettando nel lago dei frutti di genipa e aveva fatto l'amore con lei, dopodiché la donna anaconda era sparita di nuovo nel lago. Qualche giorno dopo, non riuscendo a dimenticarla, Busen torna in quel punto del lago, lancia i frutti di genipa neil'acqua e la donna serpente ricompare. Busen le salta addosso spaventandola e la donna si trasforma in anaconda e lo avvolge, minacciandolo con la lingua biforcuta. Temendo di essere divorato dall'enorme rettile, Busen la prega di tornare alla sua forma umana. Lei accetta e quando gli chiede le sue intenzioni, Busen promette di accompagnarla al lago. Dopo aver fatto l'amore e prima di prenderlo in groppa per immergersi nel lago, la donna gli offre una «foglia prospettica» per cambiare la sua percezione. Sott'acqua, Dua Busen vede gli anaconda come persone. [2]

Il fascino di Dua Busen per la donna-anaconda lo aveva condotto nelle profondità del fiume facendogli acquisire un sapere che avrebbe cambiato per sempre la storia del suo popolo. Eppure, per poter vedere quello che un tempo lo spaventava, Dua Busen aveva dovuto alterare la propria visione con la «foglia prospettica». Trasformandosi in un anaconda-persona e andando a vivere sott'acqua – dove vedeva gli esseri anaconda come suoi simili – aveva interrotto il processo che li rendeva diversi, annullando i ruoli di minaccia e minacciato. Nella narrazione, questo cambiamento di prospettiva era essenziale per la trasmissione della conoscenza, ovvero l'ingestione del *nixi pae*, che sarebbe diventato a sua volta fondamentale nella cultura degli Huni Kuin.

I diversi modi di conoscere il mondo sono al centro dell'opera di Marie Kølbæk Iversen, la cui ricerca unisce scienza, tecnologia, mitologia e tradizioni orali per capire come le creature umane e non umane coesistono e interagiscono. Nella video installazione *Rovhistorier|Histories of Predation*, l'autrice analizza le possibili forme di rapporto che esistono tra uomo, animale e macchina, tre attori che, in diversi contesti e momenti nella storia, possono occupare il ruolo di predatore. Analogamente alla vicenda di Dua Busen nella narrazione di Huni Kuin, Kølbæk Iversen si interroga su come il cambiamento di prospettiva possa interrompere il processo che distingue e definisce le creature come «prede» e «predatori». Il suo lavoro utilizza gli strumenti e i metodi di ricerca della scienza moderna per mettere in scena un gioco di specchi al fine di esaminare l'idea occidentale di «umano» e i suoi strumenti di concettualizzazione del mondo.

La ricerca di Kølbæk Iversen ha avuto inizio nel 2020, quando si è imbattuta nell'animale vertebrato più longevo conosciuto dall'umanità: lo squalo gurry o squalo artico noto anche come «tritone» (*havkal*) nella sua lingua d'origine, il danese, come in islandese e faroense (rispettivamente, *hákarl* e *havkallur*), e «sirena» in norvegese e svedese (rispettivamente, *håkjerringa e håkäring*). Se paragonato agli esseri umani, questo squalo ha tutte le caratteristiche di una creatura mitologica: la sua aspettativa di vita si colloca tra i 272 e i 512 anni, caratteristica che altera del tutto la nostra percezione del tempo.

La serie di rapimenti, saccheggi e invasioni coloniali che hanno avuto come scenario l'Atlantico negli ultimi cinque secoli – e plasmato il sistema capitalistico e il mondo occidentale come lo conosciamo oggi – può essere vista sotto una diversa prospettiva se messa a confronto con la straordinaria longevità di questo animale. Certo, lo squalo gurry si trova solo nelle acque profonde e gelide dell'Atlantico settentrionale, ma gli squali in generale occupano l'immaginario del terrore coloniale perpetrato dal traffico di persone ridotte in schiavitù attraverso il Passaggio di Mezzo: la porzione di Atlantico che abbraccia l'oceano tra Africa, America ed Europa. Alcune specie di squali che vivono al largo della costa occidentale del continente africano, abituati ad acque più calde e capaci di adattarsi alle temperature variabili del medio Atlantico, modificarono le loro rotte per seguire gli schiavisti europei e cibarsi così delle persone gettate in mare o che si suicidavano oppure si buttavano in acqua sperando di sottrarsi agli orrori della schiavitù nelle Americhe. [3] Nell'oscurità degli abissi, e in virtù della sua eccezionale longevità, lo squalo gurry può essere quindi considerato un potenziale «testimone oculare» di ciò che avvenne nelle acque del Nord Atlantico.

Essendo interamente cartilagineo, l'unica parte dello squalo gurry rimasta intatta fin dallo stadio embrionale sono i nuclei delle lenti oculari, che hanno permesso di determinarne l'età mediante la datazione al carbonio-14. Con l'aiuto di un microscopio, Kølbæk Iversen mostra i vari strati delle lenti oculari dello squalo nelle immagini che costituiscono la videoinstallazione *Rovhistorier|Histories of Predation*. L'opera triangola così tra osservatore, osservato e una riflessione sulle posizioni di potere implicite in queste diverse prospettive. Analizzare tramite la scienza le relazioni che le società occidentali stabiliscono con gli animali – sezionandoli e rendendoli altro – è anche un modo per capire come quelle stesse società vedono il concetto di «umanità.»

Con la rivoluzione industriale, gli animali scomparvero dall'occidente urbanizzato per ritornare come merci nelle società post-industriali – un destino a cui lo squalo gurry, nonostante la sua lenta esistenza nelle acque dell'Atlantico settentrionale, non riuscì a sottrarsi. Lo squalo ha così alimentato la spinta delle società nordiche ad accelerare il processo di industrializzazione nel XVIII e XIX secolo. Veniva pescato principalmente per l'olio di fegato, utilizzato per lubrificare macchinari, per i treni e come olio per lampade [4]. Così, un animale che nuota lentissimamente negli abissi dell'oceano venne trasformato in carburante per accelerare le macchine e produrre luce sulla superficie urbanizzata del mondo. Per John Berger, nel suo saggio *Perché guardiamo gli animali?,* il processo con cui le società post-industriali riducono gli animali a merci da trasformare e fabbricare come alimenti o prodotti «(...) fa parte dello stesso processo con cui gli uomini sono stati ridotti a unità produttive e di consumo isolate.» [5] Allo stesso modo, Berger mette in relazione questo processo con il ruolo degli animali nella scienza moderna, che li vede esclusivamente come oggetti da osservare, negando così la loro capacità di agire e la rilevanza del loro sguardo, sguardo che risponde al nostro. Attraverso gli occhi degli animali, veniamo visti come un animale qualsiasi. Attraverso gli occhi degli esseri umani, «noi» ci distinguiamo da «loro». [6] La moderna separazione tra natura e cultura ha favorito il processo che ha portato a quello che oggi è noto come «Antropocene», una nuova era geologica che riconosce la centralità dell'azione umana nei cambiamenti della vita sulla Terra. Gli impatti climatici, sociali, economici e culturali dell'Antropocene, uniti all'avanzata del capitalismo, hanno accelerato un processo di estinzione che vede quella che chiamiamo «Umanità» trasformata in predatrice di se stessa e di tutti gli esseri viventi.

In risposta a questi sviluppi, *Rovhistorier|Histories of Predation* analizza e mette in correlazione tre modi di vedere: lo sguardo umano, che ha bisogno di luce per formare immagini ed elaborarle nel cervello; lo sguardo dello squalo, sezionato e osservato; e il microscopio, un dispositivo tecnologico progettato per aumentare la vista a livelli che gli esseri umani, attraverso gli occhi soltanto, non possono raggiungere. La luce è un altro elemento essenziale di questa triangolazione perché ovviamente attraversa le lenti di tutti gli apparati ottici coinvolti: emessa dal microscopio, le sue onde raggiungono sia gli strati dell'occhio dello squalo sia le lenti del microscopio, per arrivare infine – grazie alla luce del proiettore nello spazio espositivo – ai nostri occhi. Inoltre, la luce e il suo simbolismo hanno attraversato tre secoli di storia nella vita di questo animale, con l'Illuminismo e il suo impatto sulla scienza e sul moderno pensiero coloniale. Anche se le immagini del cristallino dello squalo non illuminano né rivelano qualcosa in particolare, sono come punti di luce nel buio pesto, utili a delineare la geografia di un terreno sconosciuto. La luce si diffonde nelle lenti oculari dello squalo e raggiunge la nostra retina, che è tanto umana quanto limitata rispetto a un animale così longevo. Per avvicinarci alla prospettiva di questo animale, dobbiamo imparare a vedere sott'acqua e sottrarci alla luce accecante della superficie. Vedere al buio comporta anche un processo di attivazione di altri sensi e di altri tipi di sapere, processo che smantella la gerarchia stabilita dalla vista e dalle immagini mediate dalla luce che genera.

Per comprendere il presente e creare futuri possibili in questo clima di imminente estinzione annunciata dall'Antropocene, è quindi fondamentale recuperare altri tipi di sapere. In un'opera parallela a *Rovhistorier|Histories of Predation*, Kølbæk Iversen risale ai suoi antenati – in particolare alla sua trisavola, Johanne Thygesdatter, che viveva nelle brughiere dello Jutland occidentale – per ritrovare le conoscenze pagane che le erano state tramandate sotto forma di canti, registrati dall'etnomusicologo ed esperto di folklore Evald Tang Kristensen nel 1873. Queste canzoni narrano come le popolazioni native avevano lottato contro l'omogeneizzazione culturale imposta durante processo di nazionalizzazione e consolidamento dello stato danese. Per descrivere gli effetti predatori di questo processo, le canzoni fanno spesso riferimento a esseri mitologici ibridi, in parte animali e in parte umani (come i tritoni e le sirene), del tutto estranei alle nazioni e ai confini tracciati dagli uomini. Intitolato *Donnimaar,* questo progetto, che comprende musica e performance, è stato lanciato in occasione dell'equinozio d'autunno, che nell'emisfero settentrionale segna il passaggio all'inverno, quando le notti si allungano e il buio arriva presto. Kølbæk Iversen considera quest'opera un modo di celebrare «il potere del sogno di alterare il tessuto della realtà, rendendo strana e ricca di potenziale la veglia dei nostri travagliati tempi moderni.» [7]

Il sogno come strumento di comprensione della vita da svegli è cruciale per la sopravvivenza dei mammiferi, ma di pari passo con la modernizzazione ha perso centralità nella vita delle società occidentali. Eppure, quando le luci si spengono e la ragione viene relegata in secondo piano, il sogno diventa un modo di navigare nel mondo. Come scrive Jung, il sogno «prepara il sognatore agli eventi del giorno successivo»[8], e *Rovhistorier|Histories of Predation* può essere visto come un tentativo di incorporare la prospettiva dello squalo gurry: imparare a vedere nel buio più totale per trovare modi possibili di *rimandare la fine del mondo.* [9]

Gli Huni Kuin hanno appreso il sapere delle creature della foresta grazie alle visioni offerte dal *nixi pae*: quando viene ingerito, anche chi lo utilizza viene ingerito, diventando un tutt'uno con lo *Yube* e imparando a vedere il mondo attraverso gli occhi dell'anaconda. Analizzare gli occhi di uno squalo al microscopio diventa così un modo per capire il nostro modo di vedere, mettendo in discussione il metodo scientifico secondo cui per comprendere meglio qualcosa bisogna guardarlo da vicino. Nel caso dell'occhio dello squalo invece, più ci si avvicina, più le immagini diventano sfocate. Al microscopio vediamo la struttura grezza dell'anatomia di un occhio, ma mai le immagini che l'occhio cattura. È quindi necessario allontanarsi in un certo senso dall'occhio che vede solo in piena luce, e imparare a vedere l'infinito che esiste nell'oscurità, nella notte e nei sogni.

1 Bevanda psicoattiva, nota anche come *ayahuasca*, estratta da una vite e utilizzata nelle cerimonie rituali da alcune popolazioni amerindie della regione amazzonica.

2 Els Lagrou. *Anaconda-becoming: Huni Kuin image-songs, an Amerindian relational aesthetics. Horizontes Antropológicos* [Online], 51 | 2018, Online dall'11 Ottobre 2018, pp. 34-35. Accesso del 25 settembre 2022. URL: http://journals.openedition.org/horizontes/2102.

3 See Marcus Rediker, *History from below the water line: Sharks and the Atlantic slave trade*, 2008, Atlantic Studies, 5:2, 285-297. Available at: http://dx.doi.org/10.1080/14788810802149758.

4 Con l'invenzione dell'olio sintetico nel 1948, questo tipo di pesca è stato usato sempre meno fino ad essere vietato del tutto nel 1960. Si veda Camilla Bøgeskov, *Det danske fiskeri af grønlandshajen: En undersøgelse af det historiske fiskeri af grønlandshajen ved Grønland med fokus på dets udvikling samt det gensidige forhold mellem menneske og natur*, 2021, Aalborg Universitet, p. 11.

5 John Berger, *Perché guardiamo gli animali?* tr. it Maria Nadotti, Il Saggiatore, 2016.

6 John Berger, *op. cit.*

7 https://donnimaar.bandcamp.com/releases.

8 C. G. Jung, «Two Kinds of Thinking». In: *The Collected Works of C. G. Jung, Volume 5: Symbols of Transformation.* Princeton: Princeton University Press Bollingen Series, 1967.

9 Secondo il pensatore e leader indigeno Ailton Krenak, i popoli indigeni hanno vissuto varie volte la fine del mondo dall'inizio del processo di colonizzazione. Nel suo libro *Ideias para adiar o fim do mundo.* São Paulo: Companhia das Letras, 2020 [Idee per rimandare la fine del mondo], si chiede se i popoli non-indigeni riusciranno a sopravvivere.

LA TRASFORMAZIONE
YANN CHATEIGNÉ TYTELMAN

Quando il mito vero e proprio affiora nella coscienza, il suo messaggio è sempre quello. Devi cambiare vita. Ursula K. Le Guin

Al LUX di Londra, il 22 di settembre del 2017, cioè la sera dell'equinozio d'autunno, Marie Kølbæk Iversen ha presentato in anteprima il progetto che sarebbe diventato *Donnimaar*. Accompagnata dall'artista e compositrice Diana Policarpo, ha cantato un repertorio di canzoni tradizionali, alcune delle quali attribuite alla sua bis, bis, bis, bisnonna Johanne Thygesdatter. Al tramonto, nell'istante preciso che segna la diminuzione della luce del giorno e l'avanzata definitiva verso l'inverno, la voce limpida e luminosa di Marie si è proiettata verso la volta celeste. Il testo è stato cantato nel dialetto dello Jutland occidentale, la regione in cui Marie è cresciuta e da cui proviene la sua famiglia. Una delle canzoni era intitolata «Forvandlingen», o «La Transformazione». La protagonista è Donnimaar, una giovane donna innamorata, seducente e scaltra, dotata di grandi capacità magiche, che si vanta dei suoi poteri. La storia si svolge in un paesaggio nordico incantato, con folletti che danzano sui tumuli nelle brughiere ricoperte di rugiada e di brina. Donnimaar è innamorata del bel Cavaliere del Roseto, ma suo padre non approva la loro unione. Per rendere il suo amante invisibile in modo che il padre non lo veda, si offre di trasformarlo prima in un paio di scarpe, che il cavaliere rifiuta, poi in un paio di guanti, anch'essi rifiutati, e infine in un filo di lino dorato da intrecciare nei capelli. Il cavaliere acconsente. Tuttavia quando Donnimaar e il cavaliere, nascosto nei suoi capelli, si presentano al padre, questi si accorge dell'inganno e taglia i capelli della figlia, ma il suo proteiforme innamorato riesce a fuggire. «La Trasformazione» è un racconto animista di metamorfosi, filiazione ed emancipazione.

Le canzoni folkloriche hanno origini incerte, si sa. Sono il prodotto di un lungo processo di trasmissioni e osservazioni orali e gestuali, di migrazioni, variazioni, mescolanze e incarnazioni. Jacques Rancière osserva che il termine *lore*, come la parola *folklore*, è «una vecchia parola inglese che si riferisce al corpus di sapere e storie tradizionali che la gente si tramanda». Forse non è un caso che Donnimaar trasformi il cavaliere in un filo di lino e che il padre usi un coltello per tagliare la sua treccia, cioè l'intreccio che lei stessa ha creato: la giovane donna era sul punto di formare la propria tradizione, di tessere la propria «matrice del sapere», per usare i termini di Rancière, collegandosi a un'altra fonte che si trovava al di fuori del *folk*, del «popolo», cioè persone che in questo caso costituiscono il gruppo dominante e che sono rappresentate dalla figura patriarcale del padre.

Marie non ha solo recitato «La Trasformazione» ma l'ha *riportata in vita*. Trasportandola nel presente, come sulla cresta di un'onda, lascia che la canzone cambi, creando un'interessante analogia tra composizione e soggetto. La struttura evolutiva della canzone si basa su momenti precisi della storia in cui Donnimaar propone di usare i suoi poteri magici per trasformare il cavaliere in una serie di oggetti apparentemente inanimati:

> *Ti trasformerò in un piccolo paio di scarpe*
> *Ti indosserò sui miei piedi*

Più avanti dice:

> *Ti trasformerò in un bel paio di guanti*
> *Ti indosserò sulle mie piccole mani*

E conclude con:

> *Ti trasformerò in un filo di lino dorato*
> *Ti intreccerò per star vicino alla mia guancia rosea*

La forma de «La Trasformazione» è soggetta a una modifica costante e a un movimento ripetitivo, a spirale.

Gilles Deleuze e Félix Guattari vedevano il refrain – che preferivano chiamare *ritornello* – come un motivo, una forma che rivela il legame tra l'impulso vitale, fluido della nostra esistenza e la musica che si suona, e anche il legame organico che crea con gli elementi, gli esseri e le cose. In *Mille piani*, scrivono: «divenire-donna, divenire-bambino; divenir-animale, vegetale o minerale; divenire-molecolari di ogni specie, divenire-particelle. Delle fibre portano dagli uni agli altri, trasformano gli uni negli altri, attraversando le porte e le soglie. Cantare o comporre, dipingere, scrivere non hanno forse altro scopo: scatenare tali divenire.» Il filo d'oro – o legame – in cui il cavaliere viene trasformato è senza dubbio l'indizio alchemico dello status di maga di Donnimaar, ma allude anche alla materia in movimento, ai flussi e alla vita che scorre in tutte le cose nel paesaggio della storia. La guancia arrossata, *rosea,* della giovane donna non è solo un'immagine per descrivere gli effetti dell'aria gelida o il desiderio per l'innamorato, ma esprime l'emozione e mostra come una sostanza – qui, Il Cavaliere del Roseto – forma e cambia il corpo di Donnimaar, che lo ospita. Deleuze e Guattari proseguono affermando che è soprattutto nella musica che questi divenire sono più operativi. Eppure, dettaglio importante, il divenire musicale non è un modo per imitare qualcosa o per identificarsi con qualcuno. Piuttosto, Marie stessa *diventa* qualcosa o qualcun altro grazie a questo progetto, condividendo le particelle con Johanne. Le figure si allineano e si sovrappongono attraverso una ripetizione a spirale, e Deleuze e Guattari concludono dicendo che la musica non è privilegio degli esseri umani, visto che «l'universo, il cosmo è fatto di ritornelli»

Nella registrazione su vinile dei primi brani che Marie ha assegnato al personaggio di Donnimaar, la sua interpretazione de «LT» è rivelatrice. Il modo lento, delicato, arioso e quasi solenne in cui la melodia vocale scivola sugli arrangiamenti di Katinka Fogh Vindelev crea strati di voci fluttuanti, distillate, trattenute. La dolcezza quasi monotono e ipnotica della composizione sembra arrivare direttamente dalla notte in cui la canzone fu cantata per la prima volta in pubblico. Come la prima volta, il disco *Donnimaar* è uscito il 20 marzo 2022, data dell'equinozio di primavera.

Nel 2017, sulla soglia dell'inverno, «LT» pareva un incantesimo che accompagnava l'arrivo della notte, un cambiamento nel ciclo che trasformava l'atmosfera. Le parole cantate e parlate insieme erano un modo di accogliere, di immergersi in uno stato particolare, avvolgente, un ambiente sonoro che fungeva da soglia, un passaggio a un altro *modo* di essere. Nel movimento della canzone, sentiamo il movimento moderato e regolare delle ninne nanne. La ripetizione graduale, il pendolo, evocano il movimento del corpo che dondola, come in una culla, guidandoci dolcemente nel mondo dei sogni. «‹LT› è stata la prima canzone a cui ho lavorato», spiega Marie. «Mi è venuta in mente una notte. Ero da sola a casa con mio figlio. C'era la luna piena. Non riuscivo a dormire e avevo iniziato a cantare a bassa voce per non svegliarlo. Ero in una specie di trance. La melodia mi è venuta così, spontaneamente, in quello stato particolare». Cinque anni dopo, l'ascolto della registrazione in studio della voce cristallina dell'artista fa emergere le canzoni dall'oscurità iniziale. In questo spazio transitorio di composizione stellare, non ho bisogno di aprire gli occhi per vedere, o meglio per *sentire*, un'altra notte illuminata dalla luna, tra sogno e storia, in cui questa musica mi porta: la presenza di queste figure, di Marie, Johanne e Donnimaar; un filo di lino, un ruscello ghiacciato, le colline imbiancate dalla brina.

Inizialmente, la canzone su Donnimaar non aveva titolo. Fu l'esperto danese di folklore Evald Tang Kristensen ad attribuire alla canzone il titolo «Forvandlingen», «LT», quando, verso la fine dell'Ottocento, raccolse un repertorio di canzoni di Johanne durante uno dei suoi viaggi sul campo. Come molti suoi contemporanei europei, Tang Kristensen era spinto dall'urgenza nazional-romantica di catalogare i miti antichi e i canti tradizionali del suo Paese. Queste pratiche, che stavano per soccombere alla modernizzazione, prosperavano ancora nelle terre dello Jutland occidentale, dove la popolazione era rimasta fino ad allora in gran parte isolata dal resto della Danimarca. Quando Marie ha consultato gli archivi della Danish Folklore Collection, ha letto che Tang Kristensen aveva fatto visita a Johanne nel dicembre 1873 nel remoto villaggio di Sammelsted By, che si trovava nella brughiera di Ørre. Lì Tang Kristensen registrò tredici canzoni, una delle quali sarebbe diventata «LT», che lo incuriosì particolarmente: «Questa stranissima canzone magica è stata trovata solo nella memoria di una donna anziana di Sammelsted By, nella parrocchia di Ørre. Non si conoscono altre registrazioni vecchie o nuove, né in Danimarca né in altri Paesi», scrisse Tang Kristensen. Nella sua tesi di dottorato basata sulla pratica artistica, che discusse nel 2023, Marie aveva presentato una biografia di «LT» che il folklorista incuriosito aveva inviato al suo superiore, il quale – congratulandosi con lui per il suo «incredibile ritrovamento» di questa canzone «veramente strana» – lo incoraggiò a «carpire il più possibile da questa Johanne». Lo studio dell'etnomusicologia era quindi anche un'impresa colonialista. Infatti, oltre a preservare il materiale folklorico, la Danimarca dell'Ottocento stava attuando un processo politico di omogeneizzazione culturale, soprattutto nella parte occidentale della penisola dello Jutland – caratterizzato da una bassa densità di popolazione e dalla storica separazione culturale dalle isole di Funen e della Zelanda – che aveva favorito stili di vita molto diversi da quelli che lo stato-nazione danese, creato da poco, stava promuovendo per unificare il Paese.

L'unificazione della Danimarca si basava sull'emarginazione degli «stranieri» interni ed esterni, sul ricovero di donne e uomini «moralmente deviati» in manicomi specializzati e sulla cancellazione di qualsiasi tratto linguistico e culturale «aberrante» nella popolazione, come quello incarnato dai cosiddetti «Kjeltring». Sebbene il termine «Kjeltring» sia un esonimo, veniva utilizzato dalle autorità per descrivere e declassare diversi gruppi di popolazioni nomadi e semi-sedentarie, che facevano parte delle intricate ecologie delle brughiere basate sui pascoli comuni. Quella che possiamo definire la «colonizzazione» delle brughiere si basava sulla distruzione mirata delle culture e delle reti di scambio che consentivano la vita nello Jutland occidentale pre-industriale e sulla sottomissione del «popolo della notte», indipendente e non cristiano, per il quale i ruoli di genere non erano chiaramente definiti. Vennero obbligati a parlare la lingua nazionale e a battezzarsi, i loro rituali vennero ridicolizzati o proibiti, i bambini furono separati dai genitori per essere assimilati, adolescenti e adulti abili vennero obbligati a lavorare come contadini per essere «educati».

Non sappiamo se Johanne fosse *Kjeltring*, ma è certo che, nel 1873, Tang Kristensen andò a trovarla due volte in due giorni consecutivi. Il primo giorno trascrisse i testi delle sue canzoni, ma quando tornò il giorno seguente per registrare le sue melodie, uno dei suoi figli gli vietò di entrare; era un missionario, e considerava queste canzoni come opera del diavolo. Oggi le popolazioni designate come *Kjeltring* sono quasi del tutto dimenticate; ciò che rimane è la rozza parodia di una classe di persone degradate, ai margini della società. A parte le trascrizioni di Tang Kristensen, non rimane quasi nulla di tangibile del sapere e delle tradizioni di Johanne e della sua comunità. La raccolta rimane incompleta, semplici frammenti di miti e supposizioni che suggeriscono come potessero essere ben più che soltanto poveri e malmessi. Mi immagino Marie con gli occhi sgranati di fronte a tanta distruzione, che fissa il vuoto, il buio.

Cantare è un esercizio di respiro, di respirazione. Guardando una fotografia della brughiera di Ørre, penso a Donnimaar e mi dico che è nata nell'ascolto di quel silenzio, degli elementi. Sento il legame tra quei paesaggi aperti, gli orizzonti davanti ai quali le canzoni di Johanne hanno preso forma, le melodie vocali eteree che Marie ha composto. È probabile che, anche dopo che una cultura è stata uccisa, un residuo invisibile e persistente risuoni nel nostro mondo uditivo. I vasti ambienti sonori di *Donnimaar* alludono a ciò che rimane nell'atmosfera di quei luoghi. La bellezza del progetto di Marie sta nel fatto che è basato quasi interamente sulla voce, la sua e quella di chi la accompagna. Stratificando le voci, recupera e fa rivivere le voci di Johanne e altre come lei, che sono state costrette a tacere due volte.

Riflettendo sulla distruzione delle culture del Sud globale da parte delle forze imperialiste, Boaventura de Sousa Santos spiega come – ancor prima di spezzare le strutture culturali delle terre colonizzate – pensatori e antropologi abbiano iniziato a parlare dell'«Altro» per ridurre le persone a oggetto, privandole di una voce propria. Questo è il primo passo verso l'*epistemicidio*, lo sradicamento di un ambiente culturale, e verso il *linguicidio*, l'uccisione di una lingua locale. Ed è strutturalmente simile a ciò che è accaduto nelle brughiere dello Jutland occidentale: le stesse forze che hanno cercato di cambiare, industrializzare e sfruttare gli ambienti naturali, di spostare, costringere e persino annientare i corpi, sono riuscite anche a eliminare una cultura e una lingua. La forza del progetto *Donnimaar* sta quindi nell'intrecciare queste voci, presenti e assenti, in uno spazio che è esso stesso composto da un respiro, quasi reale e inafferrabile.

Si tratta di un atto di straordinaria delicatezza e potenza insieme, che potrebbe iniziare così: Johanne prende fiato. Di fronte a quest'uomo che è venuto a trascrivere i suoi ricordi, inspira e inizia a cantare. Dall'altra parte della storia, Marie osserva, monitorando le tracce della sua appropriazione. Quando espira, Donnimaar compare.

Nel 1942, mentre l'occupazione nazista della Francia era al culmine, Simone Weil si rifugiò a Marsiglia, dove, sfogliando la rivista *Les Cahiers du Sud*, scoprì la poesia occitana medievale. L'Occitania è una zona culturale dai confini poco definiti che si estende dal sud della Francia, a Monaco e in parte dell'Italia e della Spagna. Qui si parla occitano fin dall'antichità e nell'XI secolo la regione diede i natali al movimento dei *trobadour*, i trovatori.

A differenza della rivista parigina, *Les Cahiers du Sud* si concentrava sulle culture regionali e sugli scambi pan-mediterranei; analizzava le forme culturali emarginate alla ricerca di modalità alternative di resistenza, soprattutto quelle decentrate. L'Occitania è stata anche la regione in cui si è sviluppato il misticismo cataro. Caratterizzato dalla mancanza di beni mondani e da un senso di purezza, questo movimento spirituale e politico fu stroncato nel XIII secolo da una serie di sanguinose crociate.

L'articolo di Weil, «Che cos'è l'ispirazione occitana?», apparso sulla rivista marsigliese nel 1943, si concentrava sulla visione rivoluzionaria del canto dell'amore cortese, noto all'epoca come *fin'amor*. Per i *troubadour* e le *trobairiz*, l'amore era *l'opposto della forza*. La poetessa Lisa Robertson, che ha tradotto il brano della Weil in inglese, ha specificato, in un saggio che accompagna la traduzione, che proprio questa idea di «coltivare una visione intensamente eretica dell'amore» era per lei una forma di resistenza. «Grecia, civiltà senza l'adorazione della forza», scriveva la Weil. Per Robertson, ciò che rende l'analisi della Weil così potente oggi è che, con l'aiuto del *Simposio* di Platone, descrive l'amore come una «pratica sociale della relazione consensuale».

Più a nord, Donnimaar e il suo cavaliere incarnano proprio questo ideale quando la giovane donna gli chiede, senza ottenere il suo consenso, in cosa può trasformarlo. In pratica, usa uno stratagemma e non la forza, che è invece tipica del padre. Donnimaar è quindi una rappresentazione del potere come destrezza, mentre il padre incarna il potere come violenza, come forza. Scrive Robertson: «Nel nostro attuale clima politico, viviamo nel rifiuto dell'amore; la forza è normalizzata come valore socio-economico e come pratica del sé».

Ispirata da varie influenze culturali, l'arte dei trovatori non faceva distinzione tra poesia e musica. Come nella comunità di Johanne nello Jutland centro-occidentale, quest'arte poteva essere praticata da uomini e donne, ma purtroppo la maggior parte delle loro creazioni venne distrutta dall'Inquisizione cattolica. E questo non è l'unico legame con le canzoni dell'antenata di Marie Kølbæk Iversen. Citando un'intervista tra Edouard Glissant e Alexandre Leupin, Lisa Robertson osserva l'epistemicidio cataro in un contesto più ampio: per Glissant, le crociate del 1209-29 rappresentano l'inizio della costruzione di «un'Europa murata, escludente, razionalista e razzista». La storia inizia alla fine di questo processo. «La canzone è nata ed è stata uccisa», scrisse Jacques Roubaud, poeta e storico della poesia dei trovatori.

La distruzione, già coloniale e intraeuropea, delle culture, delle lingue e dei residenti, iniziò sotto il sole occitano, si estese nella notte jutlandese e continua tuttora all'interno e all'esterno dei confini europei. A Sammelsted By, le canzoni venivano cantate dopo il tramonto nella *Æ Bindstouw*, «la sala dei lavori a maglia», che non era una stanza separata, ma il soggiorno ribattezzato per la funzione serale che aveva durante l'inverno. Qui si cantava a turno, senza distinzioni di genere o gerarchie sociali – perché non ce n'erano – mentre si lavorava a maglia la lana ottenuta dalle pecore che pascolavano nelle brughiere. I canti collegavano quindi varie dimensioni, dalla voce alla memoria e al canto, e dai fili di lana al paesaggio. E nella canzone di Donnimaar, ovviamente, c'è un legame con il lino e con l'intreccio, con il lavoro a maglia. La stessa canzone cantata da Marie è una sorta di treccia concettuale; un filo per ogni mondo e ogni regno – uno per la giovane donna, che incarna il mito e l'immaginario, uno per l'antenato, che incarna la storia e la tradizione, e uno per l'artista, la sua presenza fisica e la sua biografia. Uniti in un intreccio, questi fili generano ciò che Simone Weil intende come *forza passiva*, che in ultima analisi rappresenta una forma di *resistenza* contro la forza intesa come violenza.

Le nostre vite sono un insieme di connessioni e legami sociali che intessiamo tra di noi, tra noi e gli altri esseri negli ambienti in cui evolviamo. Come ci ricorda l'antropologo Tim Ingold, siamo fatti di legami e fili, dalle fibre muscolari ai sistemi nervosi. E allo stesso modo ci colleghiamo a chi è ormai assente tramite linee, legami, lignaggi. Ingold spiega che il modo in cui rappresentiamo i legami genealogici è cambiato nel tempo: nel Medioevo venivano rappresentati da un albero con le radici che si estendevano verso il basso. Poi questa struttura è stata ribaltata in modo che le radici puntassero al cielo, verso il progresso. Più tardi ancora, ha assunto la forma di un diagramma che collega le persone della stessa linea di discendenza «punto per punto», senza mutamenti tra generazioni.

Agli inizi dell'Ottocento, scrive Ingold, «il fondatore della biologia moderna, Jean-Baptiste Lamarck, aveva visto nell'evoluzione[...] delle forme organiche la prova più evidente che creature di ogni genere stavano risalendo la scala della natura, e ogni nuova generazione accoglieva le conquiste cumulative dei suoi predecessori e le tramandava arricchite dalle proprie». È molto interessante notare che chiamò questo processo «trasformismo». Sarebbe un piccolo passo per arrivare a descrivere la trasformazione di Donnimaar come un manifesto genealogico per lo scambio consensuale tra le generazioni (piuttosto che per la cruda forza con cui si cercò di controllare i tratti ereditari della popolazione attraverso le misure socialdarwiniste dello Stato). Eppure, per Ingold il passaggio delle generazioni è soprattutto una questione di trasporto. Citando Bergson, sostituisce il diagramma e il modello basato sulle connessioni con uno basato sul concetto di traiettoria, di «un continuo muoversi, andare e venire». Prosegue, citando ancora una volta Bergson, secondo cui ogni generazione, «lungi dal seguire la precedente in una sequenza collegata di ‹spicchi› sincronici... si allunga... e tocca la successiva». Il modello che propone mostra «una serie di sentieri intrecciati», un modo di trasmettere le storie come tante «staffette»: «Il risultato è una treccia di linee che si estende continuamente man mano che le vite procedono». «La treccia della vita», scrive, si basa su «un intreccio narrativo di vite presenti e passate» in una forma di tempo condivisa e comprensibile. Ed è proprio questa connessione – la matrice, l'essenza condivisa di un simbolo politico sfaccettato – che il padre di Donnimaar taglia per separare il modello genealogico del radicamento da quello del flusso e dello scambio transgenerazionale e, in definitiva, per esprimere il potere dello Stato di separare e distruggere le tradizioni eterodosse. Nel tentativo di sanare questo taglio patriarcale, Marie ha rielaborato le canzoni della sua antenata con voci sovrapposte per permettere al passato di estendersi e riecheggiare di nuovo nel presente.

E se immaginassimo il legame tra le generazioni dal punto di vista musicale, in termini di variazioni, trasposizioni melodiche e linee fluide che evolvono come la melodia di una canzone? Le canzoni sono percorsi e modalità di connessione, linee tracciate su una mappa invisibile che viaggiano attraverso la storia e si librano sui paesaggi. Simone Weil parla di ponti: «Li abbiamo ereditati, ma non sappiamo più come usarli... Sappiamo solo che sono ponti, cose da attraversare». Li chiama *metaxu, cioè* «cose create [che] hanno per loro essenza di essere intermediarie. Sono intermediarie le une verso le altre; senza fine» scrive in *L'ombra e la grazia*. I *metaxu* sono l'epitome dell'intermedio, dell'intervallo, della trasformazione e del passaggio tra due stati, da un momento all'altro, tra esseri e tra mondi.
«Cosa è sacrilego distruggere?», scrive l'autrice: «Non privare nessun essere umano dei suoi *metaxu*, cioè dei suoi beni relativi e confusi... che riscaldano e nutrono l'anima e senza i quali, eccetto per la santità, una vita umana non è possibile.»

La treccia d'oro di Donnimaar è un ponte. Le canzoni di Johanne sono tessuti. L'opera di Marie invoca un coro infinito di voci, che ci dicono che la musica, come le canzoni, non è fatta solo di suoni o parole, ma anche di sapere.

- Marie Kølbæk Iversen, *Neo-worlds: Transformative Agency through Fright, Rite, and Myth* (dissertation), 2023.
- Marie Kølbæk Iversen, *Donnimaar*. Vredens Børn, Kunsthal Rønnebæksholm and MoBC Records, 2021.
- Deleuze, Guattari, *Millepiani. Capitalismo e schizofrenia*, tr. it. G. Passerone, Cooper 2003.
- Boaventura de Sousa Santos, *Epistemologies of the South*, 2014, New York: Routledge.
- Simone Weil, «En quoi consiste l'inspiration occitanienne ?» [«What is Occitanian inspiration?»] in *Les Cahiers du Sud*, febbraio 1943.
- Simone Weil, *L'ombra e la grazia*, tr. Italiana di F. Fortini, Bompiani 2002.
- Lisa Robertson, *Anemones: A Simone Weil Project*, 2021, Amsterdam: If I Can't Dance.
- Edouard Glissant with Alexandre Leupin, *The Baton Rouge Interviews* (translated by Kate Cooper), 2020, Liverpool: Liverpool University Press.
- Jacques Rancière, preface to William T. Lhamon Jr. *Peaux blanches, masques noirs. Performances du blackface, de Jim Crow au hip-hop Zones sensibles* (Translated by Sophie Renault), Paris: Kargo/L'éclat.
- Tim Ingold, *Lines: A Brief History*, capitolo «The Braid of Life,» 2007, New York: Routledge.
- Ursula K. Le Guin, *Il linguaggio della notte*, tr. it. A. Scacchi, Editori Riuniti 1986.

UN MONDO DOVE VORRESTE VIVERE? CONVERSAZIONE ADAM KHALIL E MARIE KØLBÆK IVERSEN

Questa conversazione tra gli artisti Adam Khalil AK e Marie Kølbæk Iversen MKI è avvenuta a Copenaghen nel giugno 2022. Una versione più breve è stata pubblicata in occasione della personale di Kølbæk Iversen del 2022, *Rovhistorier,* all'O–Overgaden di Copenhagen.

Adam Khalil, membro della tribù Ojibway, è un artista e regista di Sault Ste.Marie, Michigan, che attualmente si divide tra Brooklyn, New York e Copenaghen. La sua opera colloca nel presente le narrative indigene e guarda al futuro con forme innovative di fiction e nonfiction che sovvertono i tradizionali metodi di creazione delle immagini grazie al senso dell'umorismo, la trasgressione e l'associazione. Il contributo di Khalil al New Red Order è fondamentale, e ha anche co-fondato il collettivo COUSINS, ponendo la collaborazione e lo scambio al centro della sua metodologia artistica.

Partendo da background diversi, Khalil e Kølbæk Iversen si sono proposti di esplorare le implicazioni della ricerca delle rispettive eredità nel presente, per capire il ruolo del colonialismo in varie realtà considerate minoritarie in Europa e nelle Americhe. Il loro scambio considera anche il potenziale di una ricerca che vada al di là delle divisioni razziali e arrivi a sondare il terreno per eventuali «coalizioni tra *undercommon*» – come erano state definite da Stefano Harney e Fred Moten [1] – che guardano al di là di un presente soffocante, con l'obiettivo di evocare un «noi» fatto di lotte e problemi condivisi. Lo scopo di tutto questo è fare in modo che queste coalizioni, o complicità solidali, possano rappresentare un appello molto più potente, per porre fine a quel «mondo colpevole di aver creato gli stessi problemi che vanno contrastati», secondo le parole di Jack Halberstam. [2]

MKI Prima di tutto, grazie mille Adam, per aver accettato di fare questa chiacchierata. I nostri scambi sono stati fonte di grande ispirazione per me, non solo in occasione dei *TEDtalks on Acid* che hai organizzato di recente per la mostra del New Red Order's (NRO) *One if by Land, Two if by Sea* al Kunsthal Charlottenborg. Sono curiosa di condividere alcune delle idee che hanno portato alla mostra all'O–Overgaden perché, come molti dei tuoi lavori, il mio progetto riflette sui saperi indigeni all'intersezione di modernità e scienza per tentare di formulare una visione alternativa di futuro ed evoluzione che vada al di là della situazione di stallo del capitalismo moderno. Nella mia opera video *Rovhistorier|Histories of Predation* ipotizzo un'appropriazione dello sguardo storico di un tipo specifico di squalo, lo squalo gurry, della Groenlandia, o squalo artico, che in tutte le lingue scandinave viene chiamato tritone o sirena – l'antico nome danese dello squalo è *havkal*, ossia «tritone». Secondo recenti studi di biologia marina, questo «tritone» – lo squalo – può vivere fino a 272-512 anni. In più, attraversa tutto l'Atlantico settentrionale, il che lo rende un interlocutore immaginario o «testimone oculare» particolarmente interessante con cui riflettere sugli sviluppi storici della regione e valutare visioni di futuro alternative.
Come danese rappresento una presenza coloniale in Groenlandia, dove è stato catturato lo squalo su cui ho lavorato. Ma il progetto cerca anche di riflettere su come sono diventata danese, in un certo senso.

AK L'arco temporale che lo squalo grigio può ricoprire mi ha fatto girare la testa, ed è senza dubbio un'esca a cui potrei abboccare! Non sono certo che sia un parallelo perfetto ma ho letto un saggio di Lou Cornum sul futurismo indigeno che mi sembra utile in termini di *world-building,* costruzione di un mondo.

> *Il «Futurismo indigeno» fa parte di una tradizione alternativa alla fantascienza occidentale che tende a strutturarsi sulla tensione tra utopia e distopia. La temporalità dell'esistenza indigena trascende questi termini: non c'è pre-apocalisse o post-apocalisse, ma solo una rivelazione perpetua. Il futurismo indigeno, quindi, riguarda la lotta per un futuro diverso e un'idea di «futuro» nettamente diversa, che va oltre il conflitto tra tradizione e progresso e ci invita ad abitare il presente.* [3]

E poi mentre venivo qui pensavo... forse è un po' una sciocchezza, ma pensavo che le creature sirena o i draghi sono emersi in Europa e in Asia, ma contemporaneamente. Quindi devono essere reali, no?

MKI È un'ottima osservazione. In generale è interessante notare come storicamente ci siano stati numerosi scambi tra culture e narrazioni culturali, scambi che continuano anche oggi convergono a livelli minoritari piuttosto che maggioritari. Nell'ideazione di questo progetto un altro punto di riferimento fondamentale è stato il libro di Linebaugh e Rediker uscito nel

2000, *I ribelli dell'Atlantico. La storia perduta di un'utopia libertaria* (tr. it. di B. Amato, Feltrinelli 2018) che è qui sul tavolo vicino a me. È la storia degli *undercommons,* [4] gli espropriati dell'Atlantico, come vengono definiti nella traduzione italiana, un proletariato eterogeneo che aveva le sue origini in Europa, Africa e America:

> *«Comprendeva clowns, o cloons (ossia gente di campagna). Era priva di unità genealogica. Era volgare. Parlava una lingua sua, con pronuncia, lessico e grammatica caratteristici, fatti di slang, lingua furbesca, gergo e pidgin, parlate prese dal lavoro, dalla strada, dalla prigione, dalla banda, dal porto. Era planetaria, nelle origini, negli spostamenti, nella coscienza. Infine, la classe proletaria era autonoma, creativa; era – ed è – viva; è in movimento.*
>
> *Che cosa ha da offrirci, oggi, l'esperienza di questo proletariato?».* [5]

Per molti versi questo tema riflette l'altro punto di osservazione del mio progetto: le brughiere dello Jutland occidentale, da cui proviene la mia famiglia e dove sono cresciuta, e dove la mia trisavola Johanne Thygesdatter fu una delle informanti di Evald Tang Kristensen nel 1873. Uno dei massimi esperti ottocenteschi di folklore danese e figura cruciale del moderno lavoro sul campo, Tang Kristensen fu incaricato da Svend Grundtvig di raccogliere le canzoni e i racconti delle brughiere dello Jutland occidentale, sottoposte a una rapida industrializzazione negli anni in cui si è svolta la ricerca. Calandomi con l'immaginazione nelle brughiere nell'Ottocento, ho tentato di lavorare sulla logica linguistica e la prospettiva culturale imbastardita dei miei antenati, che era proletaria e ibrida come quella descritta da Linebaugh e Rediker, compresi i diversi dialetti jutlandesi che mescolavano scozzese, inglese, tedesco, danese, svedese e norvegese, con influenze d'oltremare.

Se vogliamo considerare il materiale che la mia antenata Johanne aveva passato a Tang Kristensen come valida testimonianza della loro cultura d'origine, basta analizzare le canzoni per scoprire che mettevano in discussione gli sforzi governativi per lo sviluppo agricolo, la nazionalizzazione e l'omogeneizzazione, nonché i concetti di proprietà della terra e l'autorità di alcune persone su altre. Il che ha senso, perché la vita nella brughiera era in gran parte basata sui pascoli comuni, e quindi non poteva che essere tragico per gli abitanti vedere la brughiera recintata e perdere l'accesso alla terra su cui contavano da sempre.

Molte canzoni del periodo sembrano riflettere sull'etica e sulle premesse dell'alleanza e dello scambio interculturale attraverso la figura romanzata delle *merperson.* Ad esempio, la canzone su Adeluds – una sorta di *mermaid* che vive in collina o in montagna – racconta di come fosse stata sedotta e ingannata da uno degli uomini del re danese, che dice di volerla sposare, mentre in realtà voleva solo sottometterla e usare la sua prole come forza lavoro. Ma prima che l'inganno venisse svelato, le si era avvicinato con un ragazzino, e Adeluds era così felice al pensiero dell'imminente matrimonio che indossò un abito dorato e si mise a insegnare al giovane a dominare il clima e le onde; a scrivere rune magiche; a far alzare e placare i venti; a provocare onde così alte da far affondare qualunque imbarcazione. Ma quando arrivarono alla nave, il capitano la prese per un braccio e le disse che non le avrebbe permesso di tornare a casa prima di aver partorito un figlio che sapesse remare e una figlia che sapesse seminare. Ma Adeluds fuggì e nonostante la barca andasse a tutta velocità e lei era a nuoto, raggiunse la riva molto prima. Appena il capitano attraccò, lei lo raggiunse e gli disse che i suoi figli non avrebbero mai remato né seminato e che, se non fosse stato per il ragazzino, avrebbe fatto affondare la loro barca. Quindi, il ragazzino è in una posizione difficile perché si trova in mezzo a culture, lotte e interessi contrastanti. Ma per me simboleggia anche il potenziale dei giovani come rappresentanti del futuro, capaci di gettare un ponte tra un conflitto mortale e un'opposizione ontologica. E penso alla *merperson* in modo analogo: una figura su cui è interessante riflettere oggi, perché abita gli spazi fluidi tra le demarcazioni nazionali e non appartiene specificamente a nessuno Stato o popolo. Tu hai lavorato anche con i *merpeople* nel contesto del New Red Order, giusto? Per Lemuria, vero?

AK Sì, stavamo indagando su Lemuria con un occhio un po' critico, perché fa parte di questo movimento new age in cui la gente crede che nelle grotte vulcaniche vivano dei vichinghi alti più di due metri. Credo che Atlantide e Lemuria siano esistite e fossero in competizione – Atlantide è scomparsa, mentre Lemuria è rimasta una fantasia potente proprio a causa dei tunnel vulcanici. Nel nord della California c'è una zona, il Mount Shasta, dove molti dicono di vedere continuamente i Lemuriani.

Abbiamo lavorato con loro per indagare su questa idea di «essere arrivati per primi», o una sorta di strana rivendicazione new age di far parte del territorio e quindi essere in linea con le preoccupazioni degli indigeni. Quando siamo stati alle Hawaii abbiamo scoperto che tra i nativi hawaiani circolano parecchi miti anche sui Lemuriani. Non ne conosco abbastanza per approfondire, ma è interessante il modo in cui una figura del genere viaggi nel mondo.

MKI Quindi i Lemuriani non sono *merpeople*?

AK Ci sono narrazioni diverse – ovviamente è difficile fare un identikit completo. A volte si sente parlare di *merpeople*, altre di fasci di luce – questa è forse la versione più new age, che oggi è la più diffusa.

Sean Connolly, un artista-architetto hawaiano presente anche nella mostra alla Kunsthal Charlottenborg, ha studiato come si sono spostati i continenti e i corpi idrici, e come in passato viaggiare da un luogo come l'Oceania all'Africa fosse molto più facile. Possiamo così immaginare le diverse migrazioni che possono avvenire se si viaggia tra gli emisferi o passando sottoterra, invece di andare intorno, o riflettere sul fatto che esistono tutte queste strane confluenze e convergenze di culture diverse in tutto il mondo come risultato del loro incontro molto prima di quello che immaginavamo fosse possibile. Questo ci fa ritornare all'idea di persone che spuntano in più luoghi, come la teoria alla base della mitologia lemuriana dei tunnel vulcanici o le gallerie sotterranee che collegano il mondo. Dove sono cresciuto gli avvistamenti di Sasquatch sono abbastanza comuni, e dalle mie parti li chiamano i «viaggiatori delle radici».

MKI Viaggiatori delle radici?

AK Proprio così. L'idea alla base dell'impossibilità di vederli o conoscerli è che ogni volta che qualcuno li avvista subito saltano nel nell'incavo di un albero. Possono percorrere l'apparato radicale come una metropolitana e spuntare a 600 chilometri di distanza in pochi secondi. Ci ho riflettuto perché l'anno scorso sono andato a fare snorkeling per la prima volta in vita mia e solo vedendo il mondo sottomarino ho pensato: «Oh, mio Dio». Cioè mi sembrava di aver viaggiato in tutto il mondo e di conoscere la geografia, ma rendersi conto che il 70% della Terra è acqua è una cosa che non avevo mai considerato prima. È un pensiero che ti fa sentire piccolo piccolo. Soprattutto con i *merpeople* là sotto che esplorano i fondali; ovvio che non sappiamo nulla di loro, no? D'altronde non hanno un particolare interesse a farsi conoscere.

MKI Ricordo di aver letto un testo dell'archeologo Neil Price in cui spiegava come si era basato sulle teorie degli storici hawaiani Sir Peter Buck/Te Rangi Hīroa e Herb Kawainui Kāne per tentare di comprendere le culture Oceaniche e Vichinghe, nel tentativo di colmare le lacune delle rispettive storicizzazioni. Mi sembra un interessante ribaltamento di prospettiva su come queste due culture apparentemente diverse, provenienti da luoghi radicalmente distanti della Terra, possano comunque avere qualcosa in comune, e permettere una comprensione generale delle culture marinare rispetto a quelle terrestri.

AK Intendi incontrare il mare o scontrarsi con il mare? Perché questo non è possibile, perché loro vivono *sul* mare, non *nel* mare.

MKI Hai ragione, sì. Ma forse potrebbe essere un altro aspetto della costruzione di comunità resa possibile dal mare – anche se non nel mare – della potenzialità dello scambio transculturale al fatto di essere tra due... In tutto il mondo ci sono così tante testimonianze di persone che vivono sull'acqua e condividono i beni comuni e ormai si sa che i cosiddetti pirati, così ci è stato insegnato a percepirli, erano in realtà persone comuni. Linebaugh e Rediker le chiamano «idrarchie».

AK Anche se il rovescio della medaglia è rappresentato da una scrittrice come Ayn Rand, un'ideologa conservatrice degli anni Sessanta e Settanta il cui *Atlas Shrugged* (pubblicato in Italia in tre volumi intitolati *Il tema, L'uomo che apparteneva alla terra* e *L'Atlantide,* tr. it. L. Grimaldi, Corbaccio 2016) è diventato fondamentale per le filosofie libertarie antigovernative, ed è molto popolare nella Silicon Valley in questo momento. Nel romanzo la scrittrice sosteneva in un certo senso che chi fosse abbastanza intelligente e qualificato e sufficientemente abile per il capitalismo avrebbe dovuto trasferirsi su un'isola al largo della costa del Paese, in modo da evitare la legge. Ma se la pensiamo come una sorta di colonizzazione del mare, è comunque sempre territorio di qualcuno?

È interessante pensare a quel libro anche in relazione alle idee di *commons* e *commoners*, – secondo la definizione di Rediker e Linebaugh, gente comune espropriata dell'uso di beni comuni, i *commons* – perché questa sfiducia nei confronti del governo o dei commons nazionali porta a pensare che si può lasciare la propria nazione per crearne una per conto proprio. Voglio dire, c'è questa sorta di sogno anarco-libertario che è allettante, ma del tutto assurdo. O come una specie di Atlantide, capisci?

Ho lavorato a un film che si intitola *Nosferasta*, in cui Cristoforo Colombo e il 1492 sono visti come qualcosa di più grandioso dei viaggi spaziali interplanetari, o forse equivalente. Ma il film riflette anche sulla fusione tra oceano e spazio e su come, prima di quel momento, fossero un po' la stessa cosa. Eppure forse non è vero, perché abbiamo appena parlato dei vichinghi e della preistoria secondo quando ci viene insegnato a scuola, le nozioni che ci vengono inculcate su dove queste persone viaggiano e come. Ma in effetti la cosa si fa strana.

MKI Si fa strana sì! Ma penso che sia proprio quando le cose diventano molto strane che possono far emergere fenomeni nuovi.
Ho letto che dopo una battaglia avvenuta ad Alken Enge intorno all'anno zero, le ossa dei caduti furono raccolte e immerse in un lago vicino. Si può solo provare ad immaginare il fetore che saliva da quelle acque e quanto fossero diventate tossiche con i corpi in decomposizione, e come, insieme alla storia traumatica della battaglia, quel luogo fosse diventato non solo pericoloso, ma anche sacro. I reperti archeologici suggeriscono che in effetti divenne un sito sacrificale, dove per secoli, pare cinque, molti tornarono in pellegrinaggio a fare delle offerte. Penso che avesse a che fare con la convinzione che gli spiriti dei caduti popolassero ancora il lago – che ora è prosciugato – e le sue sponde, e questo lo rendesse potentissimo dal punto di vista dei rituali e della magia, ma anche molto pericoloso, perché sono conflittuali nella morte come nella vita.

Se si segue questa linea di pensiero – che gli spiriti dei morti sono ancora in quel lago, invidiosi della vita umana che si era sviluppata tutto intorno – cambia completamente l'immaginario della responsabilità dei *merpeople* e degli spiriti dell'acqua: si può arrivare a pensare che siano estensioni di culture e persone che sono state annientate (da noi), e che quindi continuano a perseguitare i vivi, per vendetta.

AK Sì, sì, vero. È anche interessante pensare allo strano slittamento tra storia, narrativa e spiritualità, e come sono state isolate o separate. Pensare in modo creativo o inventare cose... anche solo questa idea di fondere gli elementi è tabù ora, perché deve esserci una risposta razionale e logica a tutto. Ma un'idea che porto sempre con me è che la storia dovrebbe essere una narrazione al servizio del presente, che questi esseri o creature mitologiche siano in realtà una sorta di credenza spirituale che si fonde armoniosamente con la storia, forse tanto bene da risultare è incredibile. Come Drexciya.

MKI Drexciya?

AK Drexciya faceva parte del movimento techno di Detroit e operava nella prospettiva di un futurismo afro-pessimista, se così si può definire. Erano un gruppo quasi segreto. Secondo la loro mitologia, i figli delle donne incinte che avevano perso la vita durante il Passaggio di Mezzo erano nati sott'acqua e avevano fondato una sorta di Atlantide Nera chiamata appunto Drexciya. Ed è da lì che vengono e da lì nasce la loro musica. E quando ho sentito questa storia mi è sembrata fantastica, perché in un certo senso fa pensare anche al fatto che un dolore o una sofferenza immani, o la vista di un trauma indicibile, possano portare alla nascita di una narrazione alternativa per comprendere o creare un mondo in cui si vuole vivere.

MKI È un punto di vista molto forte, straziante. Un ribaltamento completo della rappresentazione dei *merpeople* come creature fantastiche innocue e antistoriche.

Nello Jutland occidentale i *merpeople* non avevano la coda ma solo le zampe, quindi se si trovava un cadavere sulla riva non si sapeva se era di un essere umano o di una *merperson*. Ma c'erano vari modi per capirlo: se subito dopo la sepoltura si sentiva un gran baccano, il tempo peggiorava e la persona si succhiava il pollice nella tomba, si era di fronte a una *merperson* e bisognava riportarla in mare il prima possibile. Così si narra.

I pescatori potevano anche incontrare i *merpeople* in mare, seduti in cima a un'onda, a spostarsi una calza da un piede all'altro. Se regalavi un'altra calza ti leggevano la fortuna o ti aiutavano in altri modi diversi. Potevi anche offrire un paio di guanti. Credo che, essendo associati alle anime di chi è morto in acqua, fossero collegati agli *elverfolk,* sorta di elfi che vivono nella brughiera. Scorrendo tra il mare e le varie sorgenti e i fiumi, l'acqua è collegata al sottosuolo, proprio come gli esseri che vi risiedono. Ci sono varie testimonianze di persone che affermano di aver visto una donna – una *elver* o una *mermaid* – seduta in uno di questi tumuli, che si pettinava e metteva in bella mostra i suoi ori.

Per me è stato stimolante pensare agli *elverfolk* e ai *merpeople* come rappresentanti delle relazioni tra l'acqua e la terraferma, tra gli esseri umani e la natura. E ai *merpeople* come altri ontologici degli esseri umani ma fluidi, proprio come il terreno sotto di noi è fluido, ma su una scala temporale molto più lunga. E al fatto che tutti gli essenzialismi e le fissità sono destinati al cambiamento.

AK Di recente mi sono imbattuto in vari scritti sul potere della fede e su come la sinistra ha abbandonato la fede spirituale e ora si affidi solo al razionalismo, alla scienza e alla democrazia. Certo, si entra in un territorio paludoso, specialmente se pensiamo alla post-verità, e quindi sono sempre un po' restio a tirare fuori questa roba, ma penso anche che sia davvero utile riuscire a fare un passo indietro. Non per mettere in discussione i pilastri fondamentali della democrazia occidentale e proporre qualcosa di stravagante, ma perché è importante non irrigidirsi troppo nelle proprie convinzioni, o arrivare a sostenere l'idea che la scienza cinquant'anni fa fosse totalmente diversa dalla scienza di ora, e che continuerà ad essere così. Se lo facessimo, finiremmo per privilegiare la nostra posizione nel presente come la più giusta, o come una sorta di onniscienza.

Il motivo per cui ne parlo è che la gente si chiede, perché le proteste a Standing Rock sono state efficaci? Perché Black Lives Matter è efficace? O anche perché la «destra» è efficace? E penso che la risposta sia perché in tutti questi casi le convinzioni rivestono un ruolo centrale. Questo mi ha fatto pensare al potenziale radicale di tornare alle credenze, anche se sono laiche, per capire cosa può cambiare. E forse si riallaccia al nostro discorso sui *merpeople* e sui diversi tipi di comprensione della storia in relazione al luogo e alla mitologia. Come la storia possa essere una narrazione a servizio del presente, anche quando è un po' fantastica o inaspettata. Tutte queste cose possono cambiare il modo in cui guardiamo alla storia in generale.

MKI Sì. E aiutarci a capire se l'arte può essere il luogo dove sperimentare il potenziale delle credenze spirituali o delle narrazioni associate alla lotta politica; non per uscire dalla realtà, ma per trovare alternative per ribaltare il modo in cui viene narrata e magari arrivare a visioni diverse sul futuro?

AK In un mondo laico e razionale, l'arte offre in un certo senso un momento di sublime o di spirituale. Nathaniel Dorsey ha scritto di come il cinema e le sale cinematografiche sono diventati un po' come le chiese; lo schermo è una sorta di vetrata artistica in cui la luce si muove man mano che il giorno avanza. In quest'epoca in cui pochi credono, l'arte diventa il luogo in cui la religione si manifesta.

Penso all'intreccio della cultura e dell'arte dopo la rivoluzione sovietica, in cui si cerca di infondere un'aura sacra alle forme culturali laiche per superare, o eventualmente proporre, una nuova religione. È un aspetto pieno di contraddizioni su cui ho riflettuto molto di recente e che si ricollega al periodo che ho trascorso alle Hawaii per saperne di più sulle proteste del vulcano sacro di Mauna Kea, su Big Island, dove gli scienziati stanno cercando di costruire un enorme telescopio di trenta metri. Ho incontrato gli attivisti coinvolti nella lotta contro questo progetto, e hanno lo slogan «Pro Scienza. Pro Sacro». È così semplice ma così efficace e allo stesso tempo radicale, e mi ha aperto la mente sulla possibilità di sostenere entrambe le cose contemporaneamente, invece di metterle in contrapposizione per creare questa specie di falsa dialettica in cui bisogna scegliere l'una o l'altra.

MKI Esatto.

AK Non ho ancora capito bene dove può portare questa idea, e come, ma è stata molto utile.

MKI Mentre studiavo la relazione tra mito e rituale per il mio dottorato, ho letto il resoconto di Victor Turner sulla ritualità Ndembu nello Zambia nord-occidentale nel suo libro *The Ritual Process,* dove spiega come il passaggio di una donna o di una coppia attraverso un tunnel scavato nel terreno sia prescritto dagli sciamani Ndembu come cura per l'infertilità, ad esempio. Sia Turner che i suoi informanti contrappongono quel tipo di pratiche alla medicina occidentale. Ma poi, leggendo il resoconto dello storico H. P. Hansen sulla medicina preindustriale e sulle pratiche rituali nello Jutland occidentale, trovo lo stesso rituale: viene scavata una buca nel terreno dove far entrare i malati, come cura o sollievo.

Temo che l'effetto della diffusione di esempi come quello degli Ndembu a causa dell'etnografia accademica – insieme a quella che sembra essere l'intenzionale dimenticanza di casi nordeuropei come questo appena citato – sia che certi gruppi o etnie vengono associati all'irrazionale e altri al razionale, quando in realtà tutte le società sono state e continuano ad essere caratterizzate da aspetti sia razionali che irrazionali.

AK Mi piace l'idea dell'etnografia come una sorta di psicoanalisi per una società europea illuminista, tipo: «Qui non facciamo queste cose, ma guardate cosa fa questa gente...!». «Oh sì. Ma un tempo lo facevamo anche noi.» Per produrre un Altro discriminato per razza come Id europeo.

MKI Ah ah, proprio così. In effetti, l'Europa moderna sembra essere permeata dall'idea che le pratiche rituali o spirituali «irrazionali», risalissero all'epoca preistorica. Eppure, analizzando gli esempi di H. P. Hansen – alcuni dei quali si riferiscono all'inizio del XX secolo – molti erano coinvolti in attività rituali e magiche piuttosto elaborate fino a tempi recenti. E non credo che sia una caratteristica solo dello Jutland occidentale, dove oltre ai riti sotterranei che ricordano quelli degli Ndembo, era uso bruciare i morti e sciogliere le ceneri polverizzate in pozioni da consumare o da applicare sulla pelle. Viste da fuori, queste pratiche non sono lontane da quello che potrebbe definirsi «cannibalismo».

AK Ecco, questo è un altro esempio di come, se non si comprende l'epistemologia non si arriva a cogliere il fulcro di un fenomeno. Conosci Juan Downey? No? È pazzesco. Era un artista cileno-newyorkese attivo negli anni Settanta. Ha fatto un film intitolato *The Laughing Alligator*, che era una specie di «vaffanculo» all'etnografia e all'antropologia. Lui, la moglie e i due figli si erano trasferiti in Brasile per vivere con gli Yanomami per nove mesi, e avevano realizzato insieme una sorta di documentario familiare, in cui lui oscillava tra il tono serio serio da antropologo e un'altra voce esilarante, e non si riusciva mai a capirlo. È davvero uno dei miei film preferiti.

Nel film parla di come le ceneri dei cari estinti venissero polverizzate e mescolate in una zuppa di banane che rappresentava una sorta di architettura funeraria definitiva, e presentava questi rituali come pratiche molto concrete e forse realmente connesse. Era cresciuto come indigeno cileno bianco e dice una cosa tipo «tutto questo non è molto lontano dalle mie origini, da entrambe le parti, eppure mi viene fatto credere che ce ne sia solo una», c'è una specie di confluenza.

MKI Si collega a tutta la questione del «loro». Voglio dire, c'è di sicuro un modo di parlare del potenziale delle pratiche rituali minoritarie senza soccombere a un linguaggio divisivo: «*Loro* fanno questo ma *noi* non lo facciamo». Secondo te, esiste un modo di riconoscere la forza e il potenziale delle pratiche rituali minoritarie senza scadere nella caricatura e nel divario dell'altro da noi?

AK Certo, oh sì. Perché è anche una questione di prospettiva. Perché se parli dal punto di vista di chi ha l'autorità puoi imporre qualsiasi cosa all'altro, quindi è anche una questione di destabilizzare l'autorità, per diventare parte del tutto o formare qualcosa.

MKI Okay, quindi riconoscendo le numerose dinamiche essenzializzate ed essenzializzanti legate a questa discussione, pensi ancora che ci possa essere un posto dove il tuo background sia anche una risorsa che ti permette di immaginare o proiettarti nel futuro in modo diverso, contro il presente e la cultura maggioritaria occidentale?

AK Sì, dalla mia prospettiva di Ojibway e per il modo in cui penso e sento le cose, cerco sempre di pormi in una prospettiva rivolta al futuro, perché c'è così tanta enfasi sul passato. Ma è interessante quando la gente si rivolge a me per argomenti come la spiritualità dei nativi. Io incoraggio sempre tutti a esplorare il passato della loro identità etnica ed è qui che si fa complicato in termini di proiezione, perché le persone guardano al passato delle culture native per trovare il proprio.

MKI Sì, esatto.

AK Anche se, soprattutto grazie alla tua ricerca e al tuo lavoro, c'è una tale ricchezza di cultura, costumi, resistenza e storie all'interno del tuo background storico, ricchezza a cui ispirarsi e dare visibilità.

MKI Ma naturalmente, un ostacolo ovvio a questo lavoro è la storia del nazismo e il modo in cui i nazisti si sono attivamente appropriati delle eredità pagane nordiche e germaniche a fini ideologici ed eugenetici. Credo che questo possa essere uno dei motivi per cui molti nordeuropei di sinistra sono restii ad avvicinarsi ai costumi e alle culture minoritarie del nostro passato etnico, perché sono stati pesantemente contaminati da quel periodo della storia. È stato un fantasma anche nella mia ricerca, ma l'ho affrontato cercando di rimanere molto lucida e di attenermi alle parole e ai racconti della mia famiglia e di altre persone reali negli archivi del folklore. Non ho immaginato una sorta di fantastica utopia vichinga, che è un po' come pensare ad Atlantide o a Lemuria: non è mai esistita, ma è una fantasia forte e potente, capace di trascinare a livelli inimmaginabili di violenza e discriminazione.

Per questo cerco di partire dal basso, dai frammenti d'archivio che trovo e che posso mettere insieme grazie al sapere della zona dello Jutland occidentale dove sono cresciuta, con tutti i suoi codici non detti, e poi attraverso l'arte o l'immaginazione, o qualsiasi altra cosa, sognare come possono formare un continuum spirituale o culturale dissidente, che si oppone alle forze nazionaliste o nazionalizzanti del presente. Prima di tutto, studiando i racconti e le canzoni dei miei antenati, si capisce che non erano particolarmente entusiasti del progetto danese. Sarebbe quindi poco etico appropriarsi del loro patrimonio mitico e spirituale nel progetto danese o in qualsiasi altro progetto di costruzione di una nazione.

Per questo motivo, nel tentativo di tornare indietro e trovare strumenti alternativi che ci spingano in avanti, tendo a rivolgermi al folklore piuttosto che alle rivisitazioni mitiche del pantheon norreno. Detto questo, però, le narrazioni mitiche delle canzoni della mia antenata presentano vari temi ricorrenti legati a figure del pantheon norreno, ad esempio donne dotate di grandi poteri magici, avvolte in mantelli blu e capaci di trasformarsi in lupi e falchi – richiamo alla dea Vanir Freja, che fu la prima a padroneggiare la magia sciamanica Sejd e che si spostava attraverso i mondi e il tempo in forma di falco. Il regno immaginario evocato dalle canzoni non è quindi estraneo alla mitologia vichinga o al paganesimo norreno, ma lo affronta diversamente e per fini diversi rispetto al nazionalismo neopagano di estrema destra. Ad esempio, il motivo principale della canzone che cita l'eroina vestita da falco è lo scontro con il re danese, che fu ucciso perché aveva sottomesso il fratello di lei e poi tentato di placarla con un'offerta d'oro. A me sembra che questo rappresenti un grosso ostacolo in qualsiasi progetto che cerchi di identificare la *Danishness*, la «danesità» come una categoria etnica per alimentare un programma nazionalista e divisivo dal punto di vista razziale.

AK Be', sono assolutamente d'accordo con te. Credo che questo sia il motivo per cui cerco sempre di orientare qualsiasi tipo di background verso il futuro; perché sento che concentrarsi sul passato non solo è un'arma a doppio taglio, perché costringe a tentare di essere autentici nei confronti di un passato irrecuperabile. Ma l'altro problema, che si collega a quello di cui parli tu, è che l'eccessiva identificazione con il passato potrebbe portare, nel mio caso, alla «supremazia rossa», e allora vorrebbe dire che non siamo andati affatto oltre.

MKI Giusto. Credo sia questo il motivo per cui me ne sono tenuta alla larga per così tanto tempo. Ma le canzoni della mia antenata non vanno affatto in quella direzione, e poi non era vichinga: era una donna che viveva nella brughiera nell'Ottocento e custodiva saperi pagani. E questo è un altro esempio di come le sue canzoni si discostino da un'interpretazione neopagana di destra della mitologia norrena: la posizione delle donne nella società. Da dove vengo io, non esisteva una divisione netta del lavoro o dello status tra uomini e donne. Tutti partecipavano a ogni tipo di attività – foraggiare, allevare, macellare, lavorare a maglia, cantare – e allo stesso modo sia le donne che gli uomini rappresentavano il locus della narrazione mitica e dell'azione trasformativa. Per me, quindi, si tratta anche di utilizzare il mio patrimonio mitico e culturale della brughiera per sovvertire il modo in cui l'immaginario norreno è stato appropriato per scopi nazionalistici e divisivi in tutto l'Occidente.

Nell'ambito di questa ricerca, sto cercando di capire se sia possibile concepire una posizione in cui i diversi patrimoni indigeni possano convergere e fecondarsi a vicenda. Voglio dire, io e te siamo senza dubbio moderni, viviamo vite moderne in un mondo moderno. Ma questa vita è così pesantemente limitata dalle ideologie capitaliste, che mi chiedo se esistano punti alternativi in cui potremmo invece convergere o unire le forze grazie alle nostre rispettive eredità minoritarie. Voglio dire, in questo momento sto solo cantando, e a cosa serve...?

AK Sì, ma canti canzoni che sono quasi del tutto dimenticate!

MKI Certo, ma se dovessi fare un po' di autocritica, non potrebbe essere l'ennesimo caso di eccessivo coinvolgimento nostalgico nel passato? Le culture cambiano continuamente; alcune cose sono destinate a perdersi, e forse dovremmo lasciarle andare...?

AK Di recente ho parlato con una persona che veniva dalle mie parti, e sosteneva che invece di cercare di far rivivere le cose, di farle risorgere o mantenerle com'erano, si dovrebbe partire dall'idea che è necessaria invece la rivelazione perpetua della cultura e che le cose devono poter cambiare. Che non bisogna per forza lottare con la tradizione. Tradizione e cultura hanno qualità differenti, e mantenere viva una cultura è diverso da seguire una tradizione. Quindi penso che recuperare questi canti, che sono sì tradizionali, ma eseguiti e registrati con tecnologie contemporanee, sia un modo di perpetuare la cultura che si pone in contrapposizione con il tentativo di riprodurne un facsimile. E mi sembra che quel continuum – la catena di generazioni interconnesse che in un certo momento si toccano – sia il punto di forza di un lavoro del genere.

Ma ha anche uno strano effetto boomerang, soprattutto quando una cultura è minacciata o sta scomparendo, perché molti si impuntano su come viene rivitalizzata, e credo che questo sia un punto in cui il tutto prende una piega pericolosa. Hitler consultava i romanzi di Karl May su Winnetou – il capo Apache immaginario – perché erano i suoi libri preferiti. Si dice che leggesse quei libri come si legge la Bibbia in un momento di crisi e, secondo Gober, li assegnò persino ai soldati per la loro enfasi sul valore e sui principi guerrieri degli indigeni.

MKI Sì, credo che queste insidie siano sempre presenti, indipendentemente dal fatto che si parli di supremazie rosse o bianche o di altri tipi di nativismo. Sono fantasie dannose, che mettono in ombra i problemi reali e le lotte dei

popoli che sono stati resi precari.
AK Sì, anche in questo caso c'è il pericolo di concentrarsi troppo sul passato o sulla tradizione, perché i nativi si sentono così giustificati a dire «sbarazzatevi di tutti gli immigrati», la posizione più dura dell'estrema destra conservatrice.
MKI È vero. Un mio amico antropologo brasiliano lavora in Amazzonia con una tribù che, a suo dire, si assicura la propria continuità culturale grazie a una trasformazione perpetua; trasformazioni che trasformano trasformazioni. Gli ho chiesto se possono anche trasformarsi per diventare moderni e mi ha risposto «sì, certo, ma poi tornano come prima, con un'altra trasformazione», il che mi ha lasciata un po' perplessa, e mi chiedo se questa capacità di trasformazione possa valere anche per me, in quanto discendente bianca di una cultura oppressa basata sui pascoli comuni, o se si tratta di un talento esclusivamente amazzonico? Voglio dire, anche io vorrei trasformarmi...
AK Ecco, questo mi fa pensare al concetto di «sette generazioni». Nella mia cultura si pensa che bisogna sempre tenere presenti sette generazioni nel passato e sette generazioni nel futuro. Questo è l'arco temporale a cui fare riferimento per qualsiasi tipo di azione o pensiero, e anche per perpetuare una cultura o una comunità. Io lo trovo un concetto molto utile che mi aiuta a mantenermi lucido se penso ai movimenti politici e quando rifletto su cose che vanno al di là della nostra vita. Se si fanno i conti, a seconda dell'aspettativa di vita, questo continuum di sette avanti e sette indietro, diventa piuttosto consistente, più o meno 150-200 anni in una direzione. Pensare a sette generazioni apre un continuum di 350 anni dal passato al futuro.
MKI Credo che la mia antenata Johanne fosse indietro di sette generazioni rispetto a me... Johanne madre di Niels padre di Niels Kristian padre di Johannes padre di Maja madre di mia madre Margit. Contando anche me, Johanne e io abbiamo sette generazioni di differenza. Raddoppiandole nel futuro, abbiamo l'aspettativa di vita media dello squalo gurry, l'*havkal.*
AK Be', sette generazioni di *havkal*. Ora la cosa si fa davvero interessante. Sono più o meno 1500 anni.
MKI Esattamente. Sette generazioni di squali. È una prospettiva da prendere in considerazione. Forse è un buon punto per chiudere la conversazione?
AK Buona idea.

1 Stefano Harney e Fred Moten: *The Undercommons: Fugitive Planning & Black Study* (Brooklyn: Autonomedia, 2013).
2 Jack Halberstam: «The Wild Beyond: With and For the Undercommons» in Stefano Harney e Fred Moten, Ibid. p. 9.
3 Lou Cornum: «Who Belongs to the Land?» da *Triple Canopy*, 17 marzo 2022 (canopycanopycanopy.com/contents/who-belongs-to-the-land–accesso del 15 febbraio 2023), pp. 31-32.
4 Quello di «undercommons» è un concetto coniato da Fred Moten e Stefano Harney nel loro libro *The Undercommons: Fugitive Planning and Black Study* (Brooklyn: Autonomedia, 2013) per descrivere «il regno ingovernabile della vita sociale, il luogo in cui noi, colonizzati, queer, marginali, creiamo significato l'uno con l'altro.» Si veda: Zach Ngin: «Flights of Fantasy. On Fred Moten and Stefano Harney's Undercommons» in *The College Hill Independent*, 14 febbraio 2020, https://www.theindy.org/1878.
5 Linebaugh e Rediker, *I ribelli dell'Atlantico. La storia perduta di un'utopia libertaria* (tr. it. di B. Amato, Feltrinelli 2018).